IMAGES
of America

IRVING

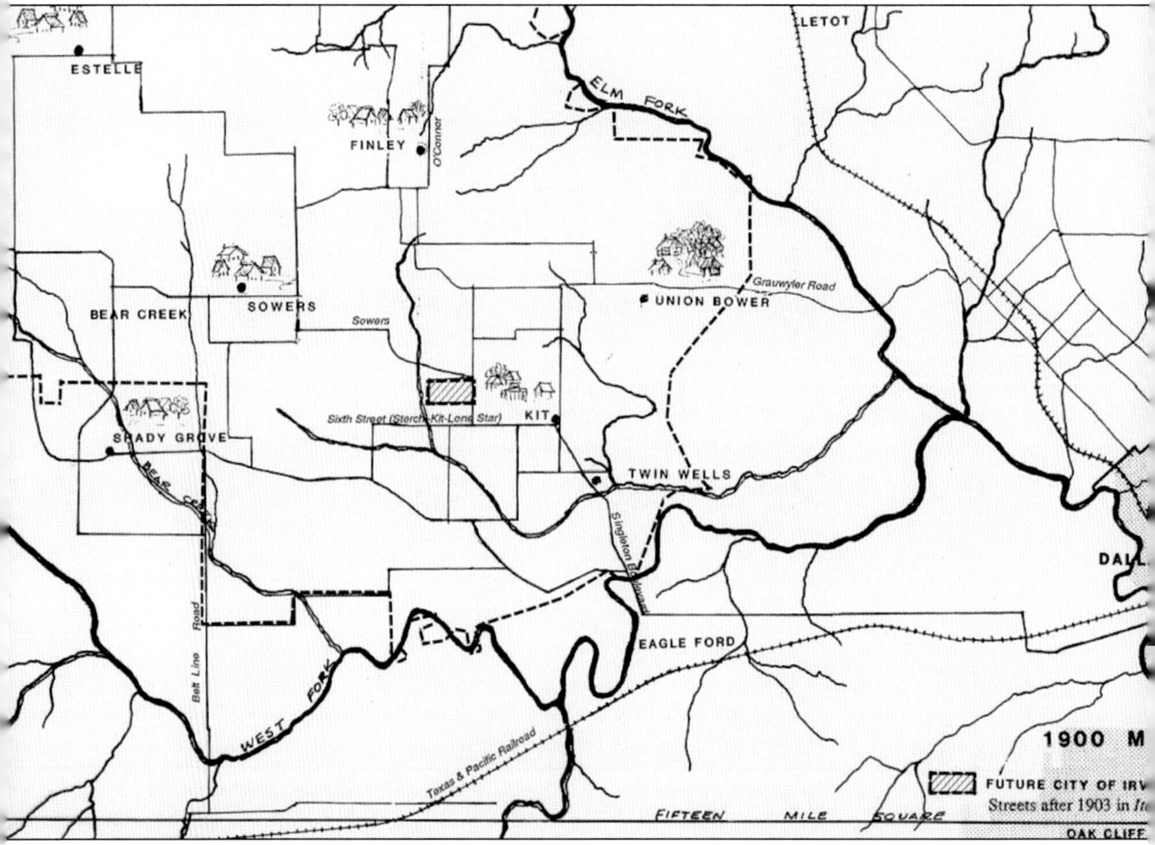

Small farming communities dotted the rolling prairies and wooded hills between the Elm Fork and the West Fork of the Trinity River during the last half of the 1800s. Settlers came into the region in the 1850s, and by 1857, Hezekiah Lucas had established the first post office at Buck and Breck, a hamlet between Dallas and Tarrant County. Shown in this 1900 map are the communities of Kit, Union Bower, Twin Wells, Sowers, Bear Creek, Elm, and Estelle before the establishment of the city of Irving. (Courtesy of Irving Archives, Irving Public Library.)

On the Cover: In 1902, J.O. Schulze, Otis Brown, and a survey crew from the Chicago, Rock Island & Gulf Railway arrived in Dallas County via horse-drawn carriages to survey the land for a railroad line from Fort Worth to Dallas. (Courtesy of Irving Archives, Irving Public Library.)

IMAGES
of America

IRVING

Roxanne Del Rio

ARCADIA
PUBLISHING

ISBN 978-1-4671-1608-4

Published by Arcadia Publishing
Charleston, South Carolina

Printed in the United States of America

Library of Congress Control Number: 2016937169

For all general information, please contact Arcadia Publishing:
Telephone 843-853-2070
Fax 843-853-0044
E-mail sales@arcadiapublishing.com
For customer service and orders:
Toll-Free 1-888-313-2665

Visit us on the Internet at www.arcadiapublishing.com

This book is dedicated to the early settlers and pioneers who set out to make a better place for themselves, their families, and others; to the dedicated residents of Irving who worked together to build communities that made this city a success; to my dear friend Julie A. Allan, a longtime educator and nurse who continues to inspire and mentor me and without whose contributions this book would not have been possible; and finally, to my husband, Pieter Vermeulen, who I thank for encouraging and inspiring me to continue writing.

Contents

ACKNOWLEDGMENTS

The Irving Archives of the Irving Public Library, the LIZ Gillispie Genealogy Department Corsicana Public Library, and the Irving Heritage Society were invaluable to this project, especially their volunteers who have contributed to the preservation of the history of Irving. I wish to thank Kevin Kendro from the Irving Archives and Dana Stubbs from the LIZ Gillispie Genealogy Department Corsicana Public Library, both of whom graciously granted permission to reproduce the images used in this book. In addition to photographs, the Irving Archives offered a bonanza of fascinating stories and information about the communities that developed the city of Irving. Unless otherwise noted, all images are courtesy of the Irving Archives, Irving Public Library.

I also wish to thank historians Norma Stanton and Joseph Rice, whose earlier work about the history of Irving served as a major foundation for this book.

Introduction

In the 16th century, Spanish settlers began their journey to the new world, known as Spanish America, in search of gold and silver. These settlers came from Spain to settle in Mexico. They would lay claim to land occupied by the American Indians. In the 17th century, Texas was known as the Spanish Southwest. By the 18th century, the Spanish settlers had established outposts in Texas and continued to fight with the Indians over the territory. The Spanish settlers not only brought with them their religious beliefs but their business savvy as well. Having learned about the importance of lucrative land grant ownership from their country, they soon sold the idea to the government of Texas. Mexico contracted with agents to find settlers to occupy specific tracts of land. The agent received start-up land for the colony. They also surveyed the land, recorded certificates of land ownership, and collected fees. Settlers were offered the opportunity to develop farmland for crops and to provide grazing for cattle. In 1836, Texas won its independence from Mexico and became a republic.

In 1841, the Texas Emigration and Land Company was contracted by the Republic of Texas to bring settlers to a 1,300-square-mile area known as Dallas County. Part of this county would become Irving, Texas. War with the Indians continued. This unrest caused a number of those who had come to settle in this area to return to their former homes. In 1842, Sam Houston, president of the republic, met with Indian tribal leaders on the frontiers of Texas at Fort Bird and negotiated the Bird Fort Treaty. The terms of the 1843 treaty included peace and friendship between nine tribes and the republic of Texas. In 1845, Texas joined the United States as the 28th state.

Transportation began to change with the evolution of the railroad system, and there was interest in connecting Texas to other parts of the United States. Business leaders of this time knew the potential financial effect that railroads would have on commerce, and in 1854, the general land grant law was signed, offering 16 sections of land per mile of track.

The Civil War was about to impact the citizens of Texas. In 1861, Texas joined the Confederacy. Only one in four Texas families owned slaves. Texas men immediately joined the war effort, traveling east to fight with Confederate soldiers. Other men stayed in Texas, defending the coastline and guarding against possible attacks by the Union. During the war, the Confederate government set up commissary headquarters in Dallas County, where food and supplies were collected for the soldiers. In addition, historian John Cochran reported that the nearby city of Lancaster housed a manufacturing company to fabricate weapons and repair artillery.

The war brought hardships for Texans, and traffic through the state's major port at Galveston was halted by the Union until 1862. Texas continued to experience trade barriers. Imports of goods from northern factories stopped, and transportation systems were impaired, which made it very difficult for cotton growers to export their crops. Trade agreements between Texas and Mexico provided some relief; however, without the major trade networks, the communities of Texas suffered from various shortages. Many settlers from other parts of the country traveled to Texas as refugees, bringing their slaves with them.

While the effects of the Civil War put a strain on Texas, Dallas County was hardly affected, with only the disruption of mail service to its communities.

When the Civil War ended on June 19, 1865, Texas became part of the Union, and all slaves were emancipated.

Texas conflicts with American Indians ceased during the Civil War years. However, several Indian wars took place in other states. In 1874, the Red River War forced the tribes off their land in Texas. Many of the Indians and leaders died during these battles, and those who survived were imprisoned or surrendered.

In 1872, the Houston & Texas Central Railroad passed through Dallas County, and by 1900, the city of Dallas had become a railroad hub serving seven railroads, including Irving. Even though the new railroad lines had been established and the industrial revolution grew within the state, Irving remained a largely agrarian-based city.

In 1903, J.O. Schulze, engineer, and Otis Brown, rodman, of the Chicago, Rock Island & Gulf Railway survey team, were contracted to survey land for a railroad system that would connect Dallas and Fort Worth. As they made their way to Texas, Schulze and Brown began to think about the possibility of establishing a town in this area. They purchased settlements that had survived until the turn of the century. These communities included Kit, Sowers, Hackberry, Union Bower, Finley, Estelle, and Elm. As Irving was established, wise businessmen Schulze and Brown began to donate land that would lay the foundation for the new town. They donated a strip of land that would be used as a depot and switching yard, along with streets and alleys. They also donated land to construct a Church of Christ, a Catholic church, and a Baptist church.

At the outbreak of World War I, Irving had been in existence for almost 11 years. German immigrants came to this area. Much of the German community lived on what is now Beltline Road. According to historian Joseph Rice, Irving did not experience a lot of racial or ethnic tensions during this time. Most residents tolerated each other regardless of where they came from. With the production of cotton by the Davis Gin and the Lively Gin, many Irvingites survived the financial effects of the war by selling cotton to the surrounding communities and cities.

The crash of Wall Street and the Great Depression also affected the citizens of Irving. Kevin Kendro, archivist for the city of Irving, shared his findings of how these events affected Irvingites. In the 1930s, Irving was a small farm town with a population of 1,528. Although Irvingites struggled economically, many of the town's residents lived on small farms and cultivated fruits and vegetables or chickens and cows. Those who did not live on farms made friends with their farming neighbors, who shared their crops with them, often using a bartering system. Since Irving was close to the tributaries and the Trinity River, many residents also fished to supplement their diets.

Farmers during this time supplemented their income by working in the local gravel pits or at the factories and warehouses in Cement City and West Dallas.

The hard times of the 1930s also saw the rise of bank robbers and gangsters. Among them, Bonnie and Clyde were notorious bandits who came from West Dallas, just down the road from Irving. The duo was known to travel along Shady Grove Road, which was out in the country at that time, and find secluded places to meet with their family members. They were also involved in a shoot-out with sheriff's deputies near what is now Esters Road and Highway 183. Their car was badly shot up, but the couple escaped through the back roads into Oak Cliff, where they stole a car and continued their getaway.

Throughout the hard times, the city of Irving continued to progress. Bus service from Irving to Dallas was established in 1930, a new high school building was constructed in 1936, and the town hired a town secretary, its first full-time employee, in 1939. Local businessman Hans Smith opened a movie theater on Main Street in 1933 that showed first-run movies six nights a week and a matinee on Saturdays.

Most of Irving's residents were not particularly well-off even in good times, and the decade of the Great Depression made meager incomes even tighter, but as some Irvingites from the time said, "We had food and we were all equally poor, so we didn't know we were poor."

In 1939, Germany invaded Poland, and World War II began. Many young Irvingites enlisted to serve. Civilian residents supported the war effort by working at North American Aviation, an airplane manufacturing company built near Irving in Grand Prairie just after the war began. This plant built the AT-6 Texan, the B-24 Liberator, and the P-51 Mustang.

Throughout the short history of Irving, communities were established around an integrated belief system based on various characteristics, such as origin of birth, religion, beliefs, and color. Irving became a thriving city of the South.

One

Tributaries of Dallas County Prior to 1900

Early settlers referred to western Dallas County as "the three forks region" because of the three major tributaries, which are streams of water that empty into a river. Two of the forks, Elm and West, merged in northwest Dallas County, forming the Trinity River. The West Fork converged in Wise and Tarrant Counties before moving into northwest Dallas County. The Elm Fork begins in Montague County and flows south into western Dallas County.

Settlers began moving into the area during the 1850s. The city of Irving was established between the West and Elm Forks of the Trinity River. During the second half of the 19th century, more settlers arrived and began small farming communities throughout the town. The communities were Bear Creek, Elm, Estelle, Kit, Sowers, Twin Wells, and Union Bower.

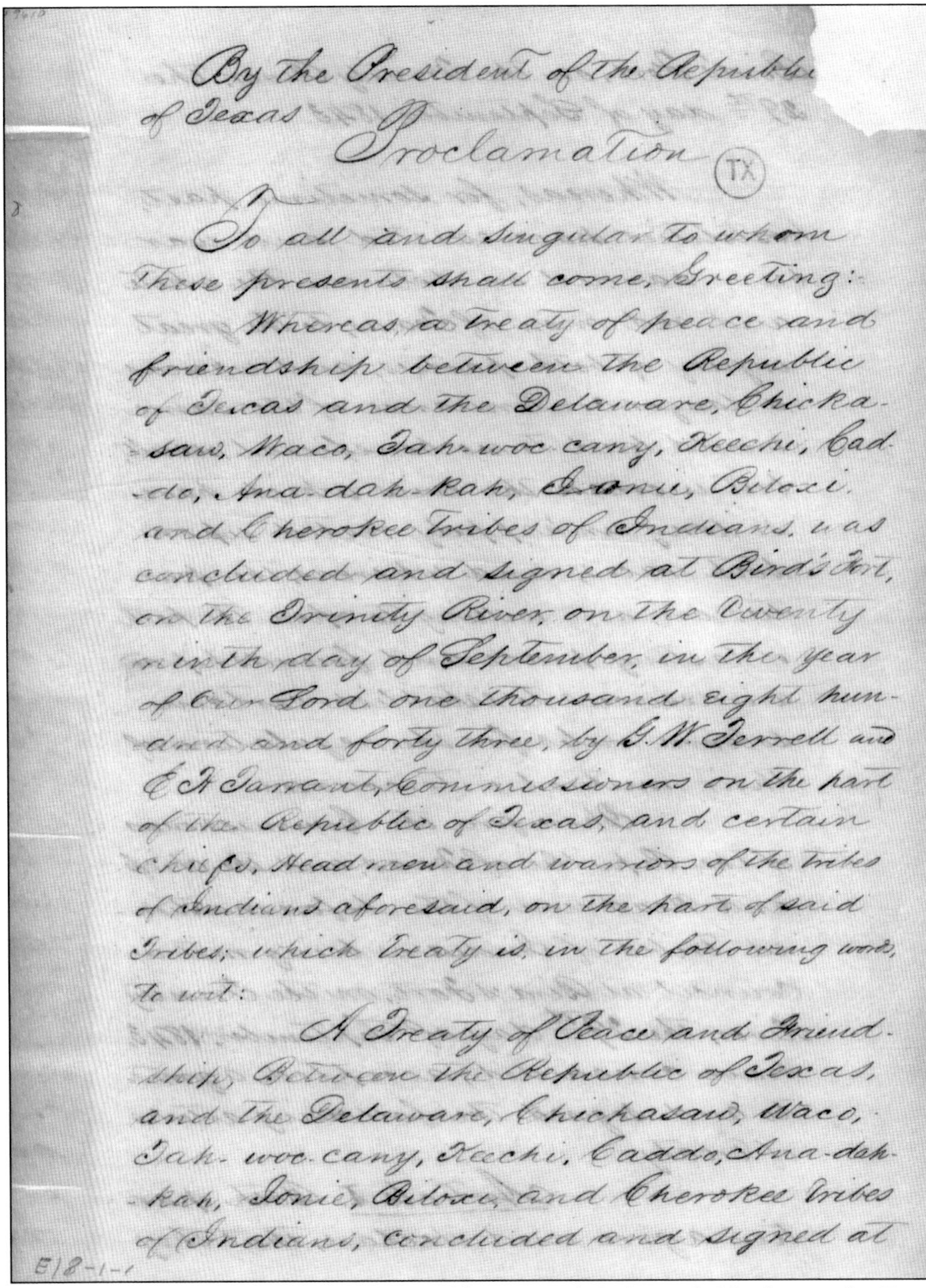

By the President of the Republic of Texas

Proclamation

To all and singular to whom these presents shall come, Greeting:

Whereas, a treaty of peace and friendship between the Republic of Texas and the Delaware, Chickasaw, Waco, Tah-woc-cany, Keechi, Caddo, Ana-dah-kah, Ionie, Biloxi, and Cherokee Tribes of Indians, was concluded and signed at Bird's Fort, on the Trinity River, on the twenty ninth day of September, in the year of Our Lord one thousand eight hundred and forty three, by G. W. Terrell and E. H. Tarrant, Commissioners on the part of the Republic of Texas, and certain chiefs, Head men and warriors of the tribes of Indians aforesaid, on the part of said Tribes; which Treaty is, in the following words, to wit:

A Treaty of Peace and Friendship, Between the Republic of Texas, and the Delaware, Chickasaw, Waco, Tah-woc-cany, Keechi, Caddo, Ana-dah-kah, Ionie, Biloxi, and Cherokee Tribes of Indians, concluded and signed at

In 1842, Sam Houston, president of the republic, met with Indian tribal leaders on the Texas frontiers at Fort Bird and negotiated the Bird Fort Treaty. The terms of the treaty, signed in 1843, included peace and friendship between the republic of Texas and nine tribes: Chickasaw, Waco, Tiwocano, Keechie, Caddo, Anadaka, Ionie, Biloxie, and Cherokee. Indians camped at California, crossing on the Elm Fork of the Trinity River. They often traveled to this area along the Trinity River to hunt game and fish. Pictured here is the first page of the Bird Fort Treaty.

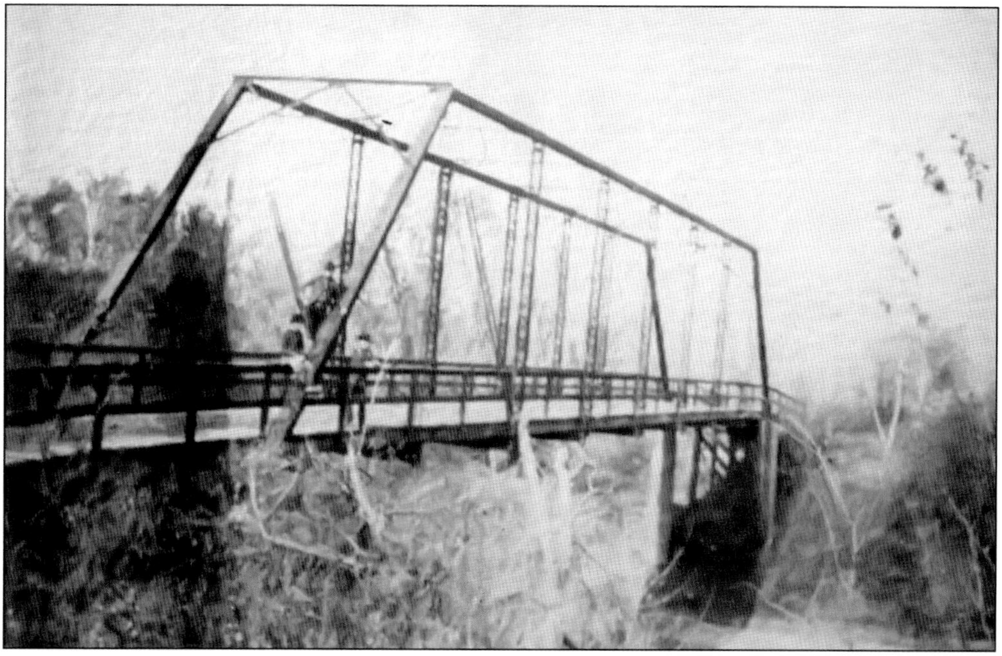

Located northwest of Dallas County, the Eagle Ford Bridge spanned the West Fork of the Trinity River. This bridge served as the major route to the town of Irving. (Courtesy of Portal to Texas History, University of North Texas.)

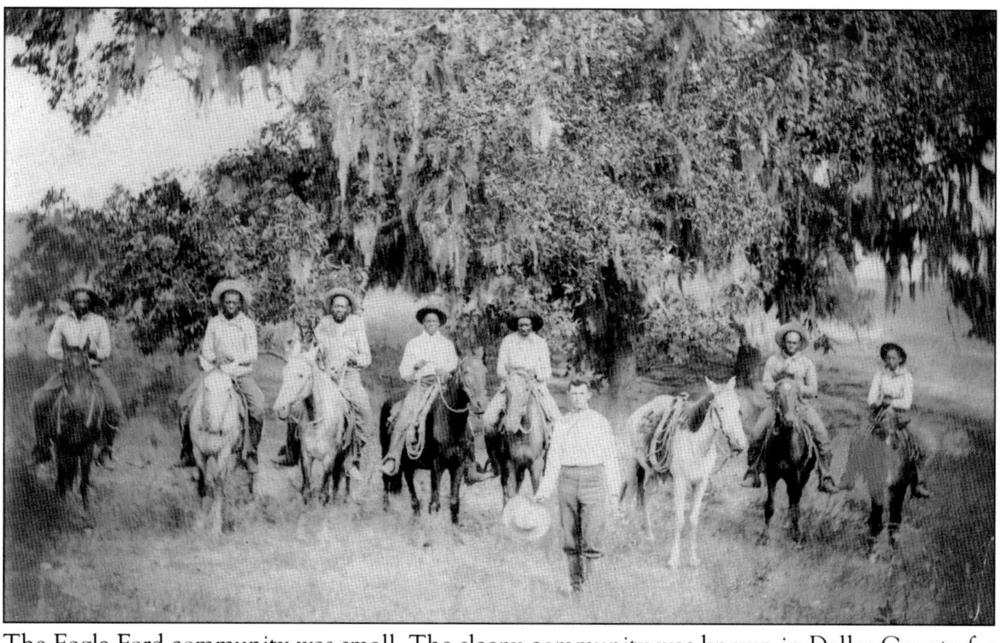

The Eagle Ford community was small. The sleepy community was known in Dallas County for having wild women, gambling, saloons, and gunslingers. The railroad came from Dallas with plans to expand to Fort Worth; however, construction came to a halt at Eagle Ford, creating a rail terminus. This terminus attracted a number of travelers, making this a popular community. When the Texas & Pacific Railway came to town, the terminus went away, and Eagle Ford went back to its quiet roots.

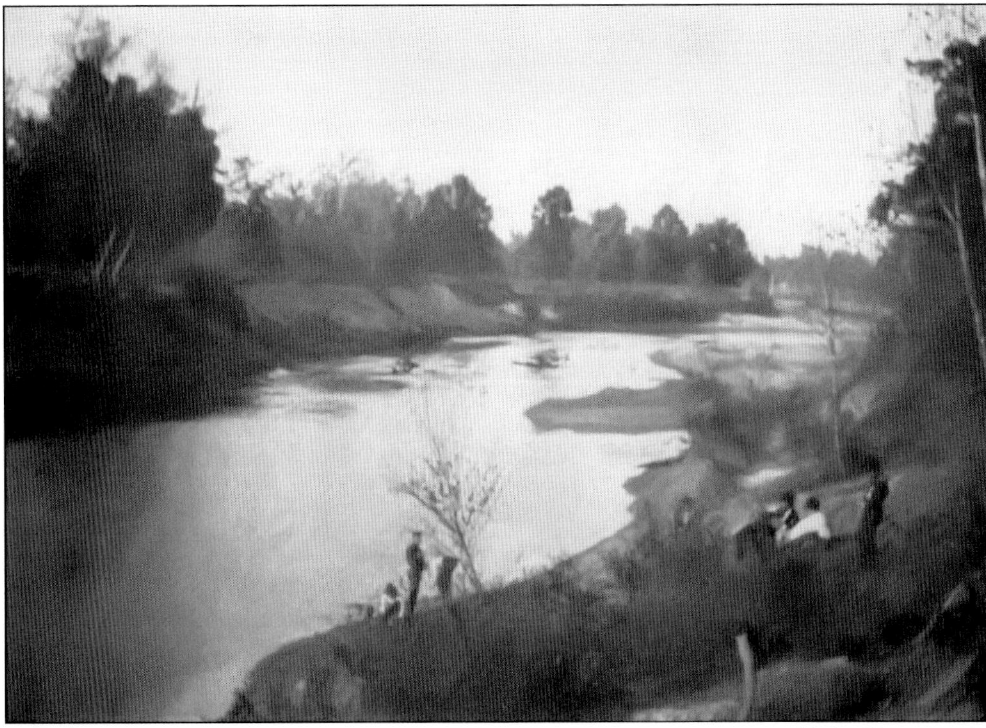

This photograph is titled "Sunday afternoon at the Trinity River." Irving was established between the West Fork and the Elm Fork that converged to form the Trinity River. Many local residents enjoyed day and weekend trips camping at various sites along Trinity River, as seen here in 1910.

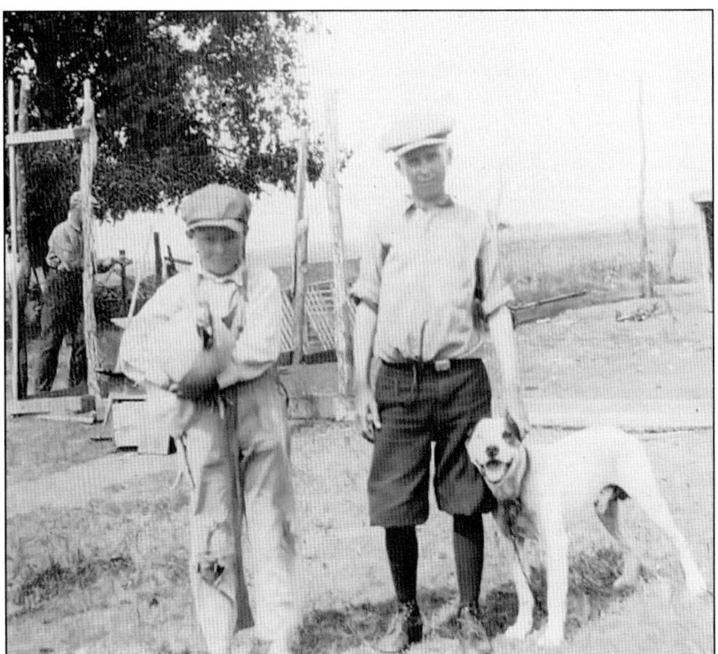

Raising poultry was common during this time. Children often adopted the chickens as pets until it was time to relinquish them to the dinner table. Farming communities ensured that these pets were fed and protected from the wild. Tommie Evans is pictured holding his prize-winning chicken.

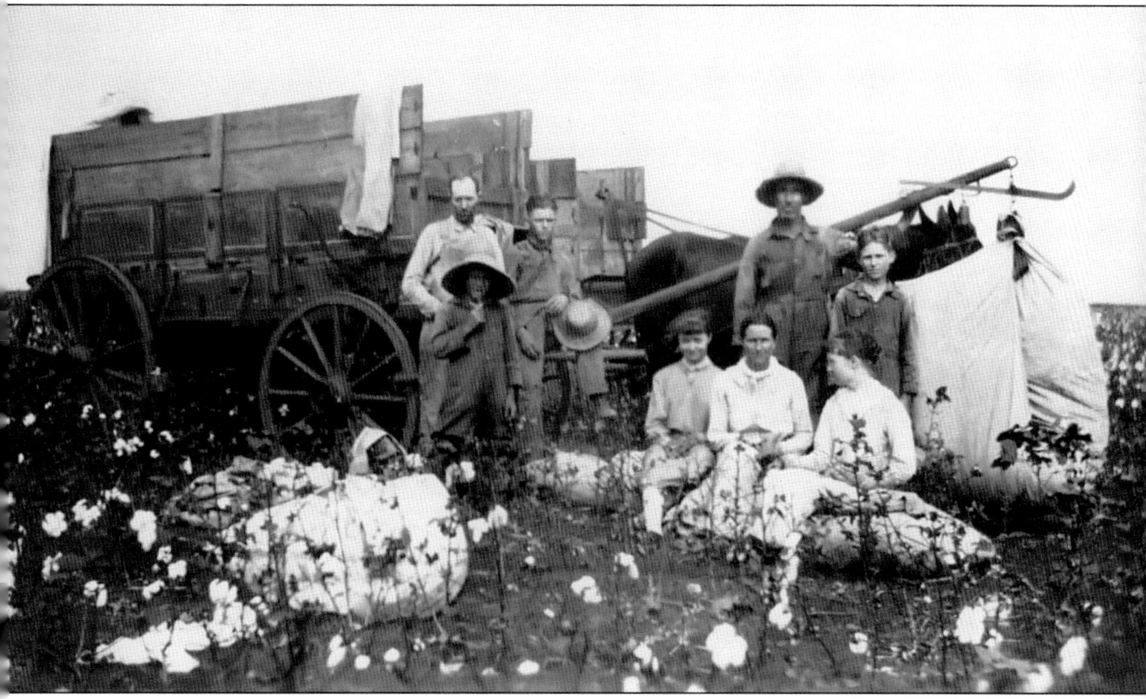

Cotton and wheat were important crops for many pioneer families in the Kit community. Families picked cotton on their farms and sold it in Dallas, recognized as the world's largest inland cotton market. Farmers could find hired hands for a dollar a day. Pictured here are cotton farmers in the Kit community. Cotton was the cash crop of the community.

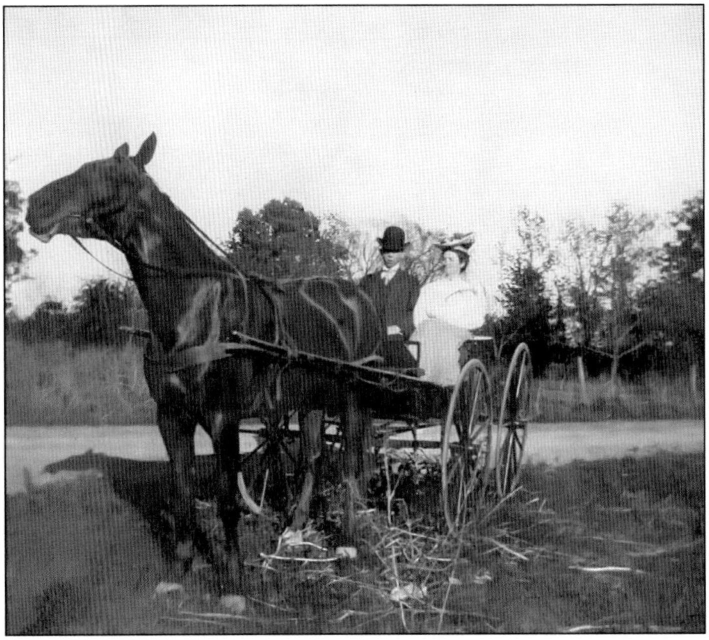

Horse-drawn vehicles were the main mode of transportation in the 1900s. Pictured here is a man and woman enjoying the scenery as they park on the side of the road in their vehicle.

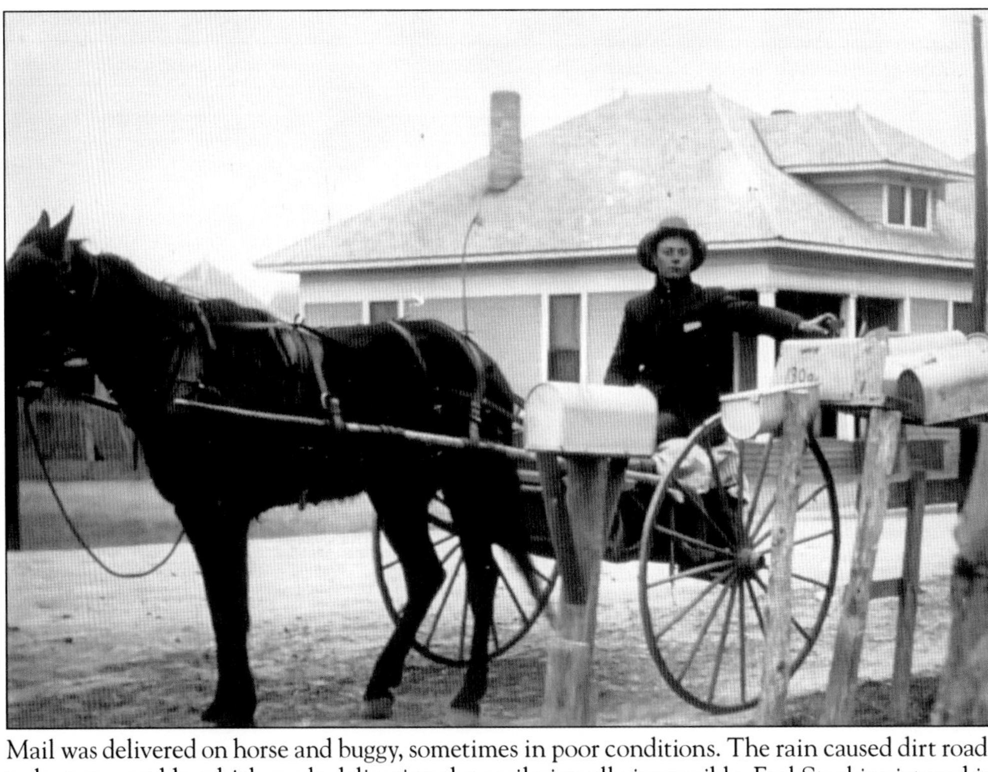

Mail was delivered on horse and buggy, sometimes in poor conditions. The rain caused dirt roads to become muddy, which made delivering the mail virtually impossible. Earl Steel is pictured in his two-wheel mail buggy.

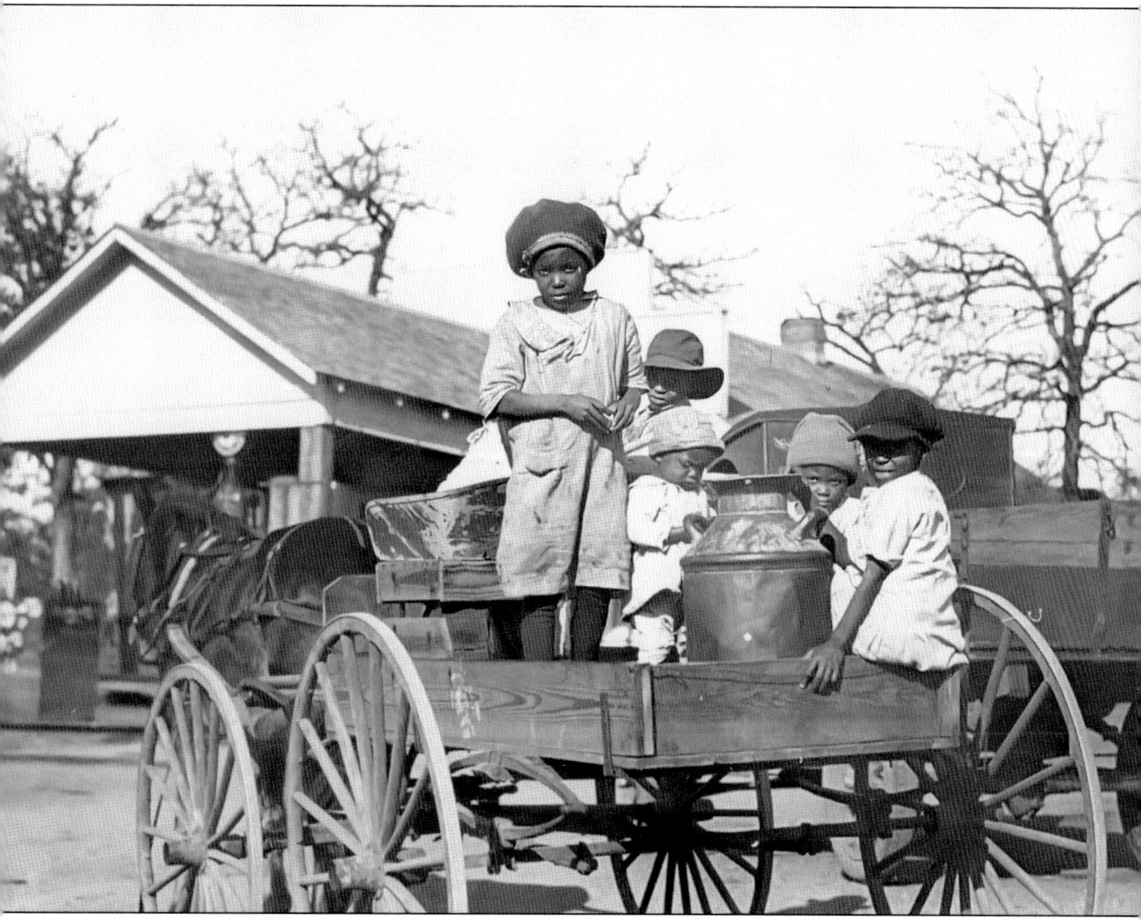

Freed slaves established Bear Creek in 1850, making it one of the oldest black communities in Dallas County. By 1900, nine black landowners had established homesteads in Bear Creek. These families sharecropped and farmed their own land. Bear Creek remained a separate entity from the rest of Irving. During the era of Jim Crow laws and segregation, African American residents settled in this community. Electricity was not available there until the mid-1940s. Among the first black pioneer landowners were Pinky Holmes and Jim Green. Children of Bear Creek are shown here posing on a wagon in 1925. These children played together and went to school together, but they were segregated from the rest of the communities. Members of the Bear Creek community stayed close to their homes during the time of segregation.

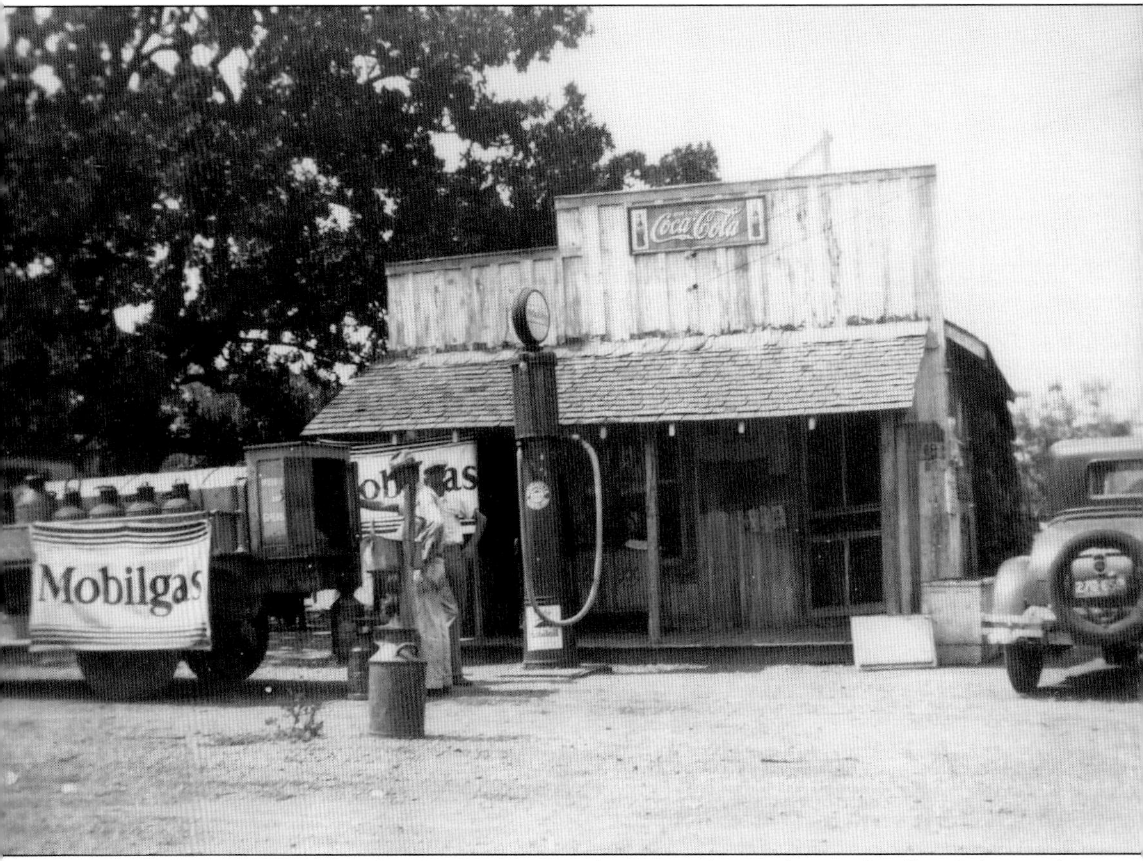

In 1850, settlers arrived in the Elm community, about 12 miles northwest of Dallas. Other settlers came from France and originally immigrated as members of the La Réunion colony, which was located right outside of Union Bower, southeast of Irving near the Elm community. When the colony failed, they moved to the Elm community. Elm farmers raised cotton, hay, dairy, fruits, and vegetables. In 1899, the first post office was established. The Finley Post Office served over 75 families until 1902, when the mail service was discontinued. The Elm community was annexed by the city of Irving in the 1950s. The Elm community store is pictured here in 1905.

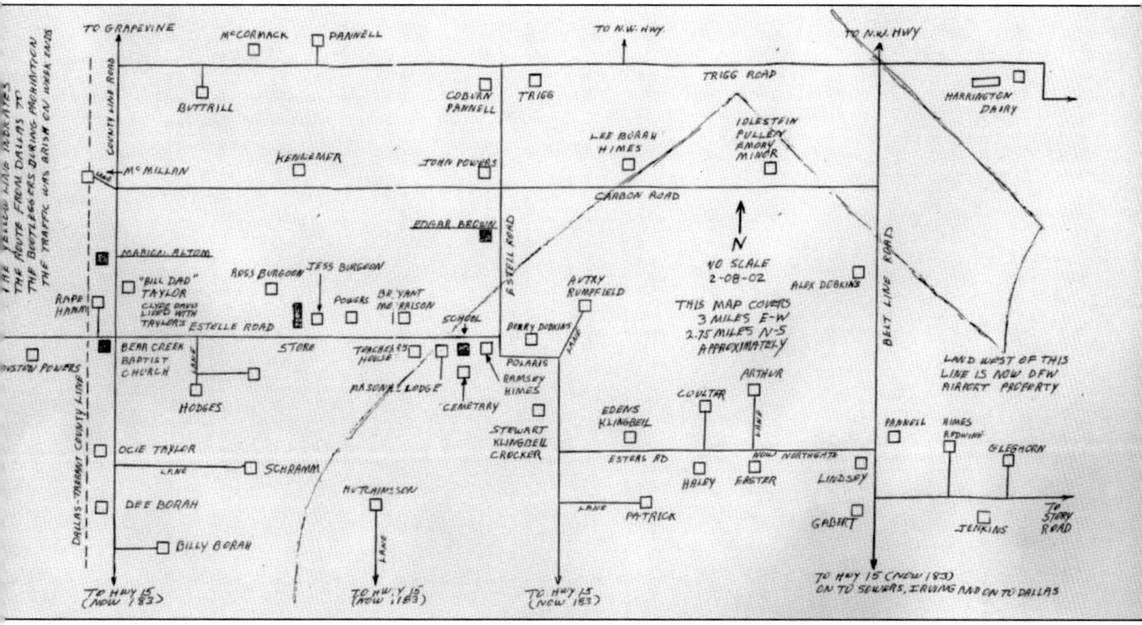

The Estelle community was established in 1881 from a land grant to Henry Burgoon from the State of Texas. Estelle got its name from Burgoon, who decided to call this area Estell after a Grapevine Prairie architect while on a journey between Tarrant and Dallas Counties. As the community was in the beginnings of its establishment, a post office location was requested. However, the US Postal Service misnamed the post office as Estelle rather than Estell, as it was listed on the application. This community was located far northwest of Dallas County. Early Estelle community farmers raised wheat, corn, and cotton, also establishing large farmlands to raise cattle. Pictured here is a map of Estelle.

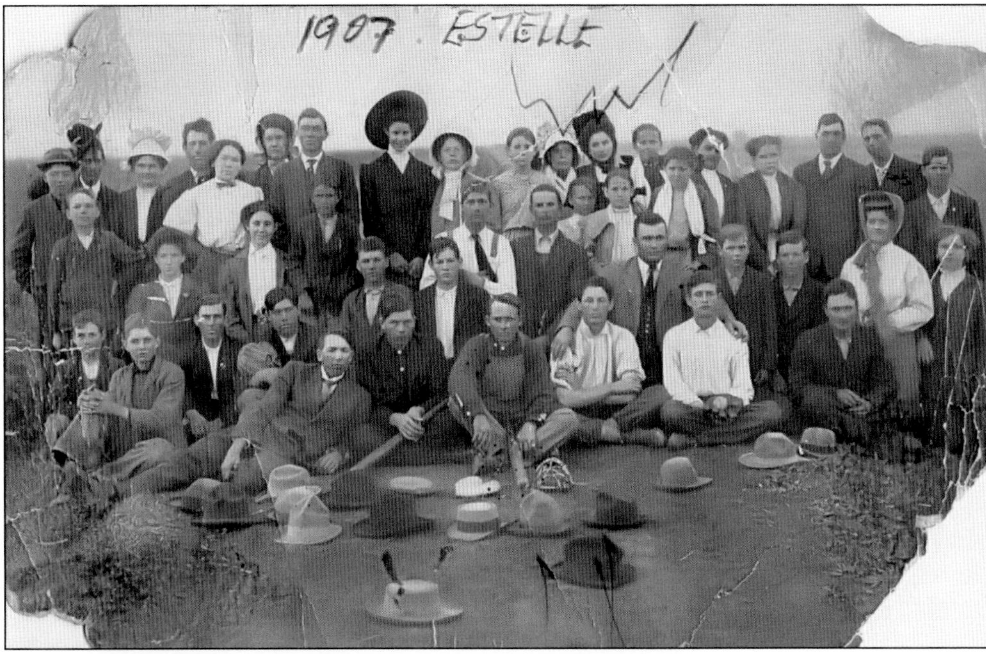

A form of matchmaking took place at this Estelle community picnic in 1907. At this gathering, single young men "threw their hats into the ring." A hat was selected by a single young woman who had prepared a picnic lunch that was shared with the lucky owner of the hat.

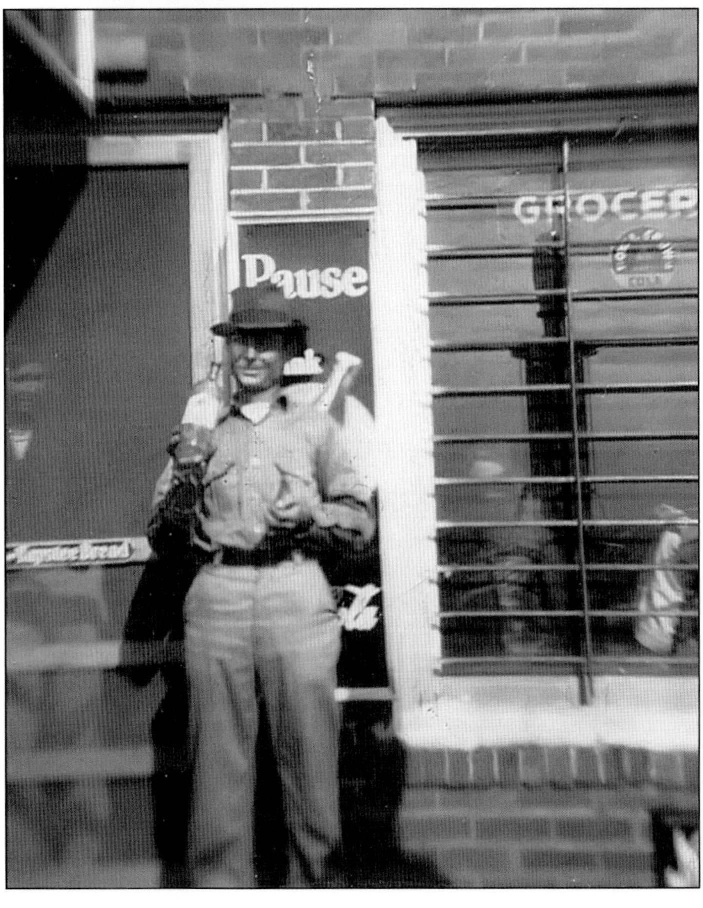

Each community provided conveniences such as a general store, post office, and specialty shops to its residents to ensure that they would frequent their community center. Pictured here is a local resident standing in front of a store in the Estelle community.

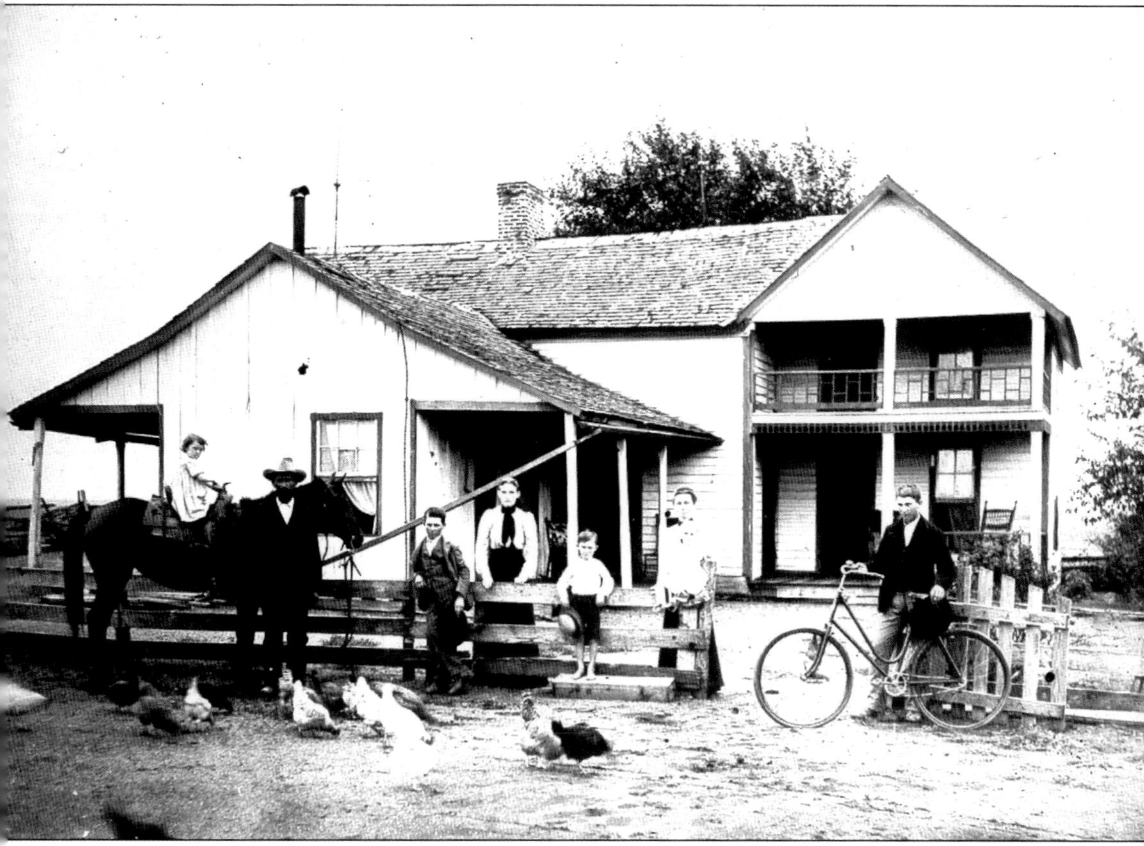

The settlers of the Kit community farmed and sold cordwood. Their farmland was generally named after the settlers who had occupied the area. This land was conducive to growing oak trees, pecans, fruits, and vegetables. The farmers provided Dallas County with produce during the early decades of the 20th century. Pictured here is Jacob Good and family.

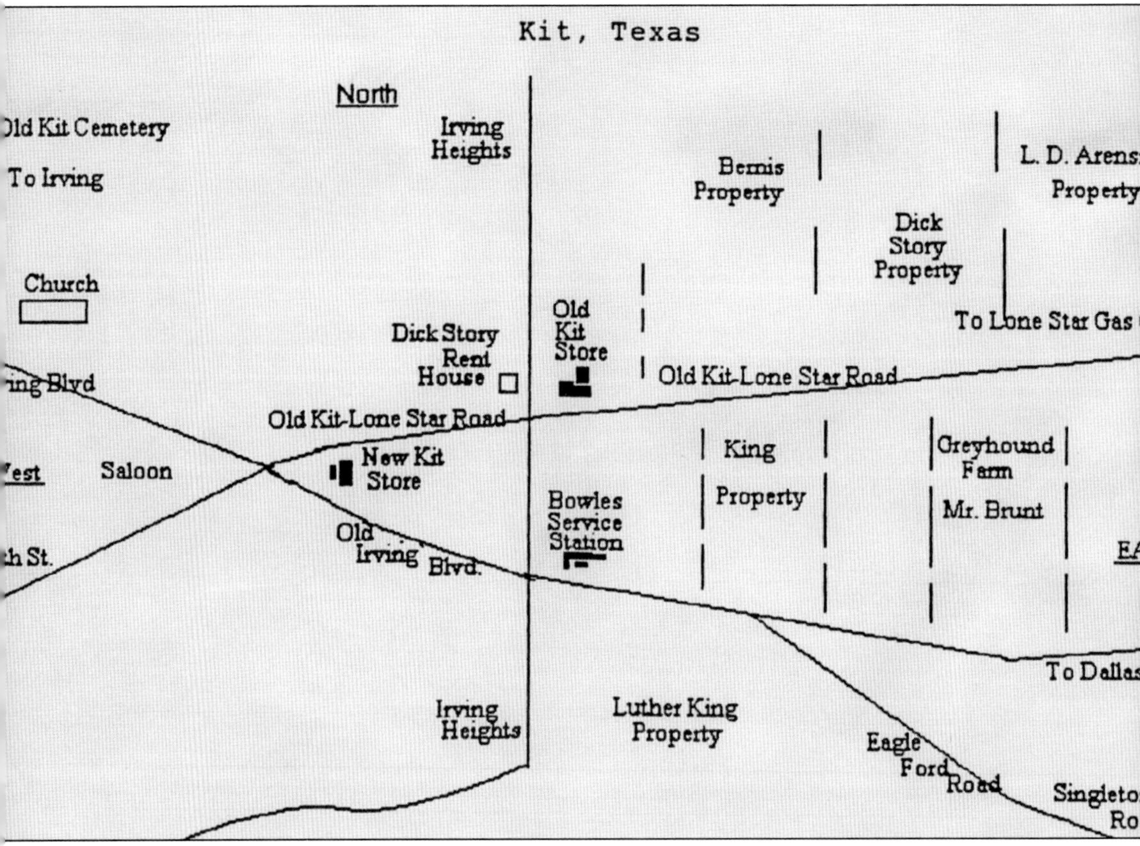

In the fall of 1855, Jonathan Story purchased land on the north side of the West Fork and west of the Elm Fork of the river and named it the Kit community. This map was drawn in the 1950s by a man who was reflecting back to how the community looked during his childhood.

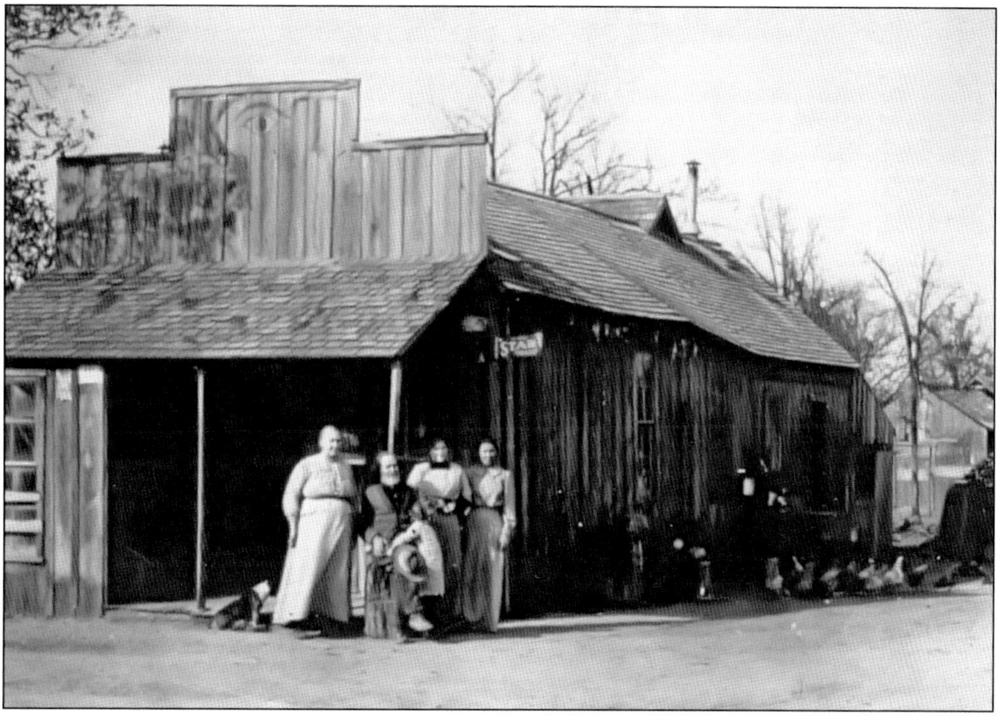

The town of Irving was founded one mile west of the Kit store. The Kit community was named by Ike Story, who ran the general store pictured here. He applied to get a post office at his store and needed a name for it, and chose Kit, the name of one of his great aunts. Story used a drawing of an eye in place of the letter "i" in the spelling of Kit, as pictured here on the storefront. The store served as the social gathering place for the community. In 1904, the post office was moved from Kit to Irving. Ike Story is shown sitting with his wife, Nancy, at left and Lillie and Opal Kinney at right in 1894. Sallie Bell is the child in front of the two women next to Ike.

In 1883, William DeHaes emigrated from Belgium in search of a better life and settled in northwest Dallas County, which would later become the city of Irving. He built the first brick home in the area. Historian Norma Stanton records that this home was used as a gathering place to host parties, picnics, and other social events. The DeHaes family is shown here in front of their home.

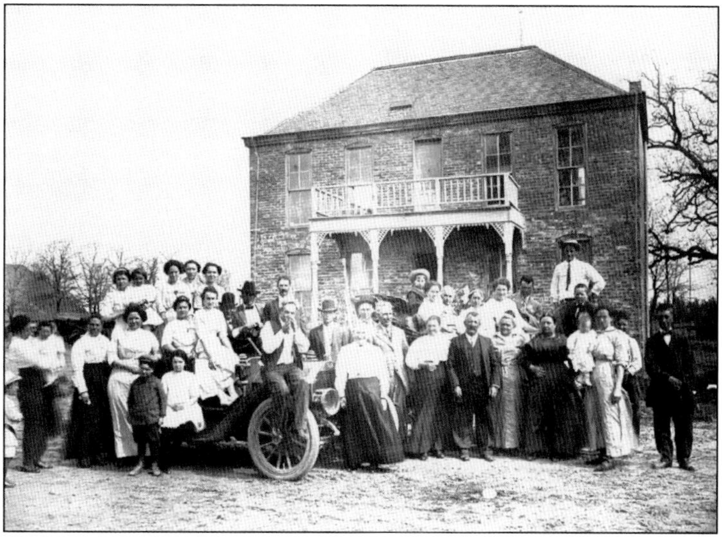

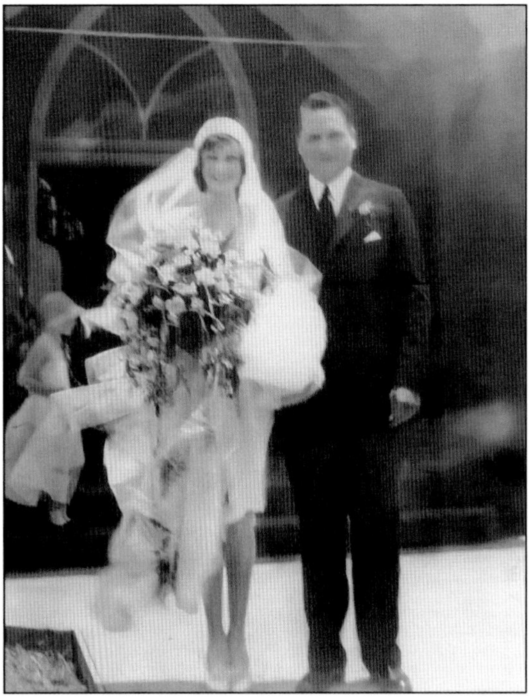

At left is the marriage portrait of Louis DeHaes and his bride, Laura. This was the first wedding ceremony to take place in the newly constructed St. Luke Catholic Church on Iowa Street, which is now O'Connor Road. This photograph was taken in 1929.

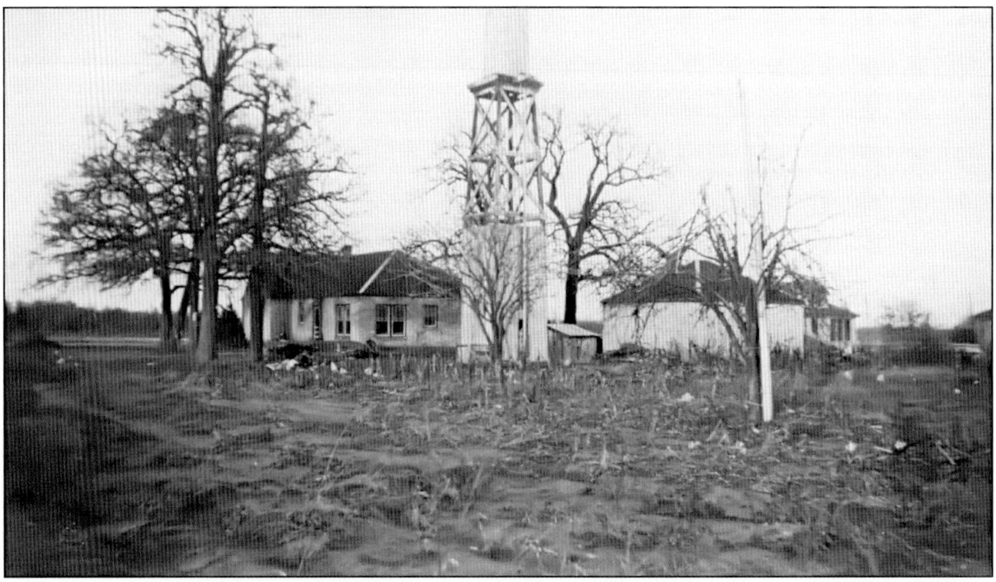

Early settlers farmed this area before it was established as Sowers community in 1856. It was named after Edmund D. Sowers, owner of the land at the time. Sowers was in the northwest part of Dallas County, about 12 miles west of the city of Dallas. In 1870, Edmund Sowers opened a general store, and in 1881, a post office was established in his store. Also during this time, a blacksmith shop, drugstore, doctor's office, and a school were built for the Sowers community, which became the largest unincorporated establishment between the forks during the second half of the 19th century, as well as a place where several dairy farms and poultry businesses successfully operated. In 1954, the city of Irving annexed the Sowers community. Pictured here is a typical farmhouse of the Sowers community in 1930.

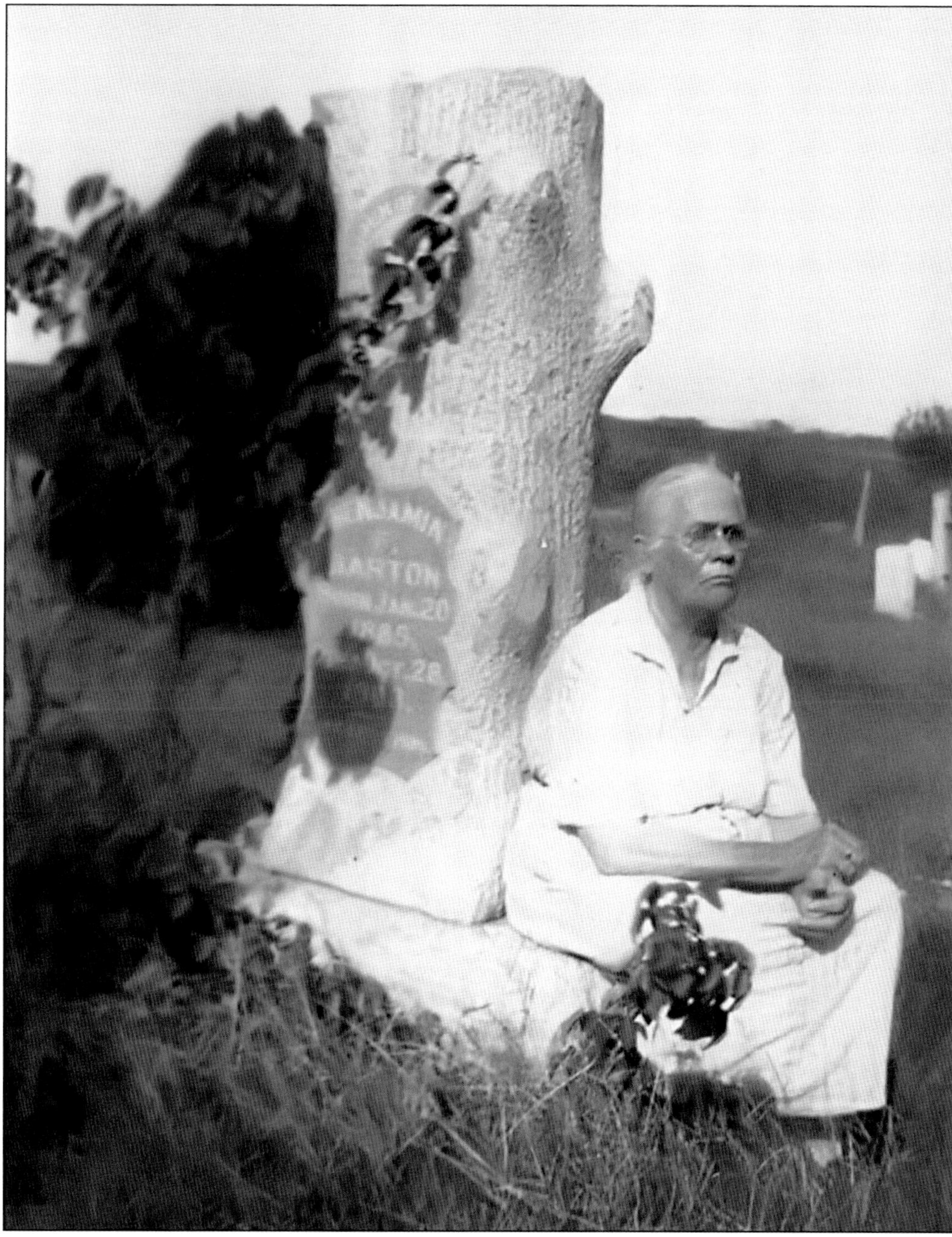

As families began to move into the community, Edmund Sowers donated land for a community cemetery. Sowers was also known to give away individual cemetery plots to community residents. While Irving was growing as an industrial city, Sowers survived as a community until 1950. This community was noted for establishing vibrant dairy and poultry businesses. The Sowers community built a school that was part of the Dallas County Common School District. The school was located along today's Pioneer Drive, near Belt Line Road. The City of Irving annexed the Sowers community in the 1950s, and the school became part of the Irving Independent School District. Today, the Sowers cemetery remains as a remembrance of the Sowers community. Mattie Barton is pictured by her son's headstone.

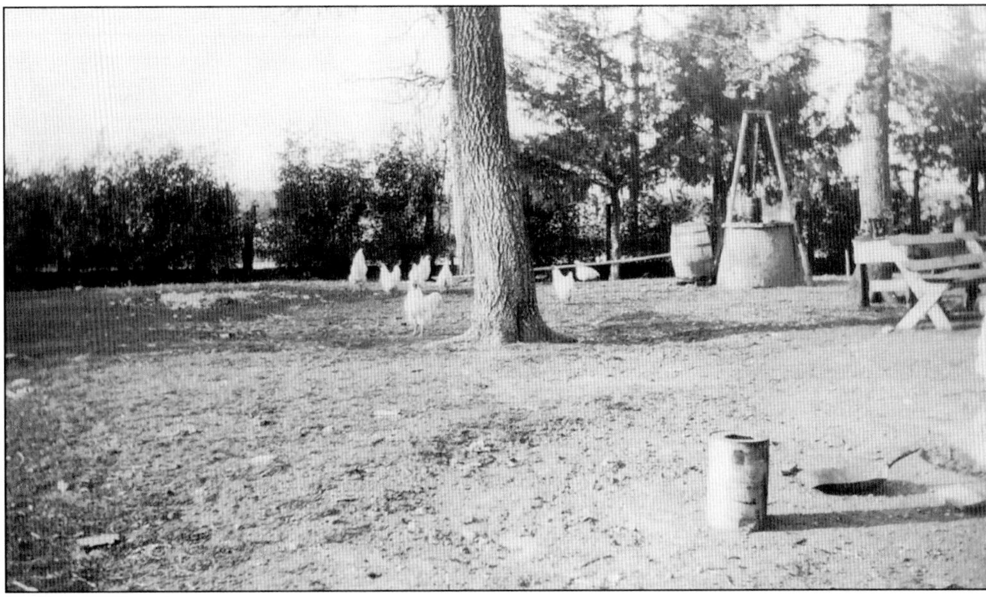

Established in the late 1800s, the Twin Wells community is today's southeastern Irving. Twin Wells was named for two early-day water wells that were built on opposite sides of the Eagle Ford Trail. The Twin Wells community was in northwest Dallas County, about eight miles northwest of downtown Dallas and two miles east of the city of Irving, near the West Fork of the Trinity River. Travelers coming from Dallas crossed the river at the Eagle Ford crossing on the Eagle Ford Trail, later Eagle Ford Road and now Singleton Boulevard.

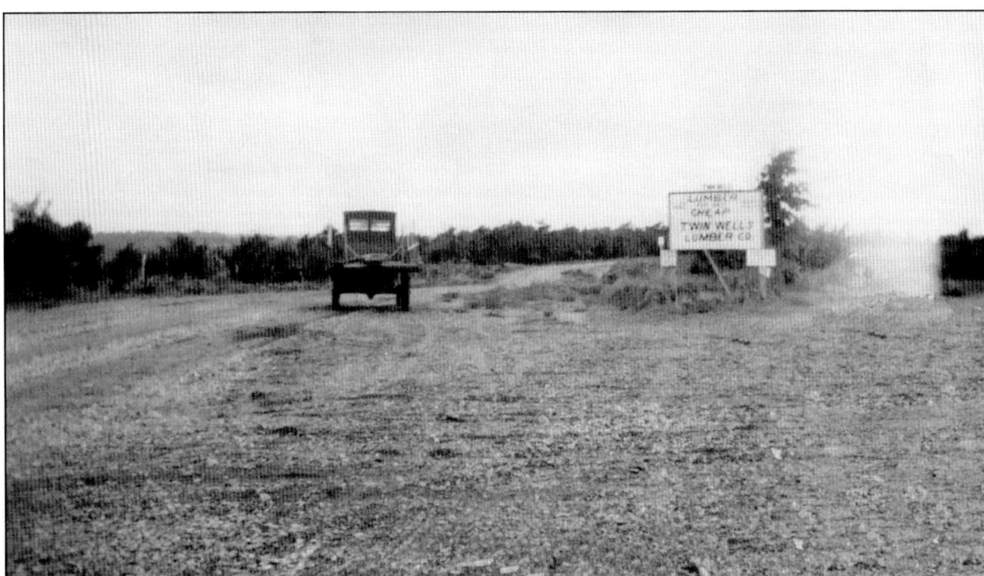

Early settlers traveling west from Dallas on the Eagle Ford Trail, which was established along the bank of the Trinity River, had to cross the West Fork of the river in order to continue on the trail. The twin wells provided the thirsty travelers with water along the way.

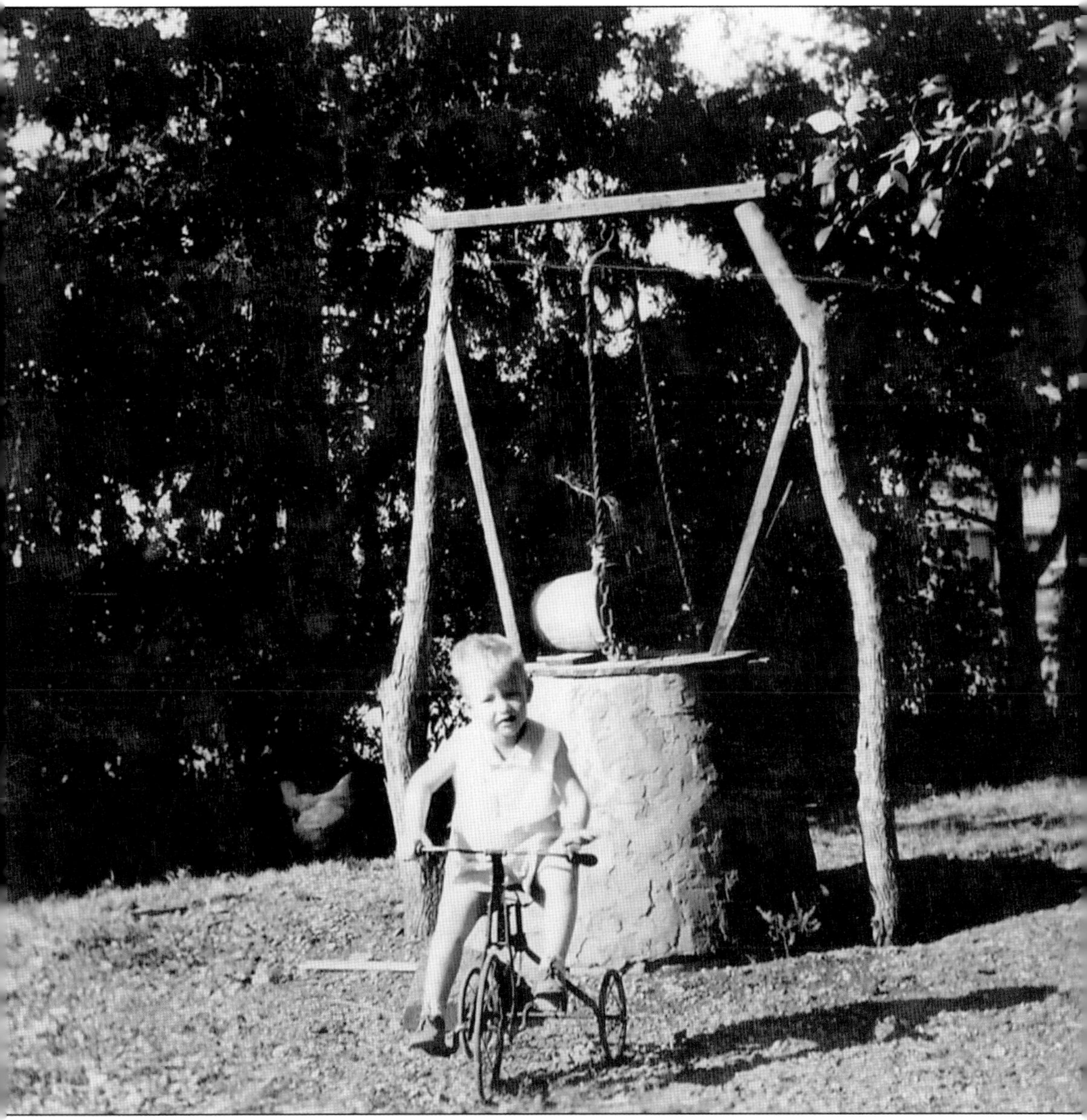

Residents of Twin Wells farmed, maintained dairy herds, and raised poultry. As the population grew, so did business and industry within the community, which included a lumberyard, a general store, and an automobile garage. In 1951, the city of Irving annexed the area. The Twin Wells community lay along the road between Dallas and Irving. Coming from Dallas, travelers crossing West Fork entered the community of Twin Wells, two miles west of the city of Irving. Harwood Hinton is pictured on a tricycle by a cistern at Twin Wells in 1930. (Courtesy the Hinton Family Collection, Irving Archives, Irving Public Library.)

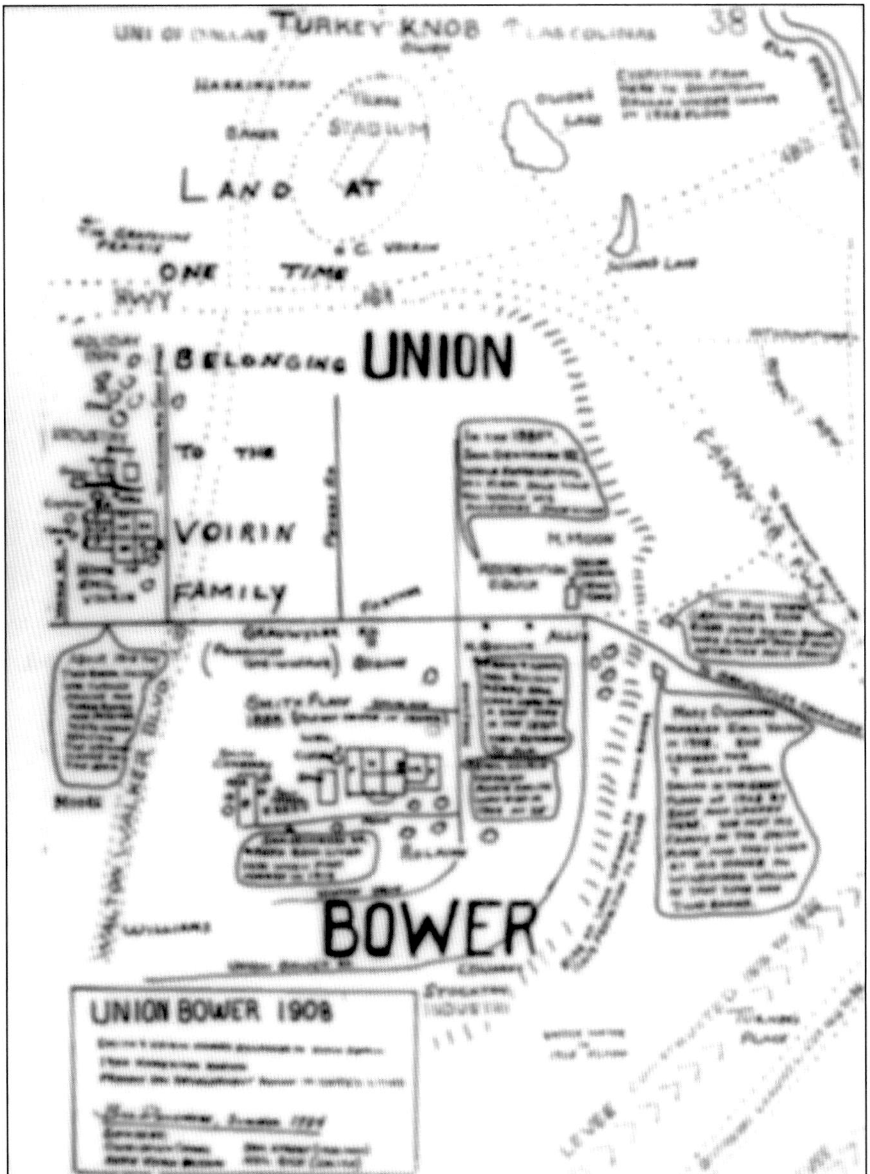

Early immigrants and their families settled in this area to relocate their colony of La Réunion, a utopian socialist community formed in France in 1855 by French, Belgium, and Swiss colonists who advocated communal production and communal distribution to the new immigrants in the United States. These immigrants spoke a different language from the other settlers and brought with them skills that the farmers did not possess, such as watchmaking, weaving, and brewing. However, they lacked the ability to produce food for themselves due to a lack of farming skills and the sometimes uncooperative Texas weather. The colony was located about three miles south of the Union Bower area. By 1859, the colony had failed, and several families moved to the Union Bower community, which had been established along the banks of the Elm Fork of the Trinity River in the mid-19th century. By the mid-20th century, small industry had moved into the community, and the population began to decline. In 1956, the City of Irving annexed the community. Pictured here is a hand-drawn map of the Union Bower community.

The Smith family is pictured in front of their home, relaxing on a cool Sunday in early spring. The Smiths were early settlers to the Union Bower community.

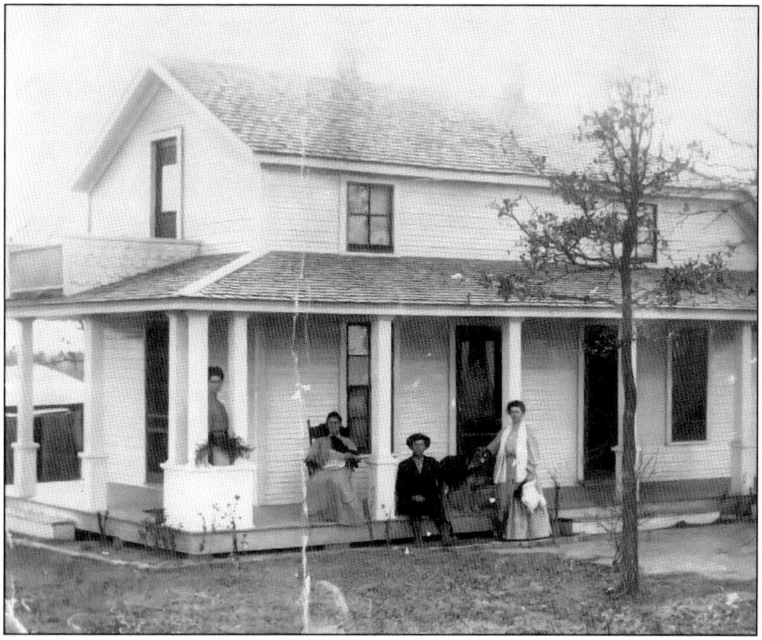

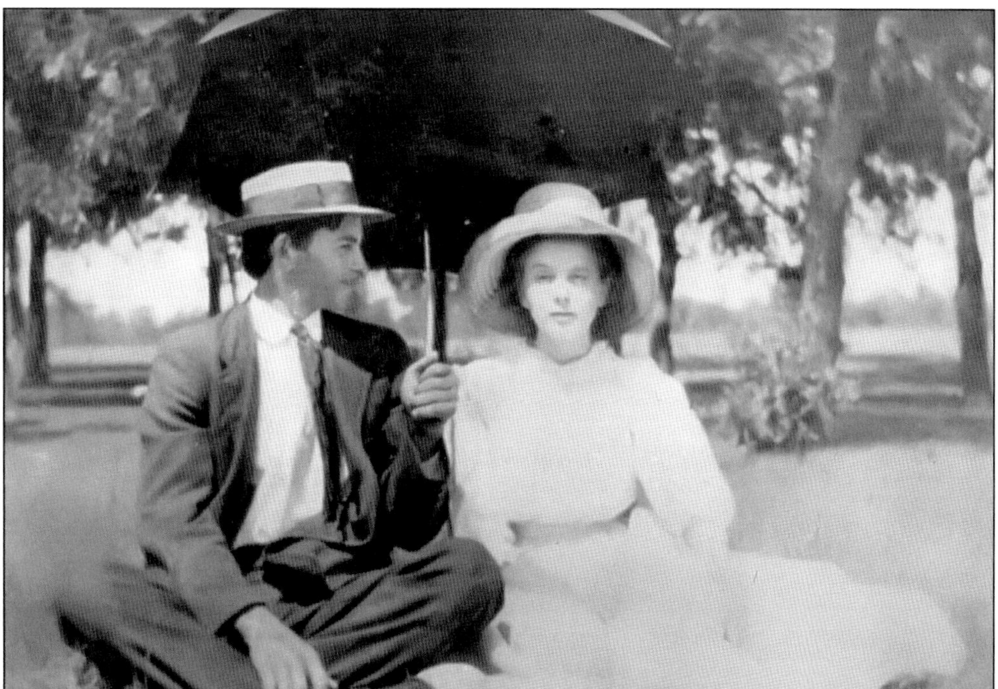

Residents from surrounding communities gathered in Union Bower on occasion for square dancing or picnics. In this photograph taken in 1910, a young couple is seeking shelter from the Texas sun at a Union Bower gathering.

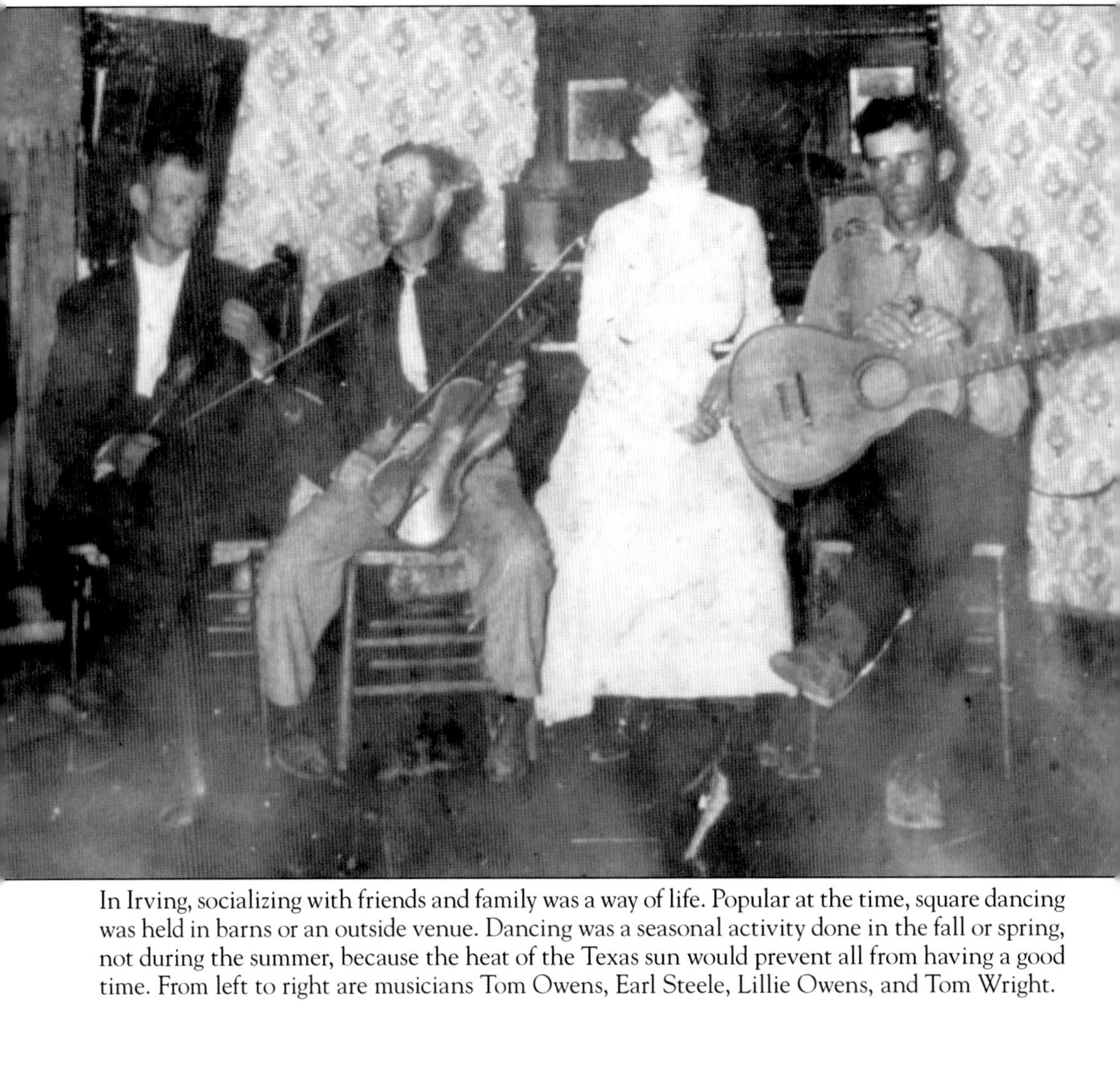

In Irving, socializing with friends and family was a way of life. Popular at the time, square dancing was held in barns or an outside venue. Dancing was a seasonal activity done in the fall or spring, not during the summer, because the heat of the Texas sun would prevent all from having a good time. From left to right are musicians Tom Owens, Earl Steele, Lillie Owens, and Tom Wright.

Two

Influential Founding Pioneers and Their Families

In 1902, J.O. Schulze (born in Iowa City, Iowa, in 1875) and Otis Brown (born in Swan Creek, Ohio, in 1879) were assigned as crew team leaders to survey a 10-mile stretch of land that extended from downtown Dallas, west of today's Valley View Lane. The Chicago, Rock Island & Gulf Railway surveyed this area for a possible railroad line from Fort Worth to Dallas. The survey crew arrived at their destination via wagon in 1902.

A month after the crew began work, Schulze and Brown decided that this area was ideal for establishing a town. Henry W. Britain owned and operated farmland midway within the 10-mile area. Britain offered the survey team camping privileges on his property. The survey team set up their tent, which would become their office and sleeping quarters. Arriving from Virginia by ox wagon in 1859, the Britain family was one of the first pioneers in what would become Irving. Britain sold the right-of-way to the Chicago, Rock Island & Gulf Railway Company for $362.25.

During that same time, Britain sold 80 acres to Schulze and Brown for $2,169.30. This would become the future site of Irving. Citizens of this newly formed town suggested that Irving was the name of a local farmer. According to historians and public records, however, the only farmer with a similar name was John Irby. Other citizens suggested that Schulze and Brown might have had a close friend or crew member with the name of Irving. Later, it was determined that the name was influenced by Otis Brown's fiancée, Netta Barcus, as her favorite author was Washington Irving. Several established communities survived and were bought to develop sections of Irving. Surviving communities include Bear Creek, Elm, Estelle, Kit, Sowers, Twin Wells, and Union Bower. Johann Jacob Grauwlyer was elected to oversee roads in Dallas County, including those in Irving. In 1914, Irving's citizens voted 27 to 16 to incorporate the town. Now the city could elect officials and pass ordinances.

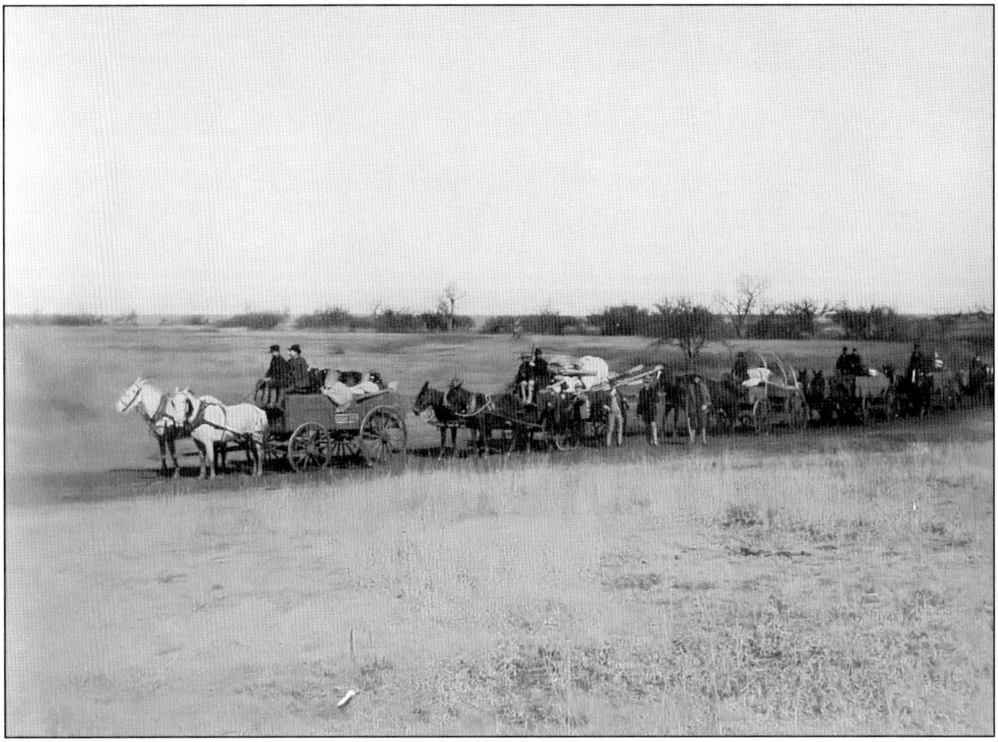

In 1902, J.O. Schulze, Otis Brown, and a survey crew from the Chicago, Rock Island & Gulf Railway arrived in Dallas County via horse-drawn carriages to survey the land for a railroad line from Fort Worth to Dallas. The crew, shown below posing for a picture, pitched tents at the corner of Henry W. Britain's Ranch.

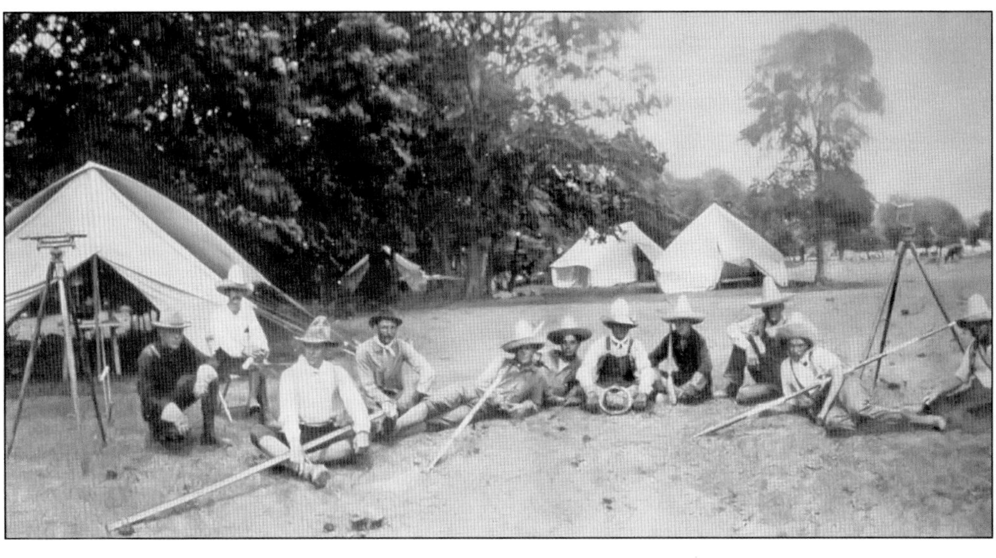

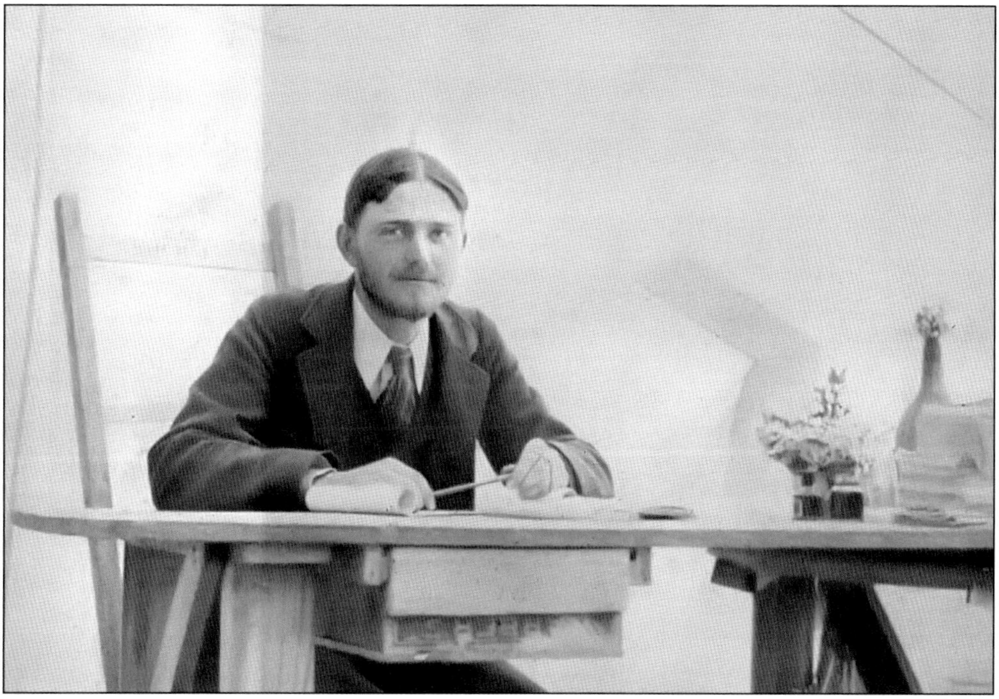

J.O. Schulze sits at the crew chief desk in his tent, which was used as both office space and sleeping quarters, around 1902.

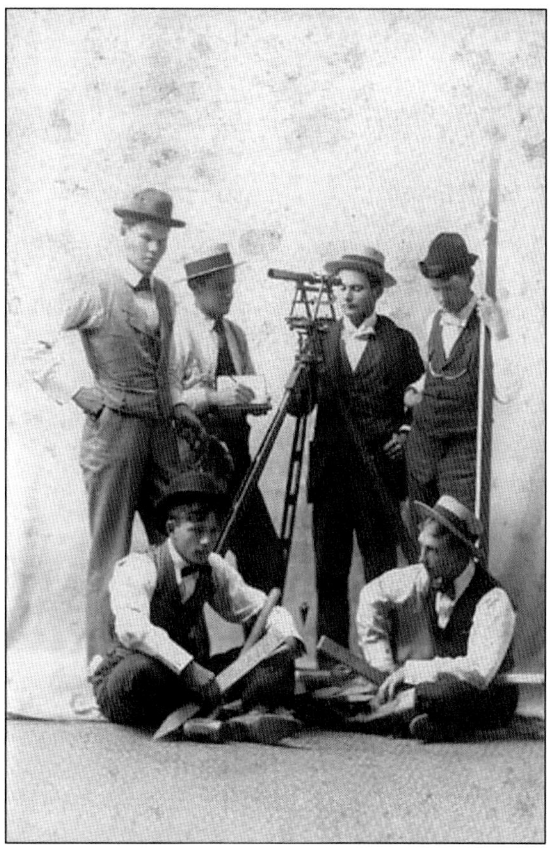

Members of the Chicago, Rock Island & Gulf Railway survey crew dressed in their Sunday best to pose with their sophisticated surveying equipment.

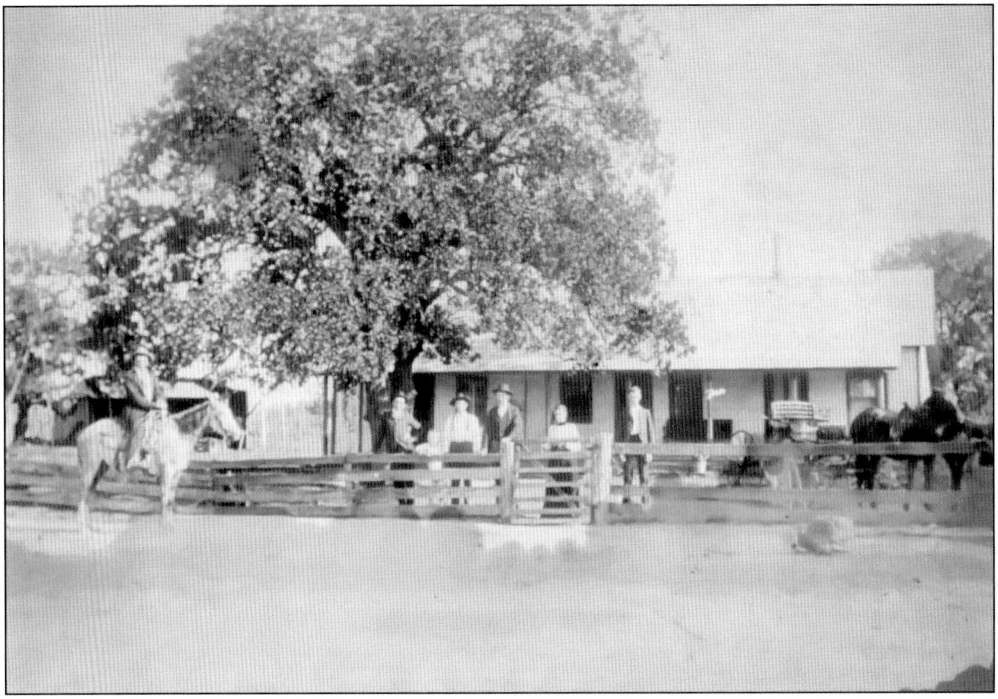

Henry W. Britain, his wife, and family members pose for a picture on their ranch in 1902. The Britains were ranchers who raised cattle and horses.

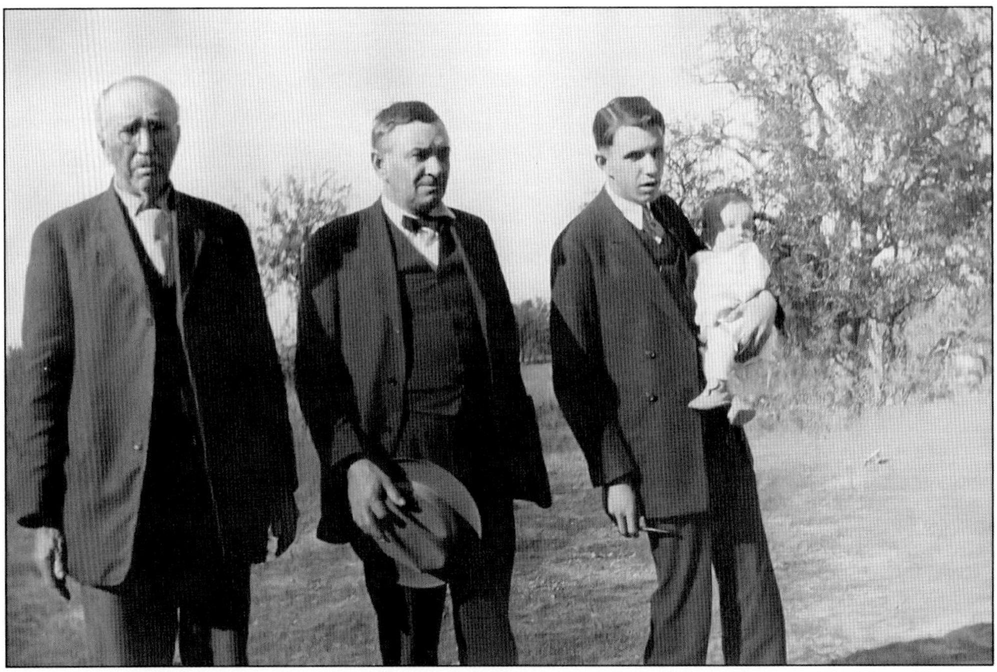

Pictured in 1927 are, from left to right, Henry W. Britain, David Earl Britain, Earl Lee Britain, and Henry W. Britain Jr. The Britain family sold land that would one day become Irving.

Netta Barcus and Otis Brown are shown happily posing for the camera just before their marriage in 1903.

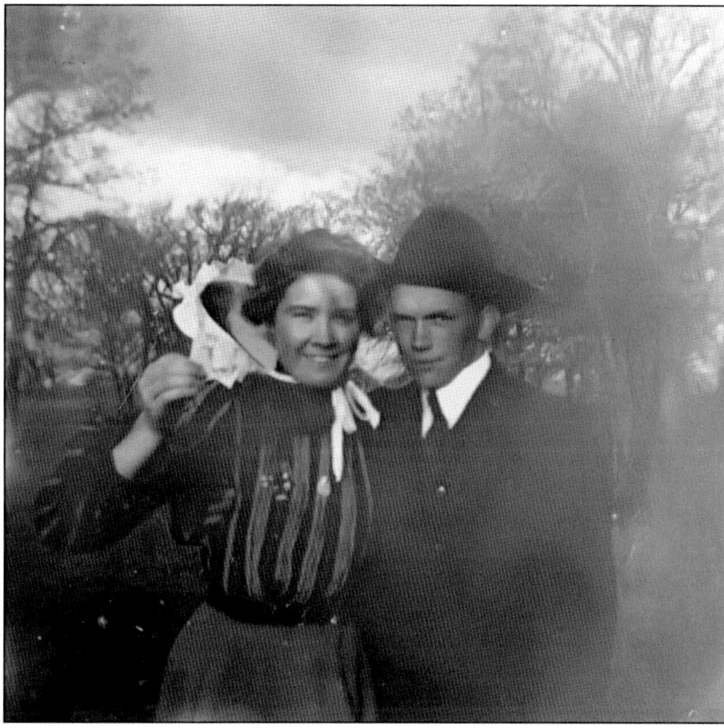

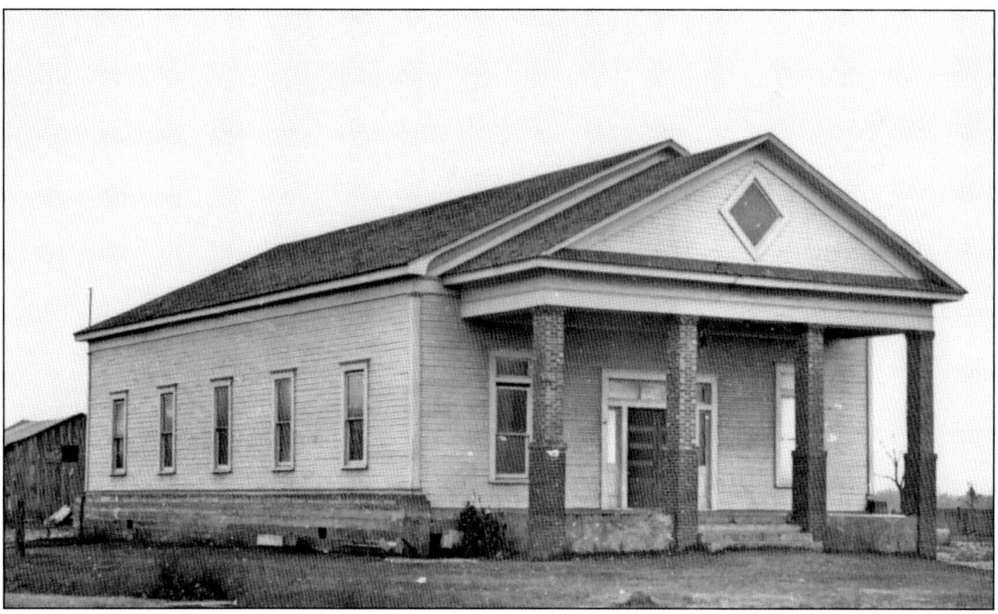

In 1904, founders Brown and Schulze donated land to build three churches in the new town of Irving: First Baptist Church, Delaware Street Church, and St. Luke's Catholic Church. According to historian Joseph Rice, Rev. L.M. Keeling was pastor at the First Baptist Church. Pictured here is the First Baptist Church, built at Main and Fourth Streets.

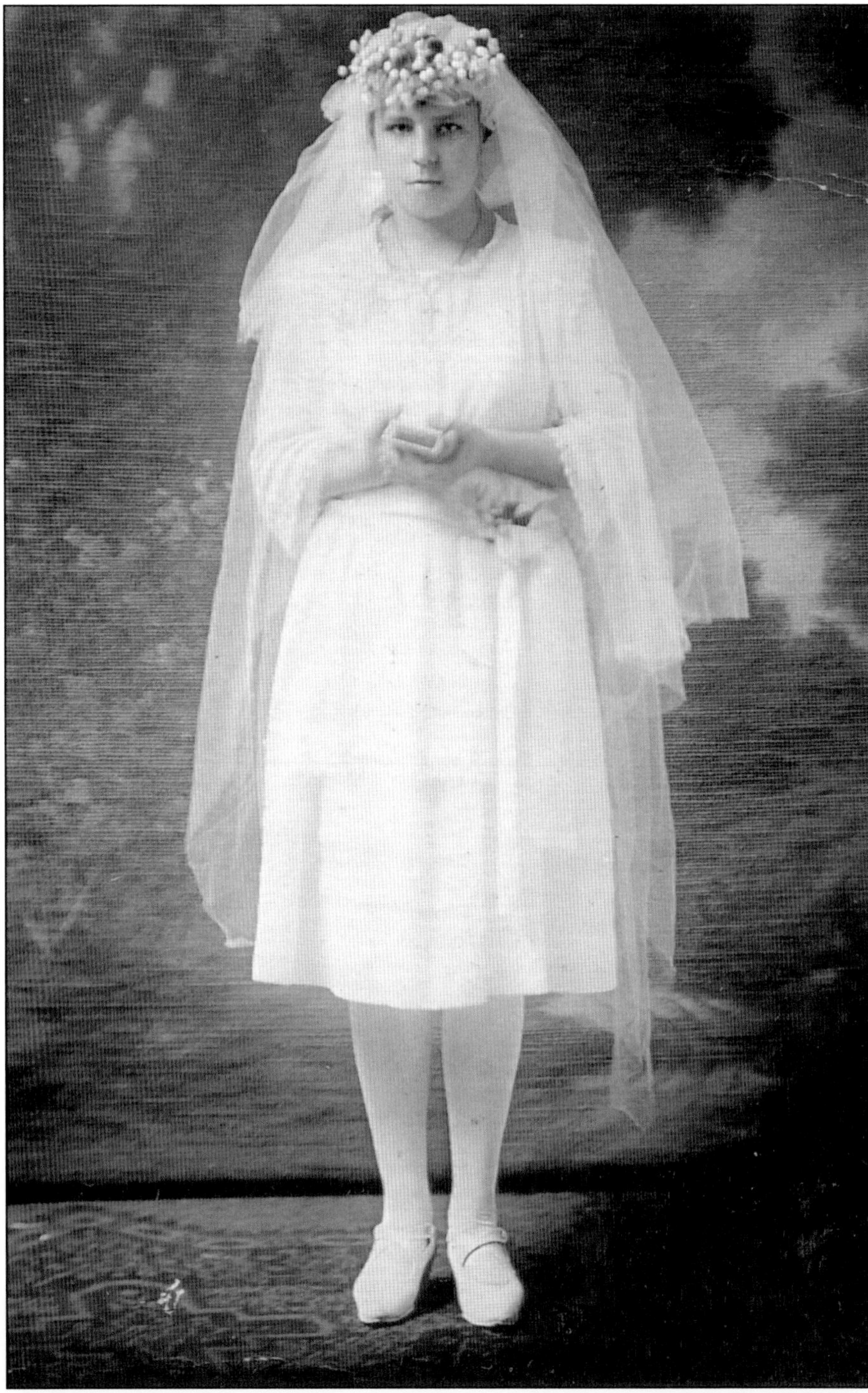

Catholic families made sure that their children followed the strict teachings of the Catholic religion. They attended Sunday masses, sent their children to Bible study, and attended mass on other holy days throughout the year. Strict Catholic families did not eat meat on Fridays during Lent, and it was not uncommon for some families to refuse to serve meat on Fridays during the rest of the year. Clemence Estelle Walker is pictured at her first communion in the 1920s.

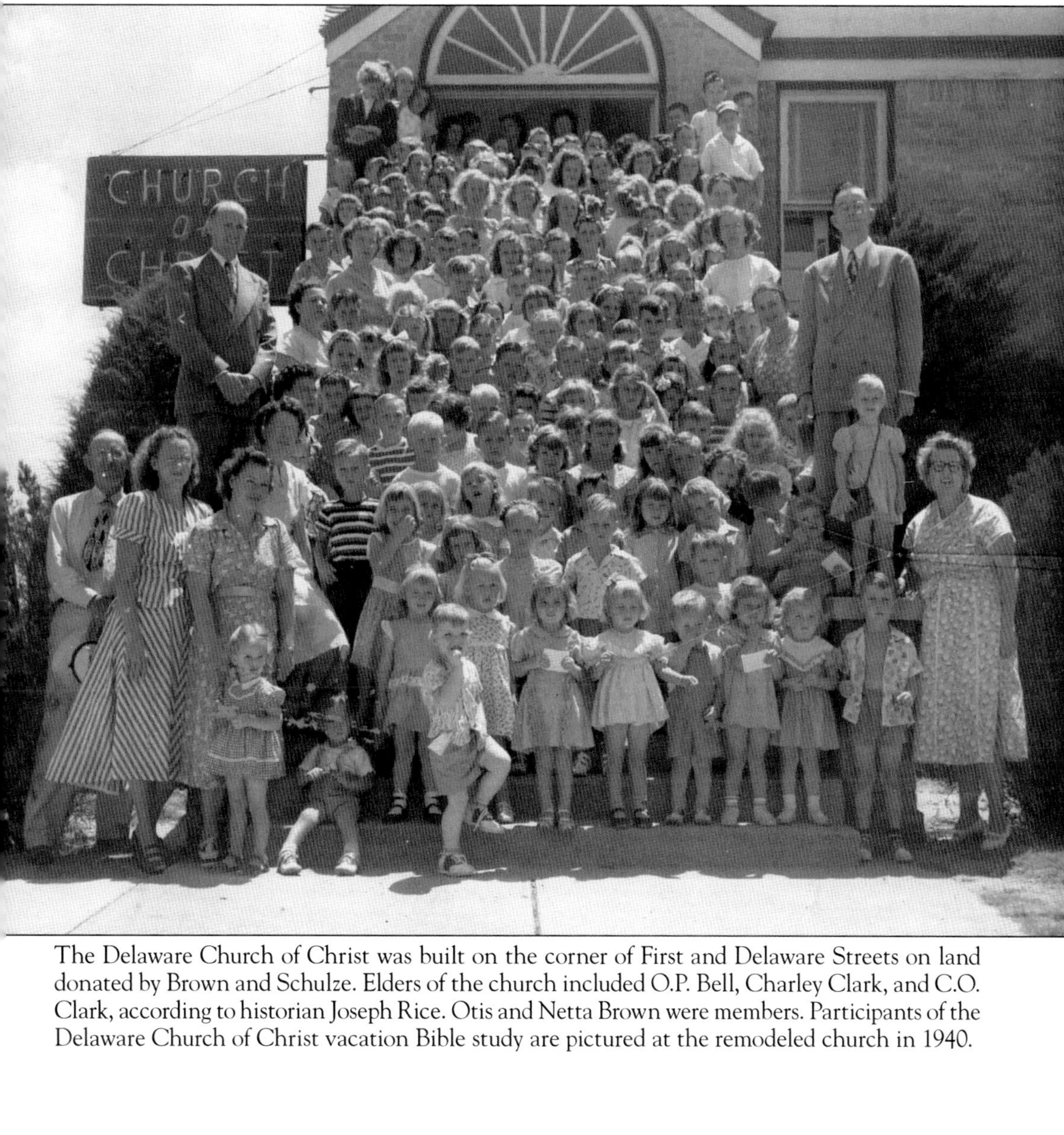

The Delaware Church of Christ was built on the corner of First and Delaware Streets on land donated by Brown and Schulze. Elders of the church included O.P. Bell, Charley Clark, and C.O. Clark, according to historian Joseph Rice. Otis and Netta Brown were members. Participants of the Delaware Church of Christ vacation Bible study are pictured at the remodeled church in 1940.

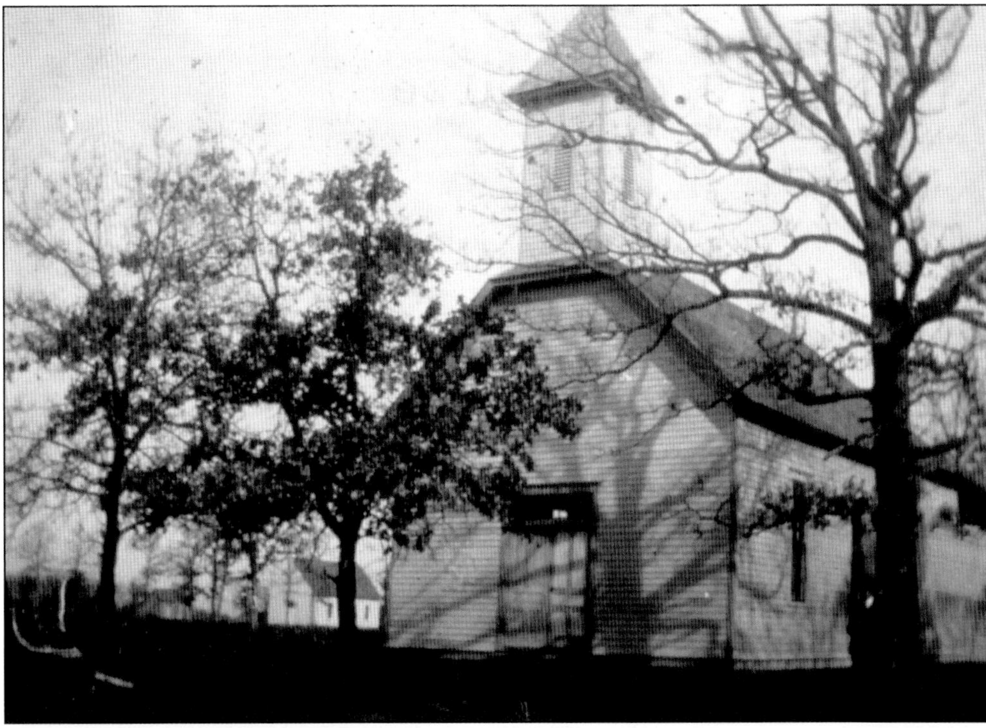

The first St. Luke's Catholic Church was built in 1904 on the southeast corner of Second and Jefferson Streets on land donated by founders Brown and Schulze. Several French families from the defunct La Réunion colony founded the parish. A parish list from 1890 includes the names of DeHaes, Chassang, Beaufford, Boinard, Isidore, Lanotte, Joffre, Rogers, Vacher, and Moulard. Prior to 1904, masses were held in private homes. (Courtesy of the Estelle Bates Collection, Irving Archives, Irving Public Library.)

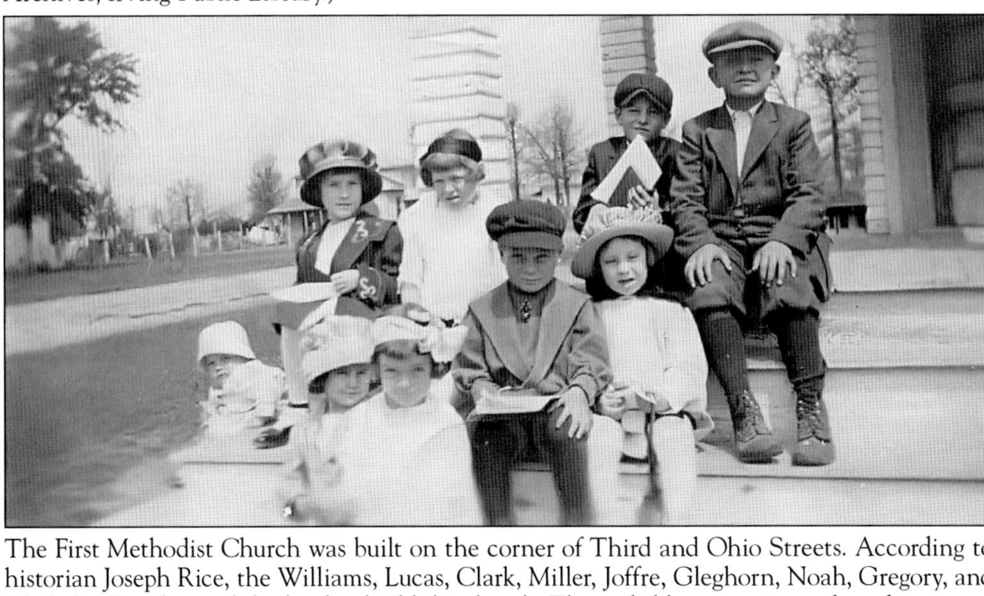

The First Methodist Church was built on the corner of Third and Ohio Streets. According to historian Joseph Rice, the Williams, Lucas, Clark, Miller, Joffre, Gleghorn, Noah, Gregory, and Clark families donated the land to build the church. These children are pictured on the steps of the church in 1914.

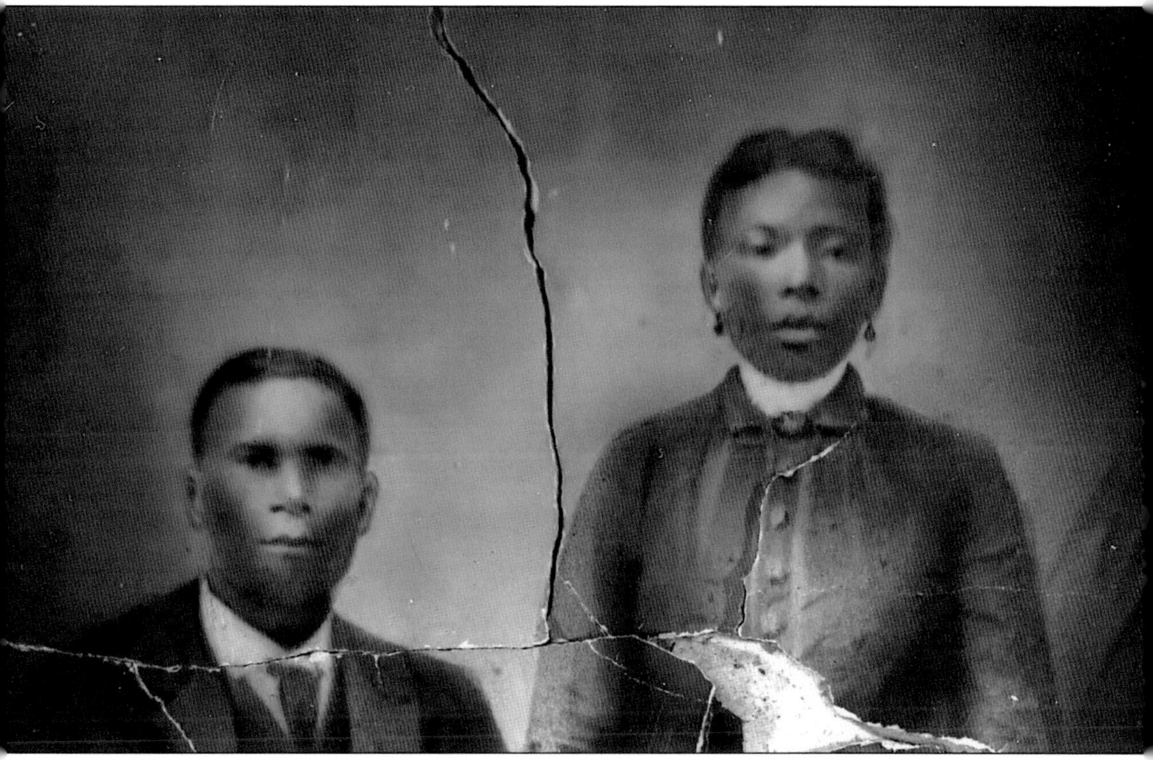

Bear Creek settlers began arriving in western Dallas County in the 1850s. Pioneers included the Casters, Borahs, Sowers, and Haleys. Jim Green, who was among the first African American landowners in this community, bought his land in 1878. Soon after, other pioneers followed: the Chivers family, Ben and Rose Dilworth, Alex King, Elizabeth Lawson, Collins and Rachel Patton, D.W. Ellison (Ellerson), Sam Sweat, the Trigg family, and Minnie Sheldon (Shelton). During the Civil War, sharecropping replaced slave labor. After the Civil War, free black soldiers moved to Bear Creek, where they were united with friends and families once separated by slavery. Pictured here are early pioneers Ben and Rose Dilworth, who migrated to Bear Creek in 1880. According to historian Joseph Rice, the Dilworths left Austin bound for Bear Creek with their 17 children and the clothes on their backs. They worked side jobs from Austin until they reached their destination. By the time they arrived at Bear Creek, Ben and Rose had lost three of their children to illness.

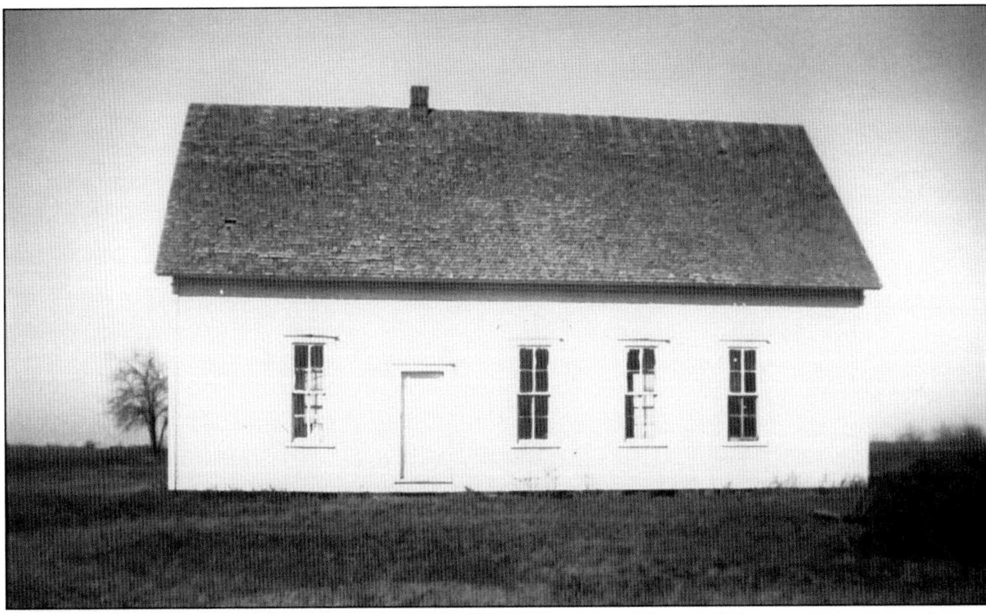

Religion and spirituality were important to the free salves. Many of their songs were religious in nature. Jim and Pinky Green established the first one-room freedom school that was used for worship services in this community. Pictured is the Bear Creek Church in 1895.

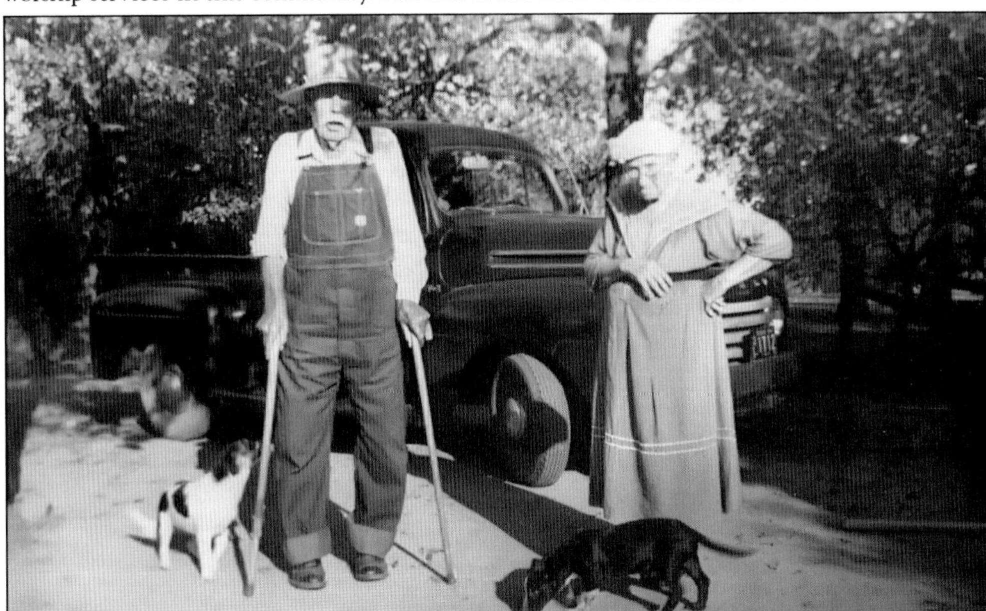

Settlers first came to the Elm community during the 1850s. Elm was located about 12 miles northwest of Dallas and, after Irving's founding in 1903, about two miles north of Irving. Nicholas Farine was one of the first settlers of this community. Before arriving at Elm, the Farine family settled in the La Réunion colony, located in a section of Dallas called Oak Cliff. When this colony failed in the late 1850s, the Farine family moved southeast of Irving, a little farther north in the Elm community. The Farines helped establish the Elm community. Pictured here are Will and Fannie (Farine) Story.

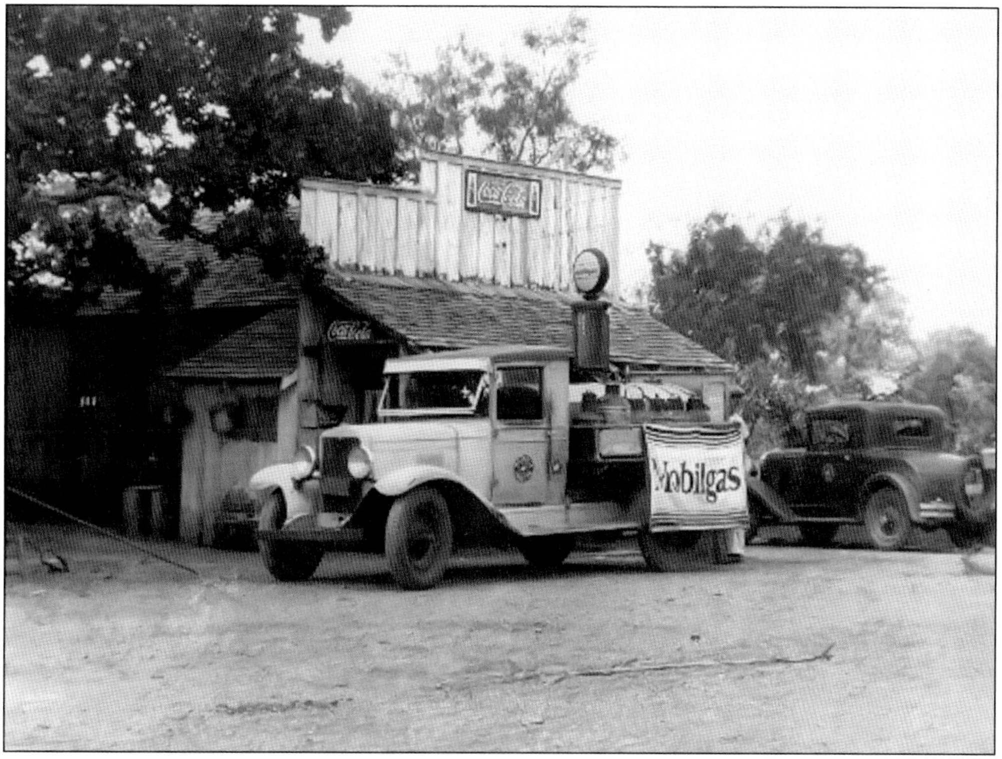

Many residents of the Elm community who drove their cars instead of riding the train needed gas from Philip and Lou Farine's store on O'Connor Road, located in the Elm community in the early 1920s. The Mobilgas truck is shown filing up the pumps at the store.

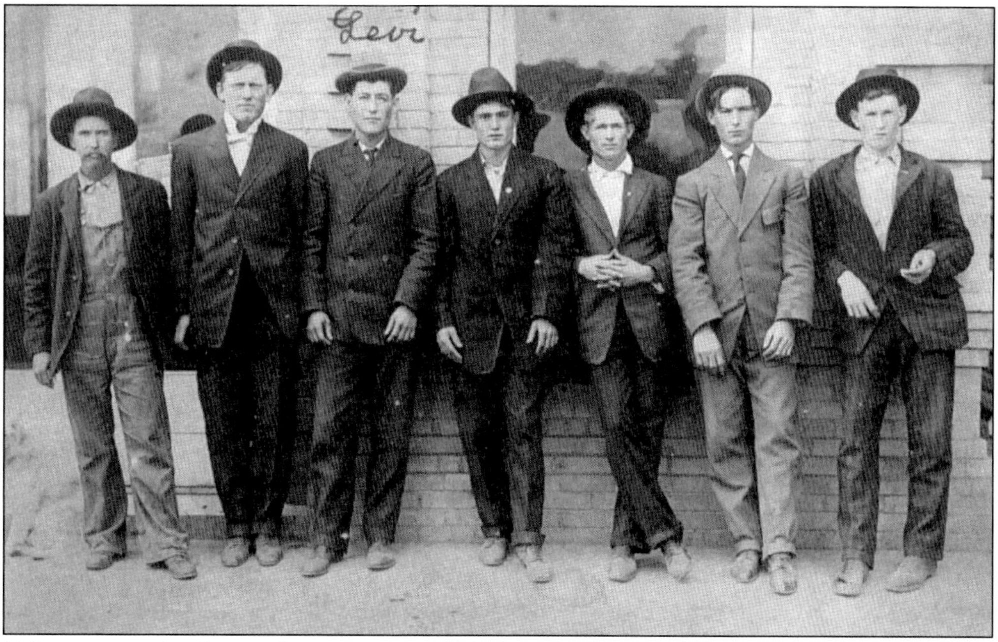

Other pioneer families in the region were the Tolers, Metkers, and Storys. Levi Story (third from left) is shown posing with friends in Irving.

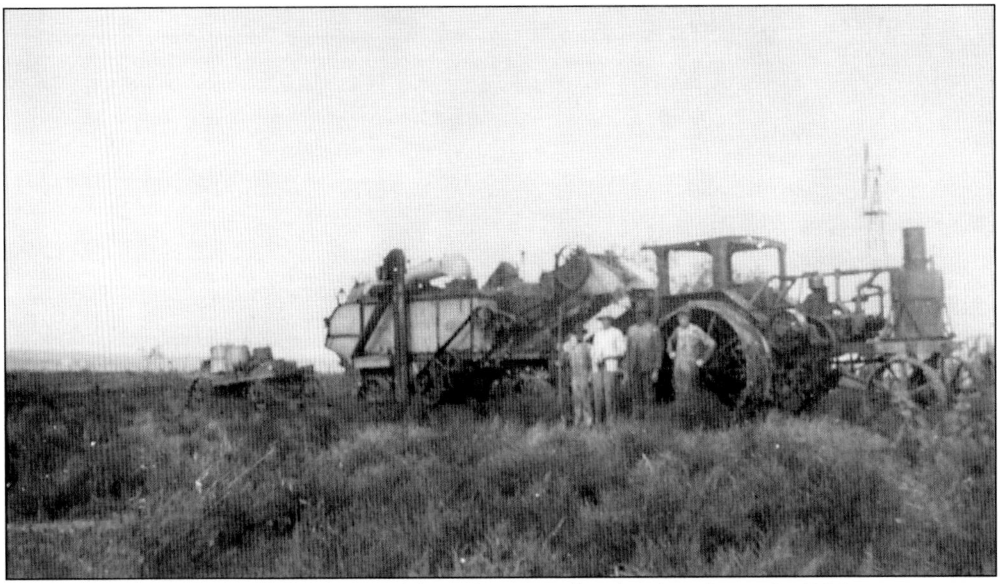

Pictured here is a steam tractor in a field on the Story farmland in the early 1900s.

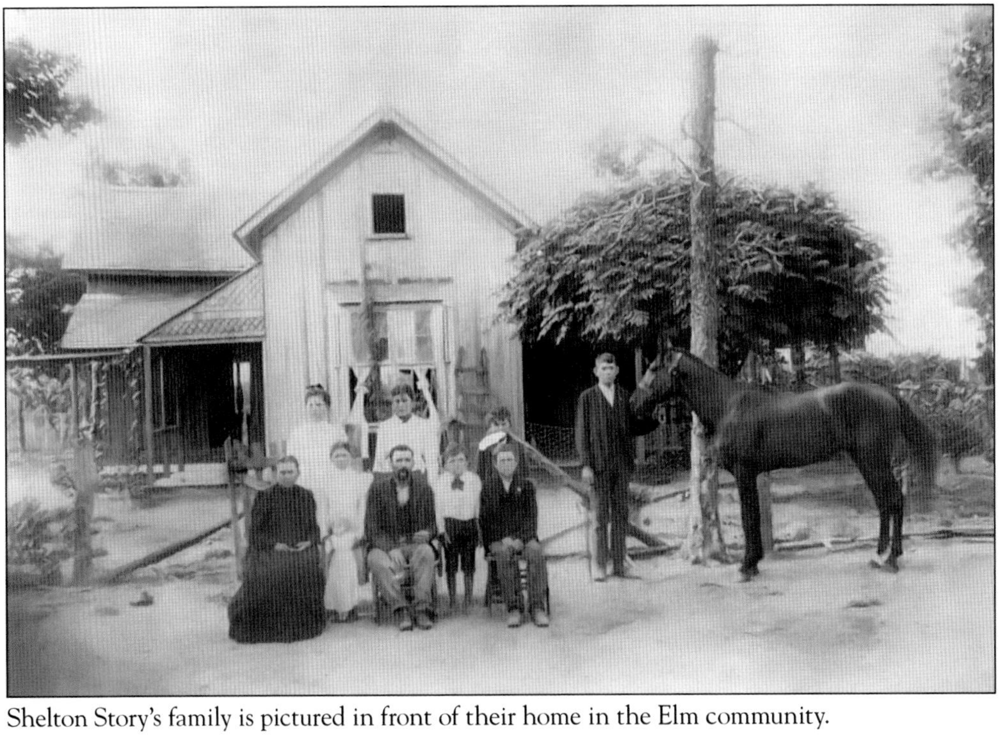

Shelton Story's family is pictured in front of their home in the Elm community.

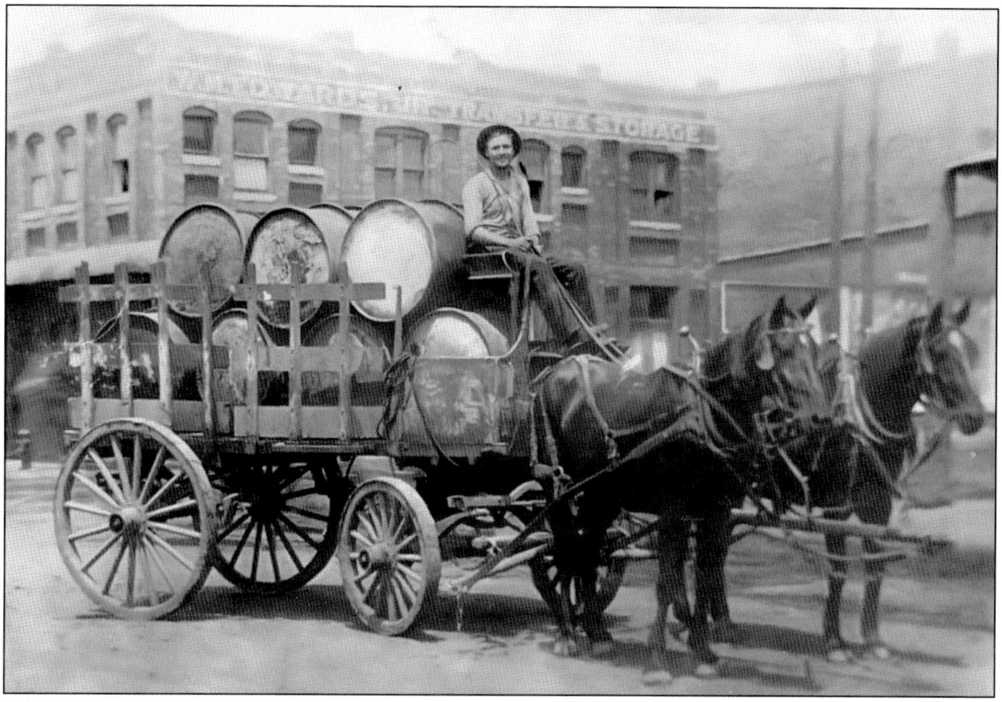

John Finley Mills came to the Elm community with his sister Jane shortly after the Civil War. He opened a general store during the 1880s and later served as postmaster for the area. The post office, known as the Finley Post Office, was open from 1899 to 1902. Finley Mills is pictured on a wagon.

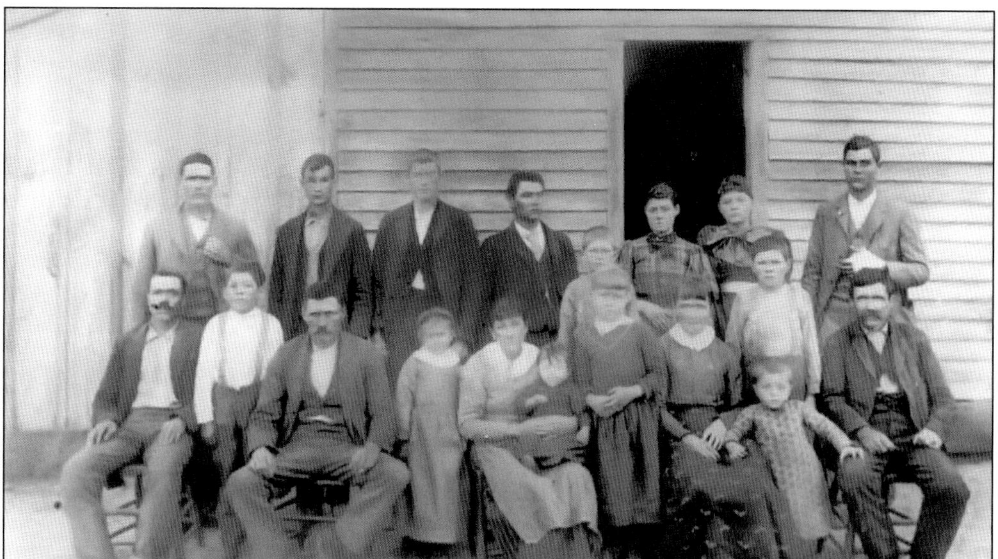

Stephen Toler was a person of influence and a major contributor to the success of the Elm community. Toler farmed and raised nine children in the community. He was one of five men who donated $25 for materials to construct a community school. Toler (sitting third from left) poses with friends and family for a portrait in 1895.

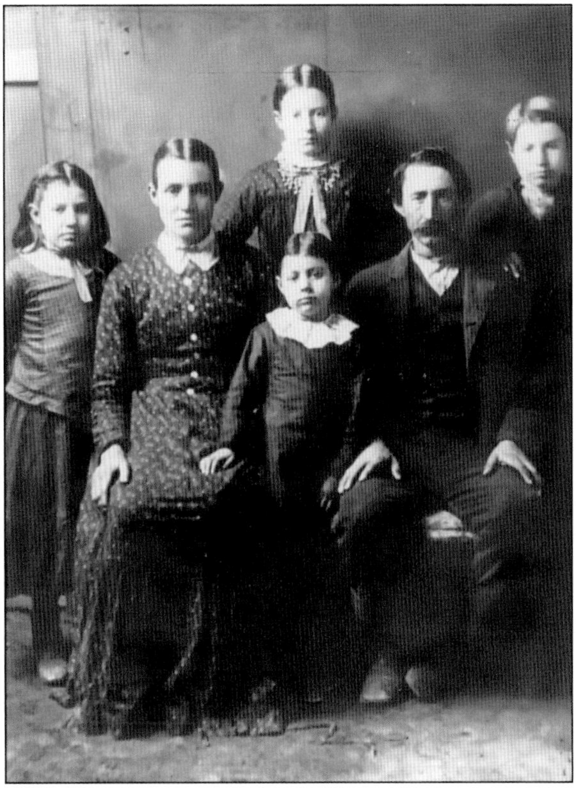

Henry Burgoon and other early pioneers established Estelle with a large land grant. Later, Bryant and Ryan Harrington came to the Estelle area after the Civil War. Others who helped build the community were the McCormick, Lucas, Good, Arthur, and Borah families. The Borahs had large land holdings in the community on which they farmed and later established a large dairy farm. Uleseyes O. Harrington and his wife, Mary Ellen Caster, are pictured here with their family in 1904.

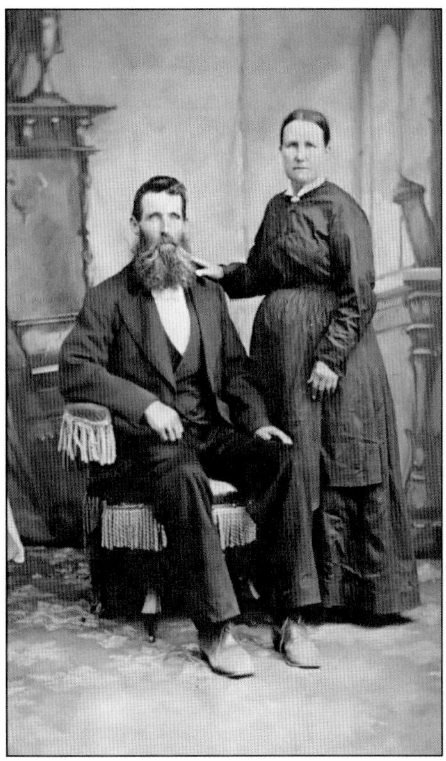

Jonathan and Saphronia Story and their children moved to Texas from Illinois in 1855. They bought 320 acres of land in what would become the Kit community northwest of Dallas County. Pictured here are Jonathan and Saphronia Story.

Other settlers included Henry W. Britain, who owned a ranch in the area on the western edge of the Kit community. He sold 80 acres of his land to two members of a Chicago, Rock Island & Gulf Railway survey crew in 1902. The land was about one mile west of the Kit community store. The two young railroad surveyors, J.O. Schulze and Otis Brown, would become the founding fathers of Irving.

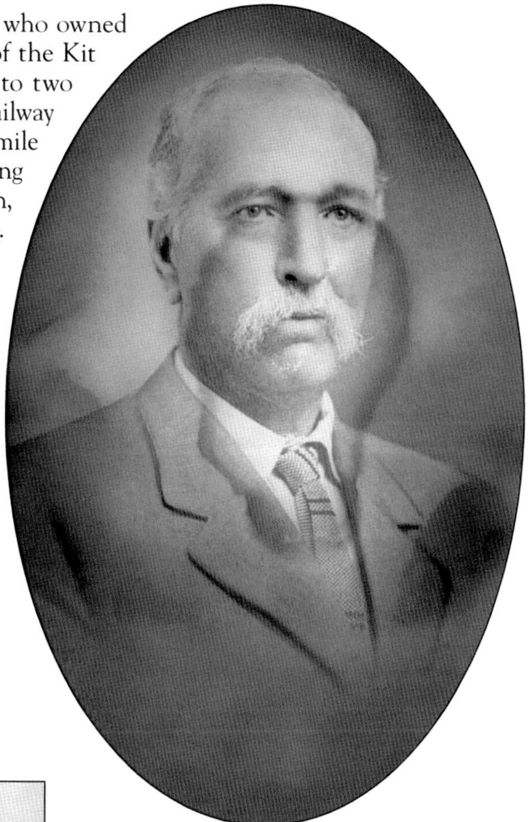

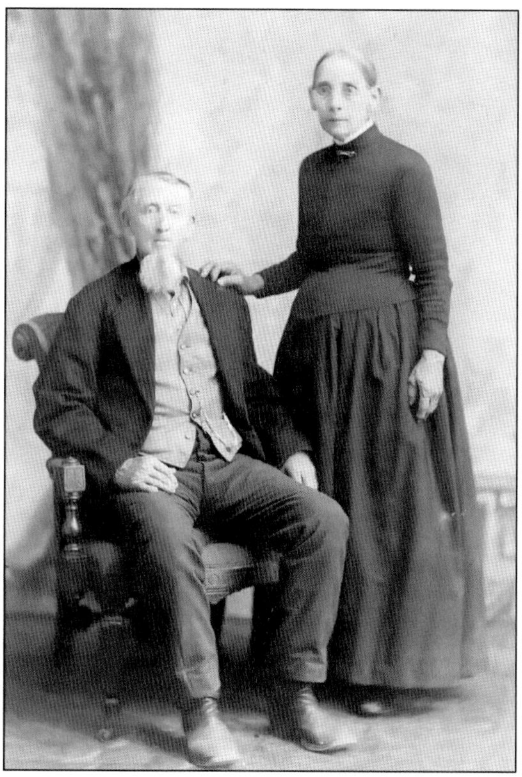

The Sowers community was located in the northwest part of Dallas County, about 12 miles west of the city of Dallas, and was established by founding pioneer and settler Edmund D. Sowers in the late 1850s. Sowers came to the area from Illinois in 1856. By 1876, he owned close to 1,000 acres of land in the area. Pictured here are Edmund and Freelove Sowers.

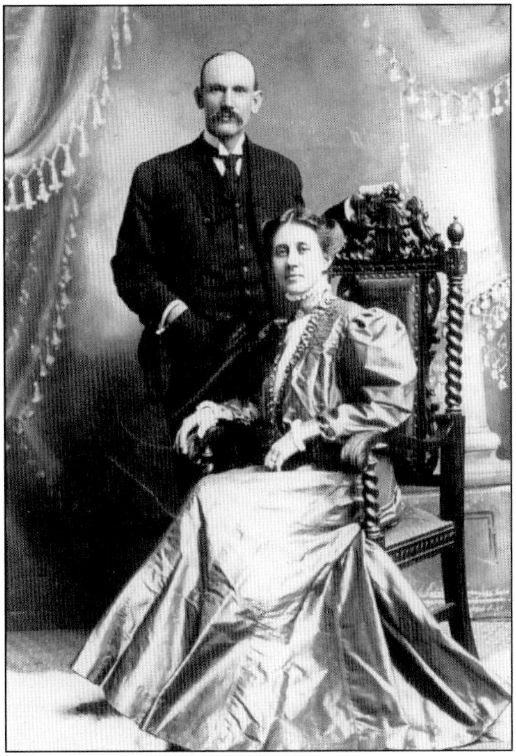

Included among the early settler families were the Haleys and the Casters. John Haley is pictured here with his wife, Anne Good Haley. Dr. John Haley, brother of Tom Haley, was one of Irving's earliest pioneer physicians.

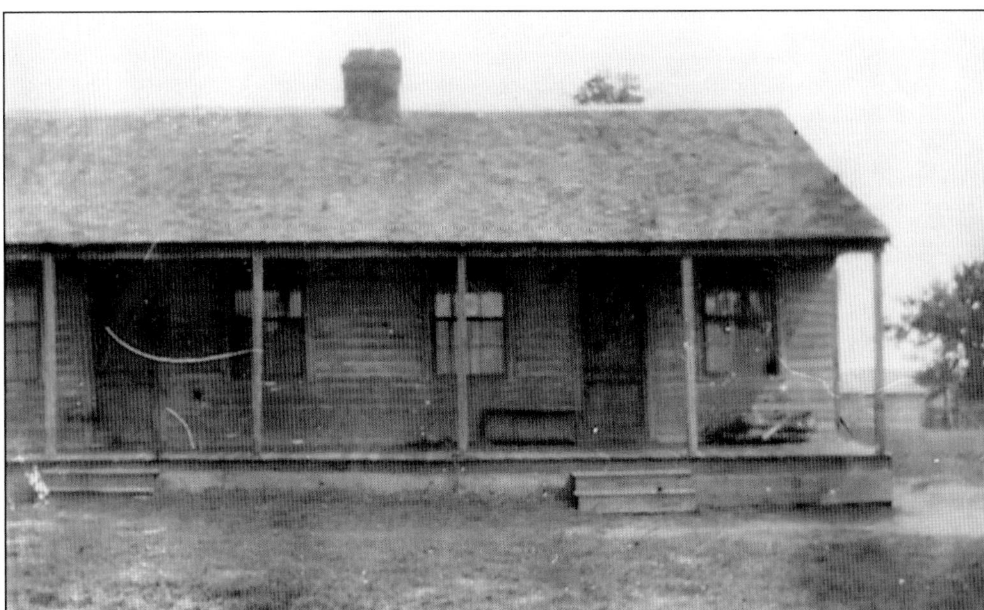

Pictured here is the Haley home in the Sowers community. Built with local lumber, the home was much improved from the original log cabin structures.

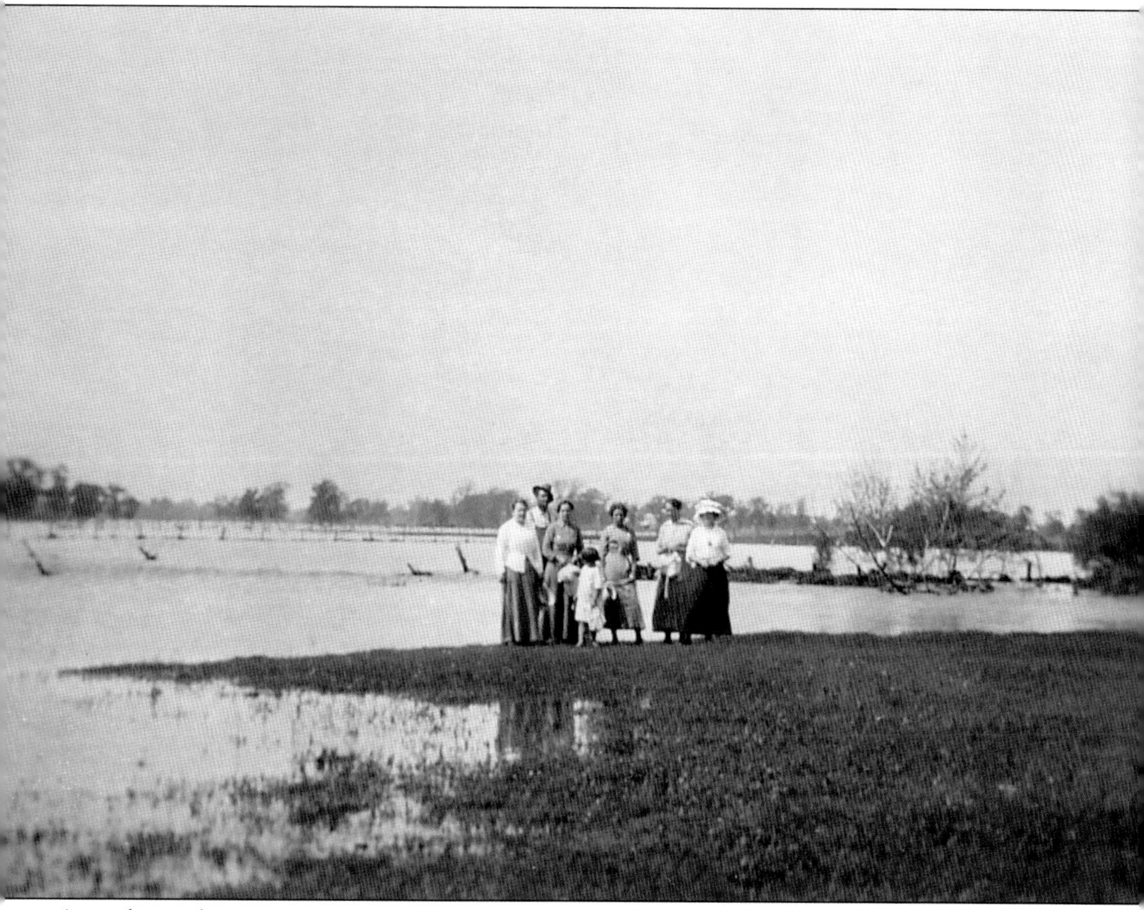

According to historian Norma Stanton, the Britain home was built near Twin Wells so that they could have access to a water system that fed into the well on their property. These wells were used to refresh travelers and their working animals. The Trinity River is shown here in its flood state, just a short distance from Twin Wells.

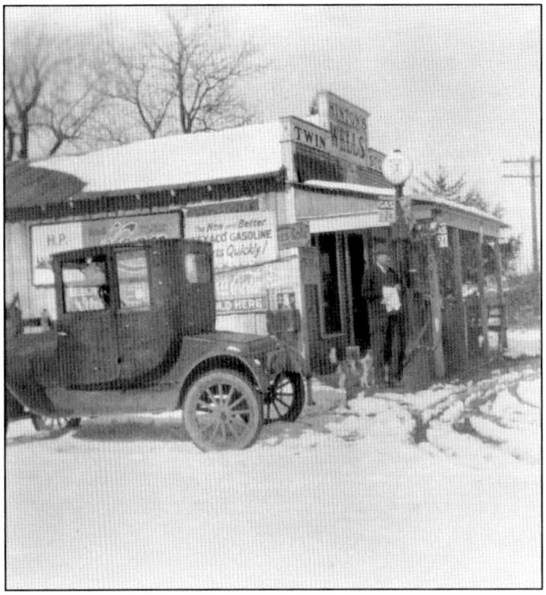

Harwood P. Hinton Sr. was born in Marshall, Texas, in 1870. He moved to West Texas to live with relatives in 1891. In 1909, he traded his chicken farm for 63 acres in the Twin Wells community in northwest Dallas County. Hinton then traded part of his 63 acres for a store in Irving, which was about two miles west of his land. In 1924, Hinton opened a store and lumber company that greatly contributed to the success of Twin Wells. The store was built along the old Eagle Ford Road between Dallas and Irving, north of the Eagle Ford Trail crossing on the West Fork of the Trinity River. Harwood Hinton is pictured in front of the Twin Wells store in 1930. (Courtesy of the Hinton Family Collection, Irving Archives, Irving Public Library.)

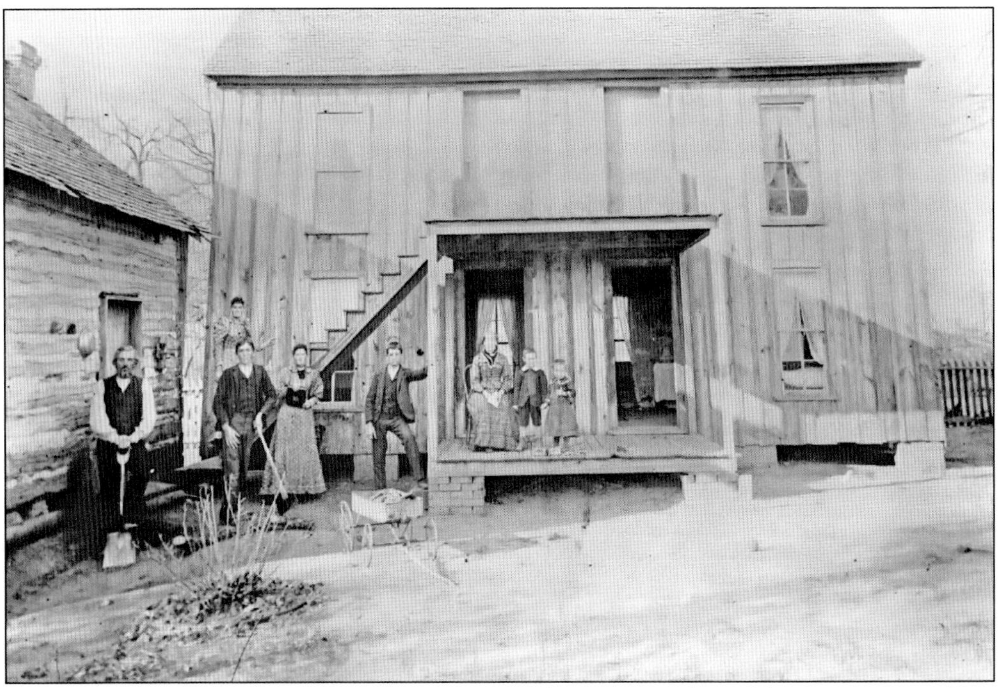

Lucy Sanaterre married Charles Voirin in late 1867. They were members of the La Réunion colony. They settled here from Europe to help found the colony, and when it failed, they moved to this area. The Voirins bought 160 acres of land for $122 and one half cent in 1869.

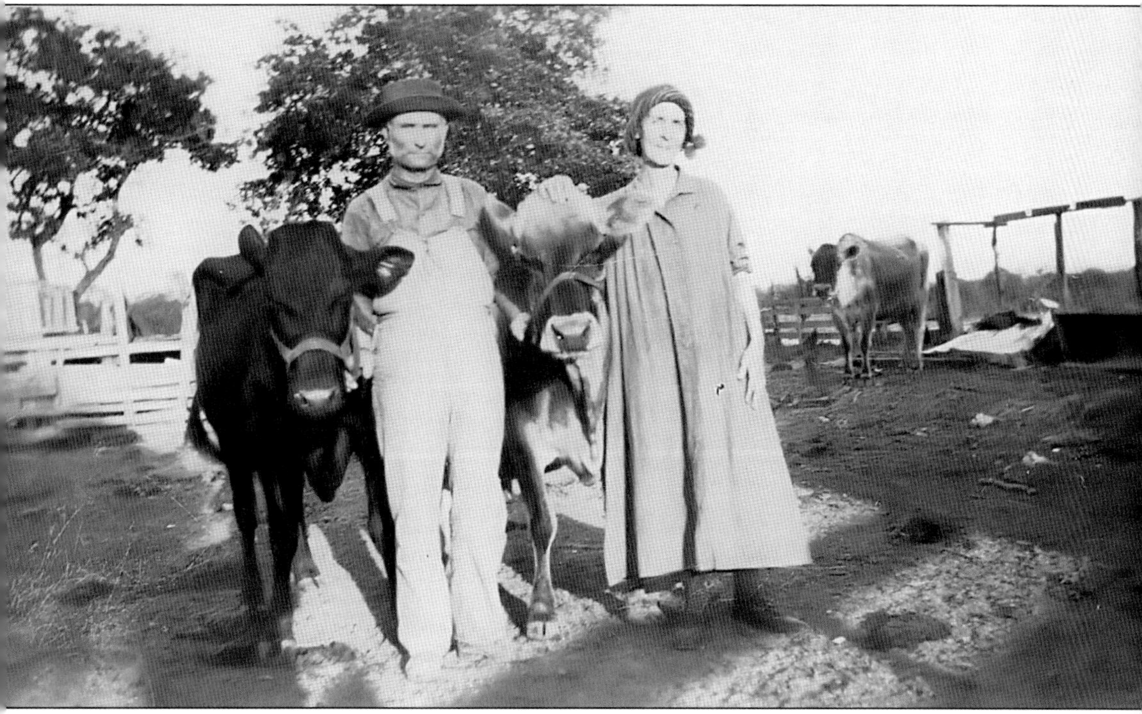

Mr. and Mrs. Childress are pictured with dairy cows on Harwood Hinton's mother's farm in the Union Bower community in 1926.

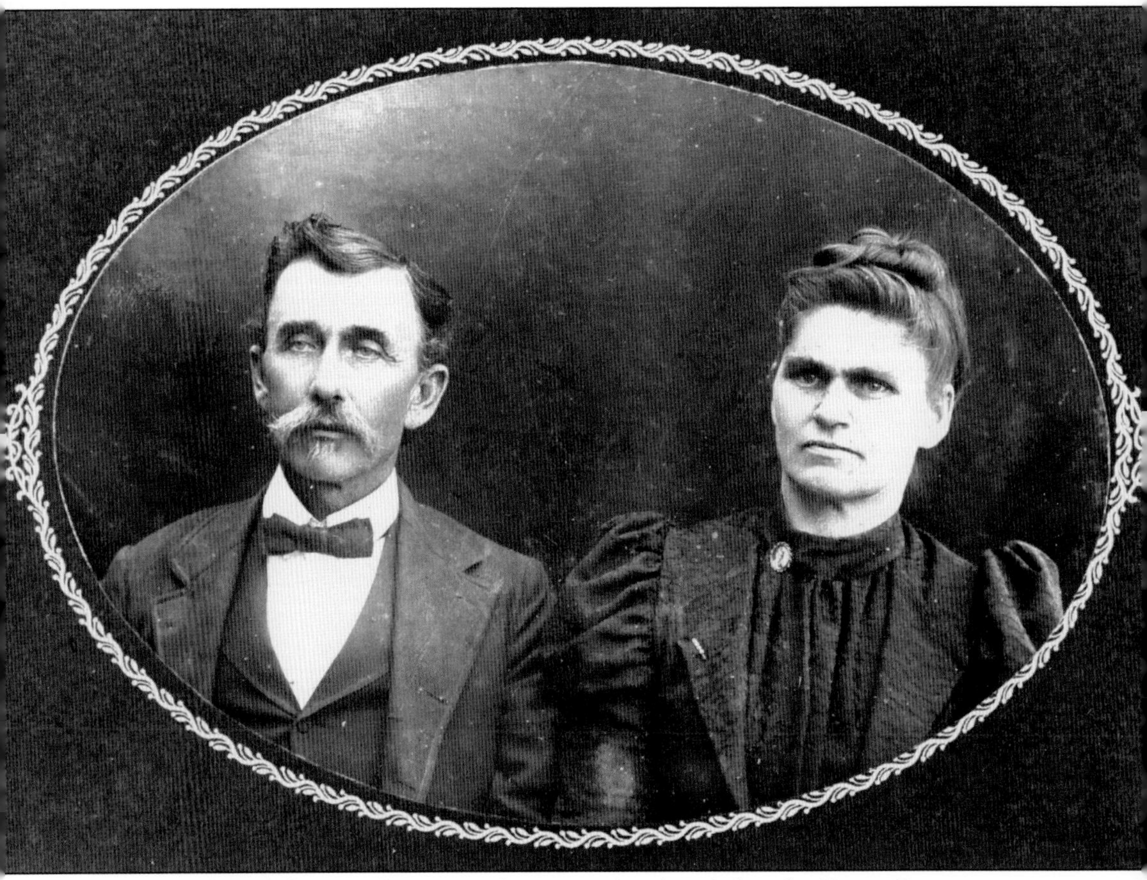

Families of the defunct La Réunion colony moved and settled in the Union Bower community. Among them were the Lanottes, the Joffres, the Farines, and the Voirins. In 1879, William and Virginia Smith moved to the area from Pennsylvania. The Union Bower community was named after a school located in a town in Pennsylvania where William Smith taught. Although the Smiths were not the first pioneers to the community, they were able to bring stability and unity to its residents by working toward the same goals. The Smiths donated land for a community cemetery after the death of their young daughter. William and Virginia Smith are pictured here in the late 1800s.

Three

Inspiring Contributions of Irving Women

Women in this society were assigned gender-based roles that resulted in performing household functions such as cleaning, cooking, and caring for their children while enduring life's hardships on the prairie. Many female settlers in Irving came from Missouri, New York, and other parts of the world where their communities had established indoor running water and plumbing systems, sophisticated medical services, electricity, and other modern amenities. Early female settlers also had a keen eye for fashion. They brought with them the latest fashions influenced by European designers. At this time, Irving did not have such amenities or fashion. Irving was made up of dirt roads and a precarious water system. The hot Texas sun and dirt of the prairie made it hard for the women to work in their fashionable attire, but they did so gracefully.

Around the turn of the 20th century, women continued to work side by side with their families to cultivate the land and prepare it for harvest. It was forbidden for women to pursue a career even if was to help support their families. Women were not allowed to vote or have control of their property or their children. Texas women could not serve on juries or act as lawyers or even witness a will. They had a difficult life on the prairie; however, they became more independent as time went on.

As Irving was flourishing as a city, World War I commenced. While the men were away at war, the women were expected to perform jobs formerly done by men. Women were expected to take care of their families, maintain their farmland, and make ends meet. It is estimated that, between 1880 and 1910, women in the job market went from 2.6 million to 7.8 million. Soon, women pursed teaching and nursing careers. Then clerical work, such as bookkeeping, stenography, and sales jobs, became increasingly popular.

Female settlers continued to endure the adversities of prairie life. Women of this time did not hold the same status of men but closer to that of a slave or free black in society. Soon, women began to realize they should hold the same status as men. They had worked hard to hold their families together. Women began to organize and formed groups like the Young Women's Christian Association. These women's groups focused on literacy and social reform. When women were given the right to vote on August 26, 1920, they rose up and worked alongside their male counterparts to influence the development of their communities and the prosperity of the city of Irving with their inspiring contributions.

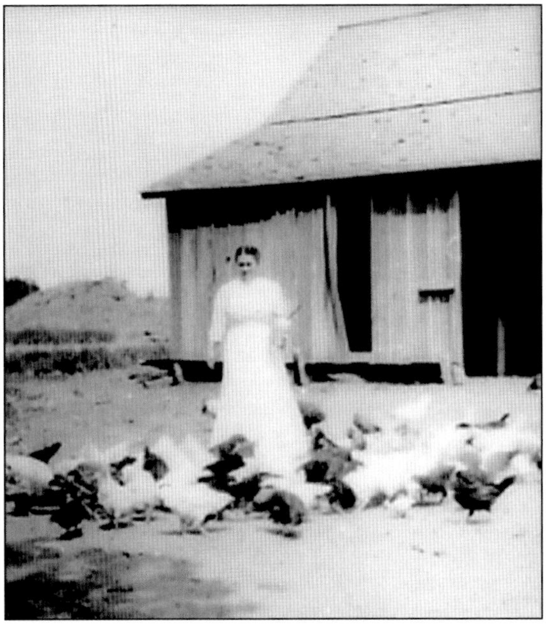

Life was tough for the settlers. The wives of settlers were responsible for making sure the daily chores were completed, including cooking, cleaning, and caring for their children. In addition, wives were responsible for maintaining the farmland right alongside their husbands. Developing the hot Texas prairie land was difficult. This photograph of "the chicken lady" was taken in the late 1800s or early 1900s.

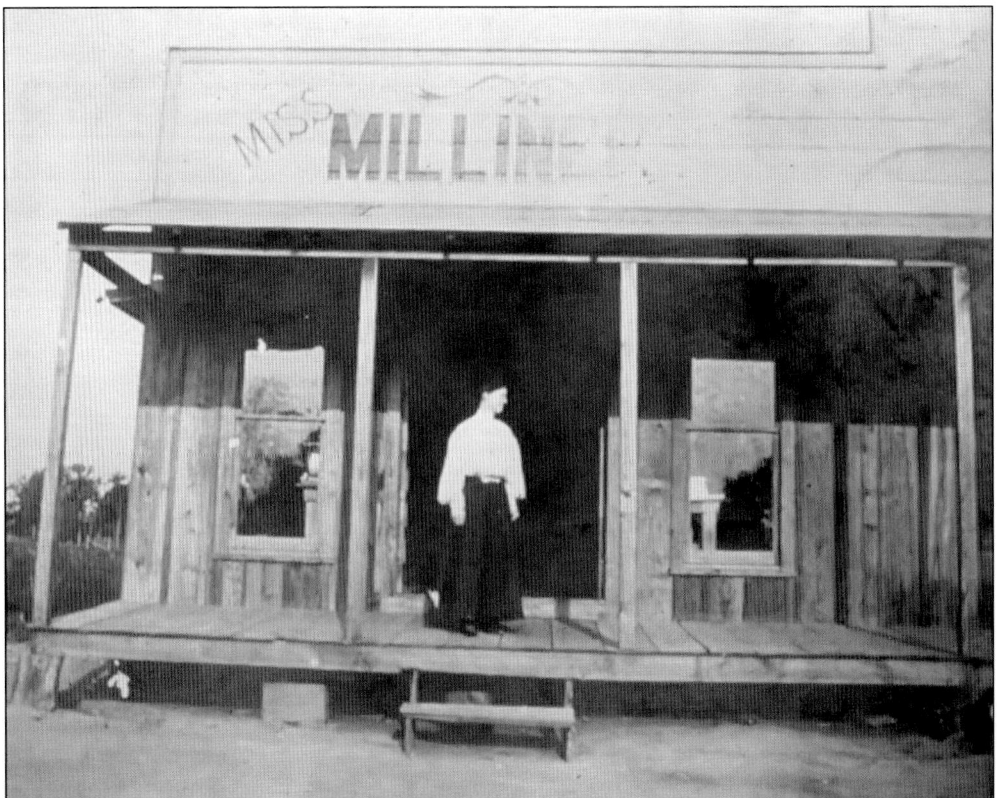

Fannie Hicks was one of Irving's early female business owners. Miss Hicks dressed in the latest fashion, as seen here in 1905. She wore a shirt collar with a floppy artist bow and a flared skirt modeled after the Gibson Girl style. Her store was in the 100 block of South Main Street.

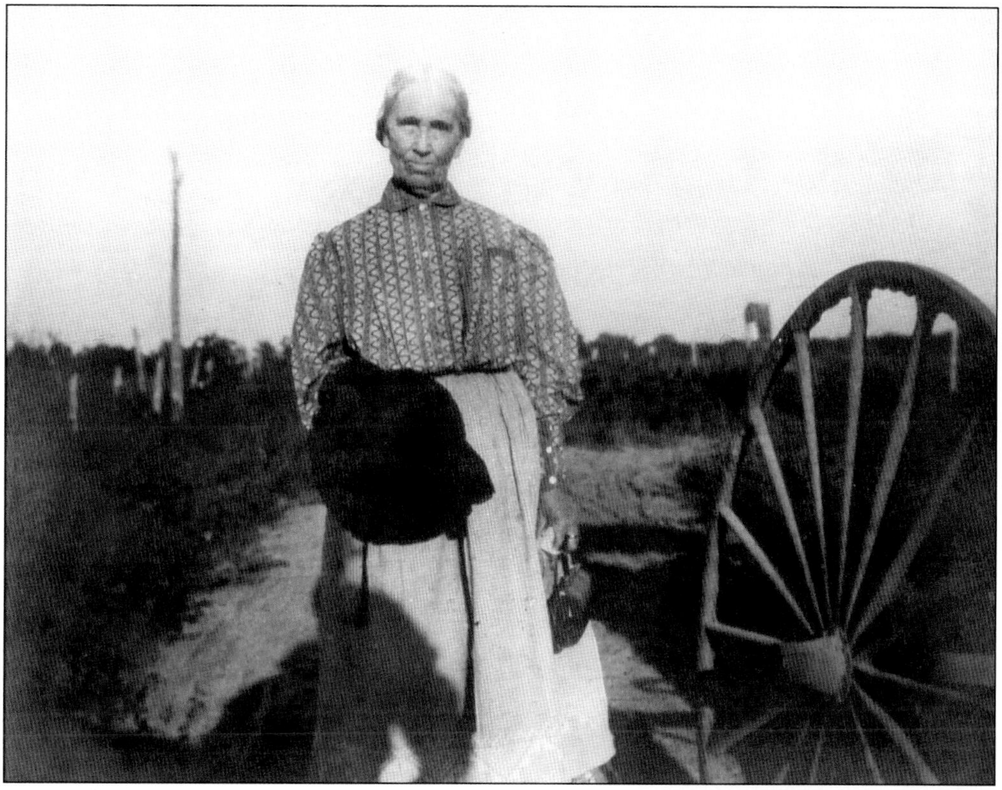

Lucy and Charles Voirin's hard work and dedication helped shape the Union Bower community. Lucy Sanaterre Voirin is pictured here in the late 1800s. Her bronzed face and gentle smile is representative of all the early women settlers who worked hard under the Texas sun for their community.

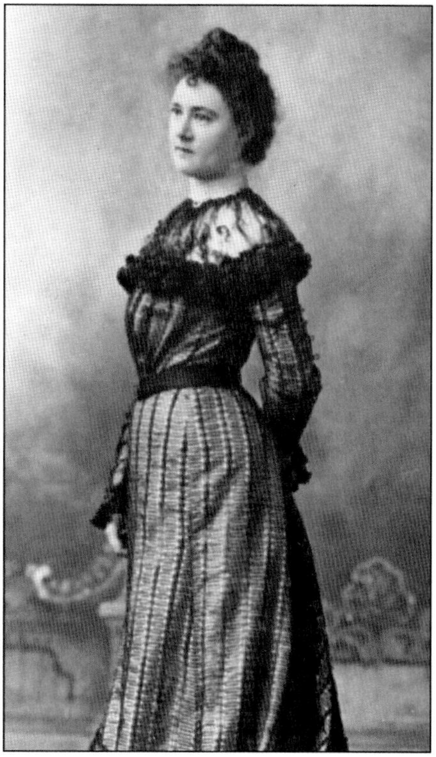

Agnes Suepel was born to a prominent family in Iowa City, Iowa. In 1903, Agnes married J.O. Schulze. As a young city, Irving lacked the resources and the comforts of home she was accustomed to. She struggled to stay and help her husband develop Irving, but when their firstborn fell ill, she returned to Iowa in 1904 to provide her son the latest advances in medicine.

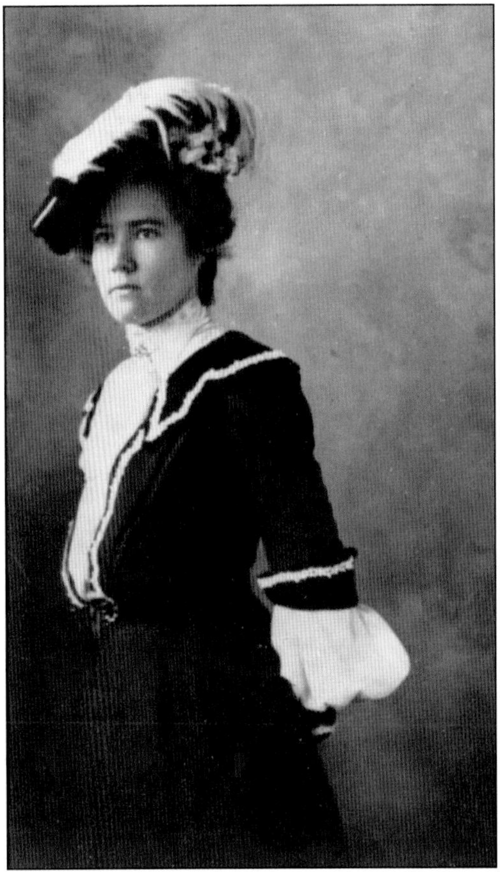

Netta Barcus is shown modeling a bodice featuring pouches of cascading lace. The straight sleeves of the late 1890s evolved into bloused garments that gathered at the wrist. High lace collars that reached to right under the chin elongated the neck. Barcus served as a teacher for the Kit community school. She was a boarder at the Britain farm during the time that the survey crew was camping there. In June 1903, she married Otis Brown, one of Irving's founders. During World War I, she served as chair of the Red Cross Irving Chapter, rallying a group of women to knit mufflers, socks, and sweaters for the soldiers. In addition, the group made dressings for the wounded soldiers. Because of her efforts and dedication, her chapter received a nomination signed by President Wilson for their charitable contributions to the wartime efforts.

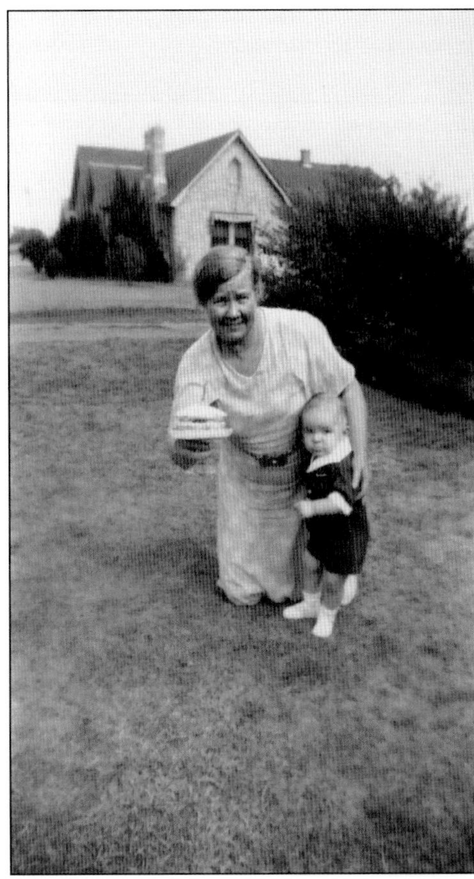

Netta Barcus Brown, wearing a dress with less frill and fashion, is pictured with her grandson Charles Brown in front of their house in 1936.

Here, 12 of the brightest girls are shown displaying their Edwardian hairstyles. Although these women might not have been from Irving, they provide an example of women's hairstyles in the early 1900s. To produce this effect, most women curled their hair using curling tongs. If the tongs got too hot, they would singe the hair. Thus, women were glad when Nestlé came out with a new line of permanent wave products. Women would sit attached to Karl Nessler's machine for up to 12 hours to acquire the right amount of waves. What sacrifices women made for beauty.

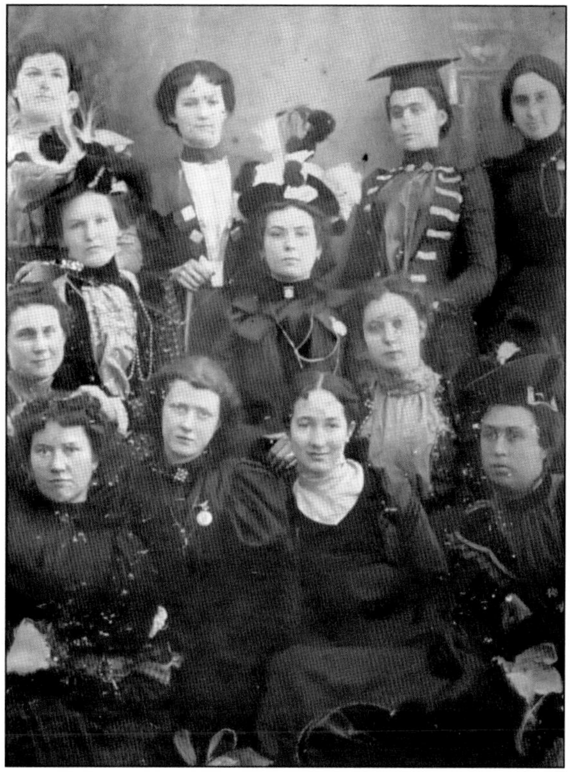

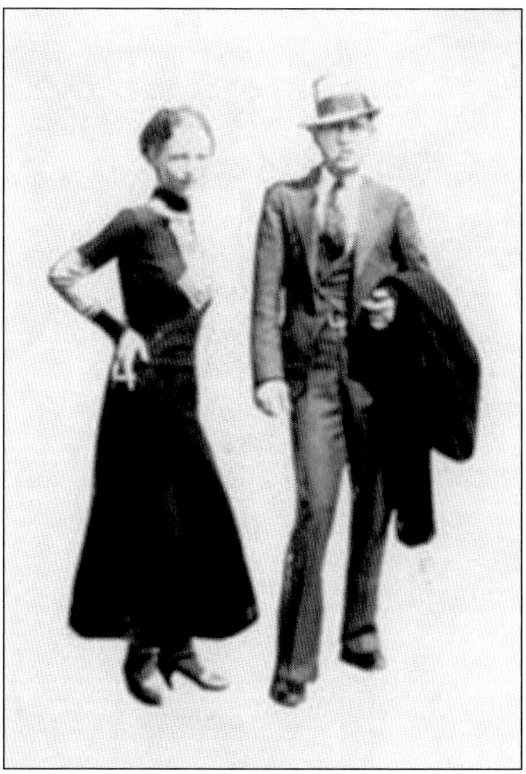

Bonnie Parker (left) is pictured in the latest fashion. In the late 1920s, a new woman was born. She smoked, drank, danced, and voted. She cut her hair, wore makeup, and went to "petting parties" where lots of kissing took place. She was a flapper, known to be giddy and take risks. Bonnie Parker was the epitome of this day and age. Risky and brave, she is known as a modern-day criminal. Together with Clyde Barrows, their criminal ventures as they roamed through Irving and Dallas County are legendary. Bonnie and Clyde escaped capture during a gun battle with Sheriff Smoot Schmid and Deputy Ed Caster in the area of what is now Highway 183. (Courtesy of Portal to Texas History, University of North Texas.)

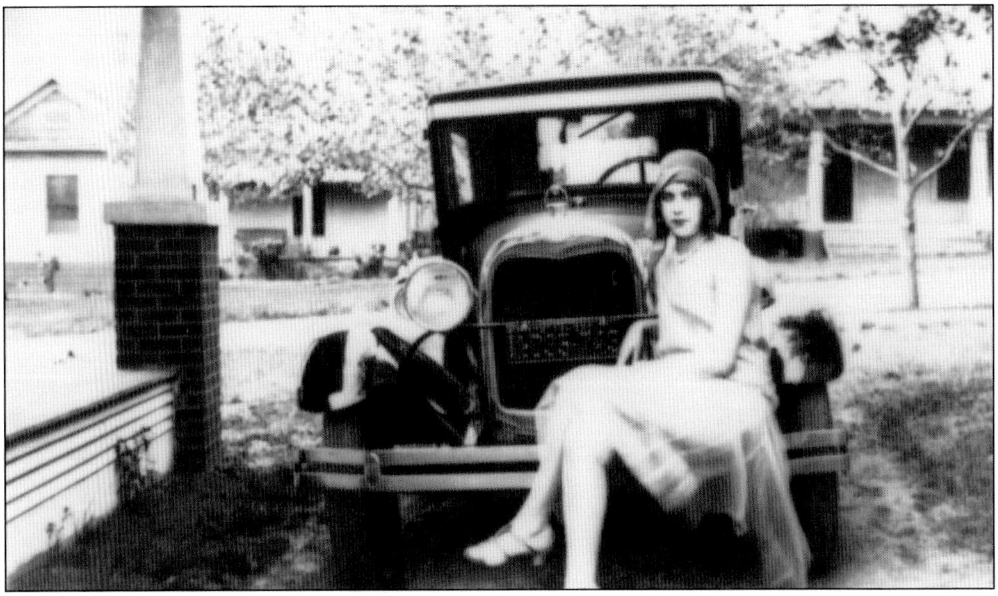

Grace Story Watts, daughter of Will and Fanny Story, is shown posing in the latest flapper fashion of 1929. The flapper movement consisted of radical and somewhat shocking changes in women's clothing and hairstyles from the early 1900s, when the fashions were conservative and less revealing. Flappers not only insisted on riding in cars, but they also drove them. Cars were fast and treacherous and perfect for the flapper disposition. The helpless days of women were over.

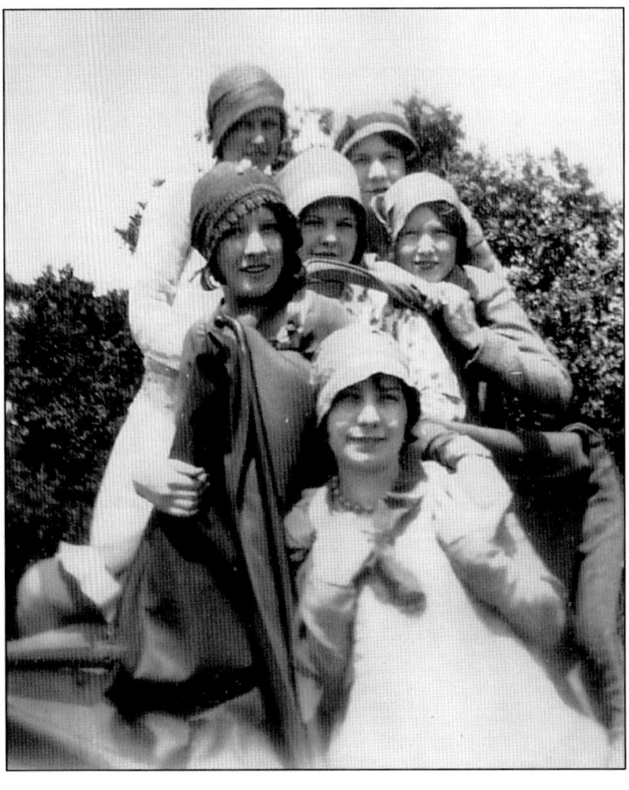

During the flapper era, almost every article of clothing was lightened to make movement easier and less confining. At left is a group of strong-minded women dressed in cloches.

Lorene Lucas is pictured here with her diploma. The shortened hem of her skirt, designed to fall just below the knee, was characteristic of a flapper. Many women rolled and twisted matching stockings. As an educated female, Lorene no doubt believed she was now able to triumph over the world.

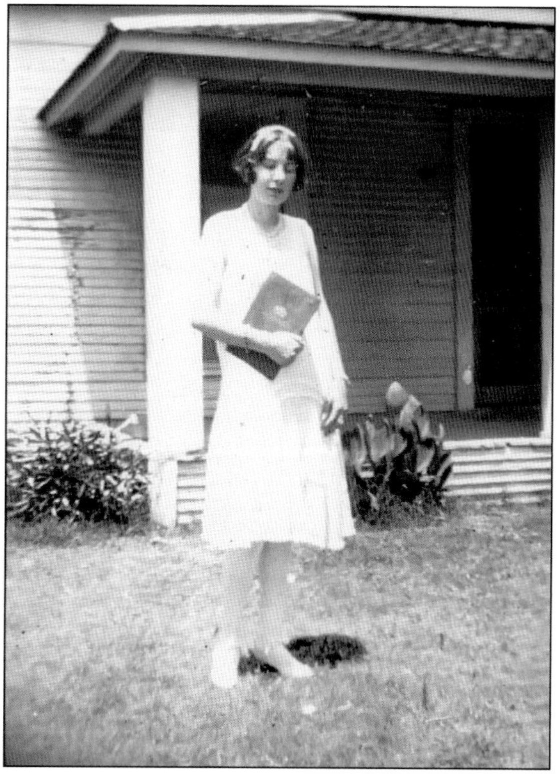

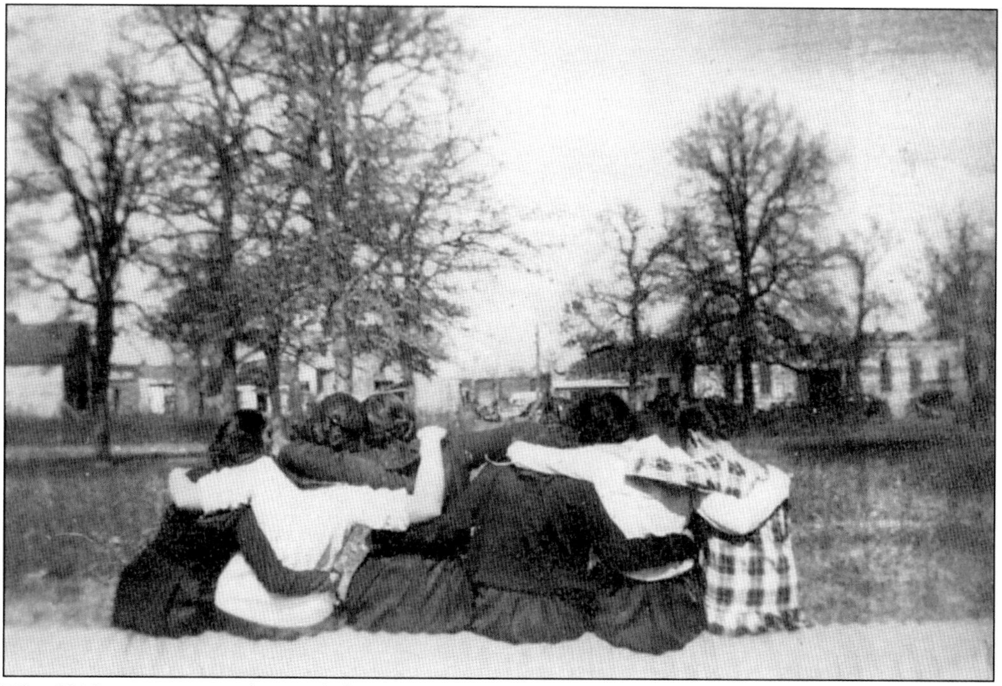

The 1920s was a time when girls became self-confident and defiant about the traditional gender roles. Women were motivated to learn a trade, earn a degree, or start a career. They completed high school and often attended trade school or college. Pictured here are six seniors of 1920.

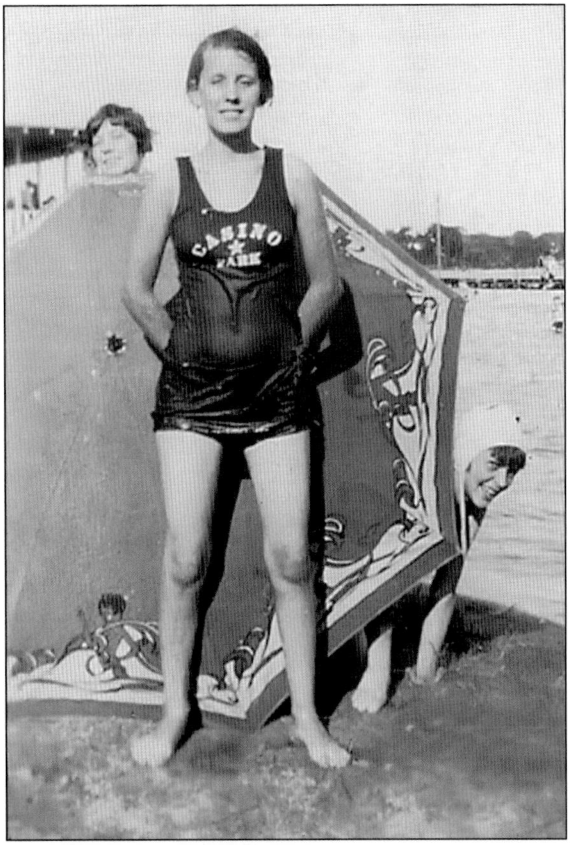

By the early 1920s, women's bathing suits had been reduced to a long top that covered shorts. Sometimes women of this time wore matching stockings in the smoldering heat of the Texas sun.

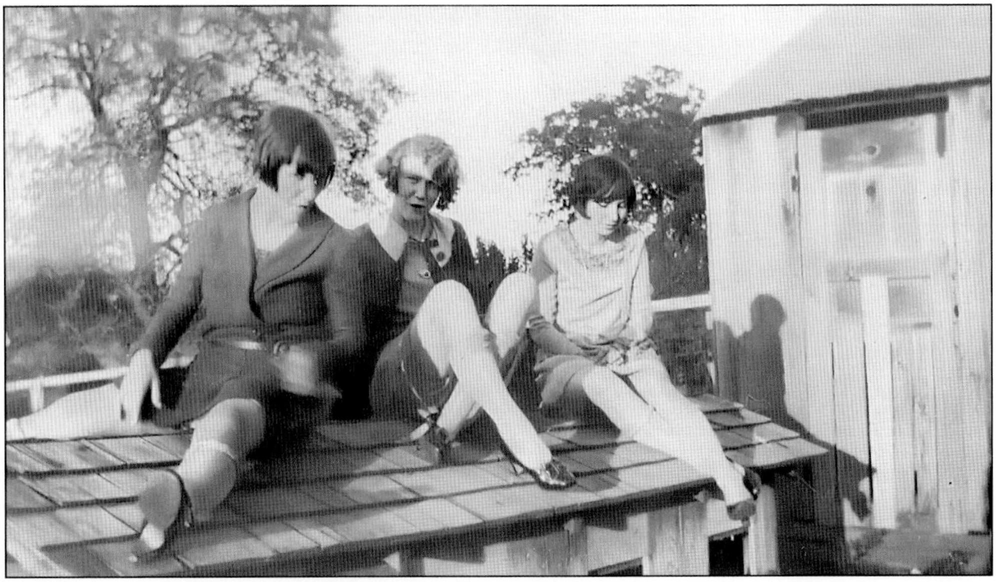

Stockings were made from silk, which did not stretch and required garters to stay in place. Garter straps clipped to the top of women's thigh highs, and the straps were attached to girdles or corsets. These flappers are rebelling against wearing girdles and corsets by rolling their stockings down instead of pulling them up to attach to garter straps.

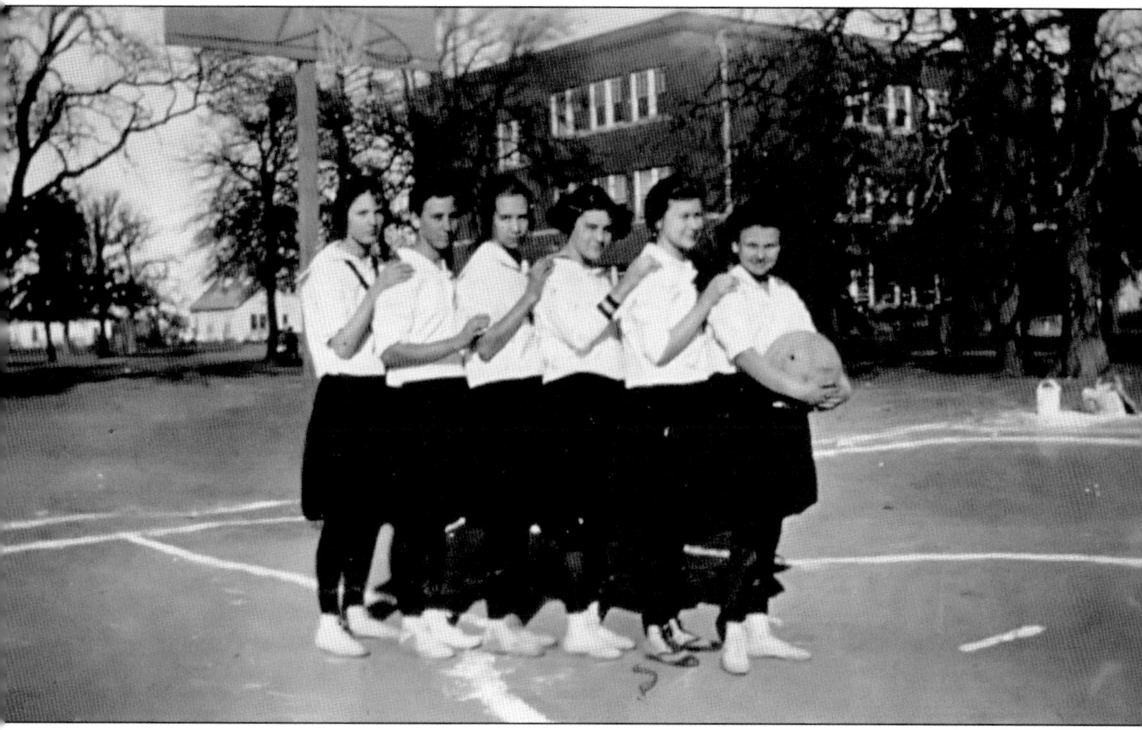

Pictured here is the 1922 Irving High School girls' basketball team. During this time, girls were allowed to play some sports only if they dressed modestly and played on school property. From left to right are Mae Mitchell, Exie Cunningham, Delma Crowe, Wilma Harkey, Lillian Embree, and one unidentified team member.

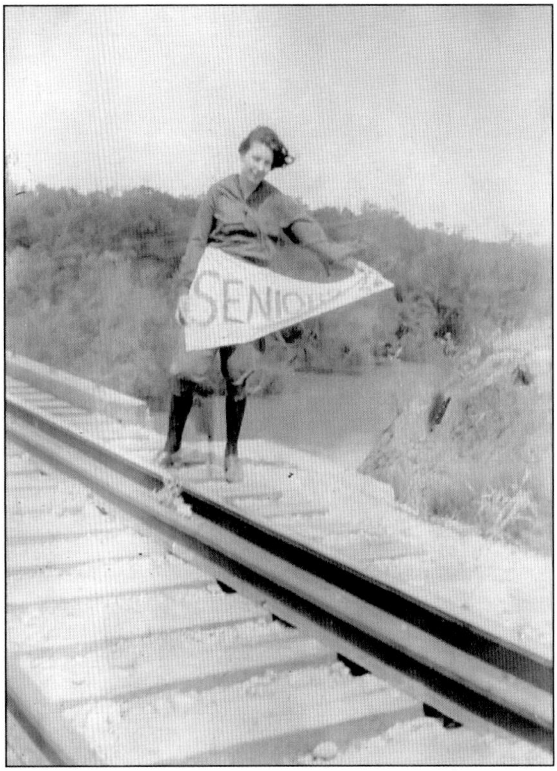

The outer clothing of flappers is still extremely identifiable even during playtime. The famous French fashion designer Coco Chanel developed a style called *garçonne* ("boy" with the feminine suffix), prompting girls to look more like a boy. The girls of Irving were educated and fashionable. This photograph is labelled "girl on track with pennant."

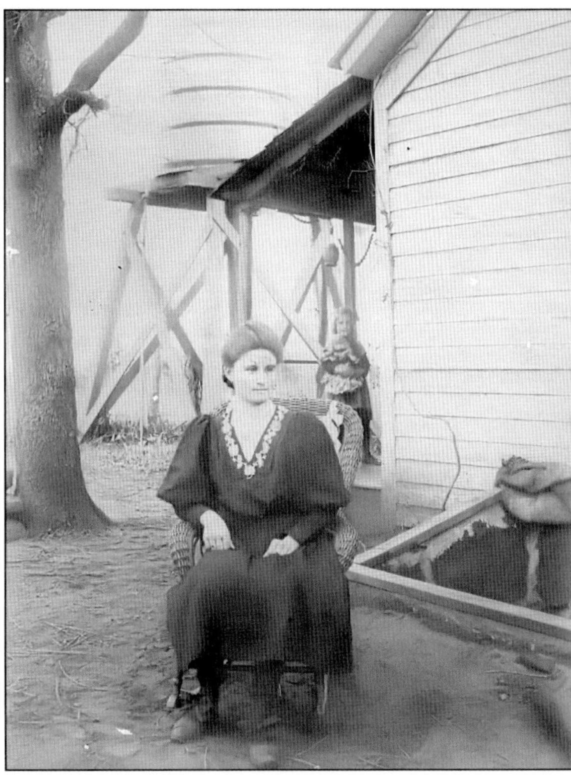

Belle Bidault, pictured sitting beside her house, moved from France to Texas in the early 1900s. A number of immigrants from Europe came in hopes of freedom from religious persecution.

In 1919, Dr. Monroe Gilbert married Dorothy Bald Brandon in New York. The following year, they immigrated to Texas, where they began a medical practice. Both Dorothy and Monroe contributed a number of hours and resources to help residents in need of health care. Dorothy Brandon Gilbert is shown modeling the latest fashion of the 1930s, with the longer bias cut, inverted pleated skirt, and soft sleeves and yokes. The sharp and snappy style was tailored with crisp lines and an emphasis on clinging fabrics around the hips.

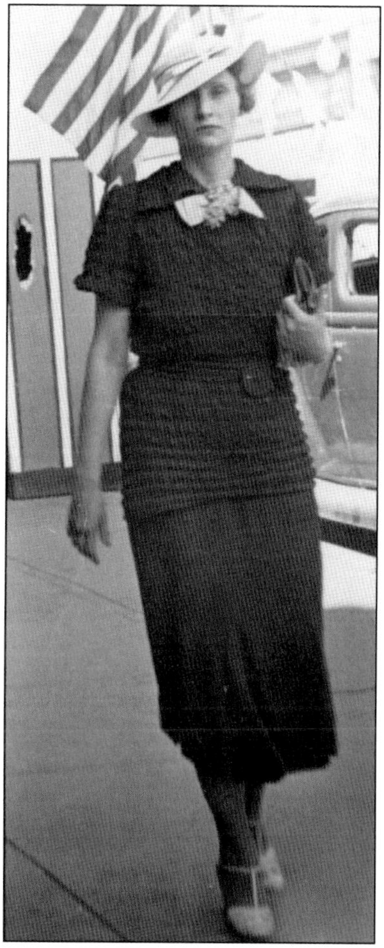

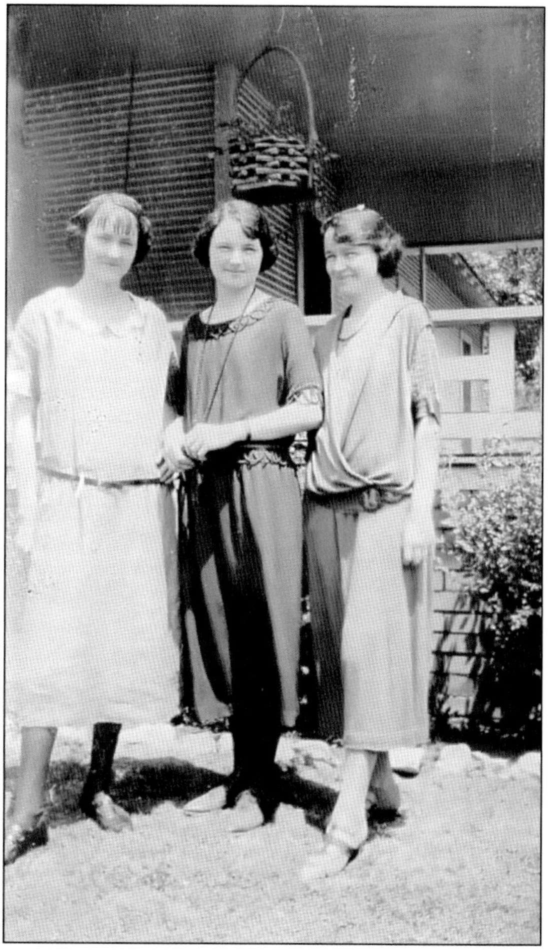

Three of Tom Haley's four daughters are pictured here in 1930. From left to right are Vera, Bess, and Flora. Vera Haley married C.C. Anderson, the City of Irving's first full-time employee. Vera taught for 42 years in the Irving School District. Bess and Flora also taught for many years in the Irving schools. (Courtesy of the Haley-Miller Collection, Irving Archives, Irving Public Library.)

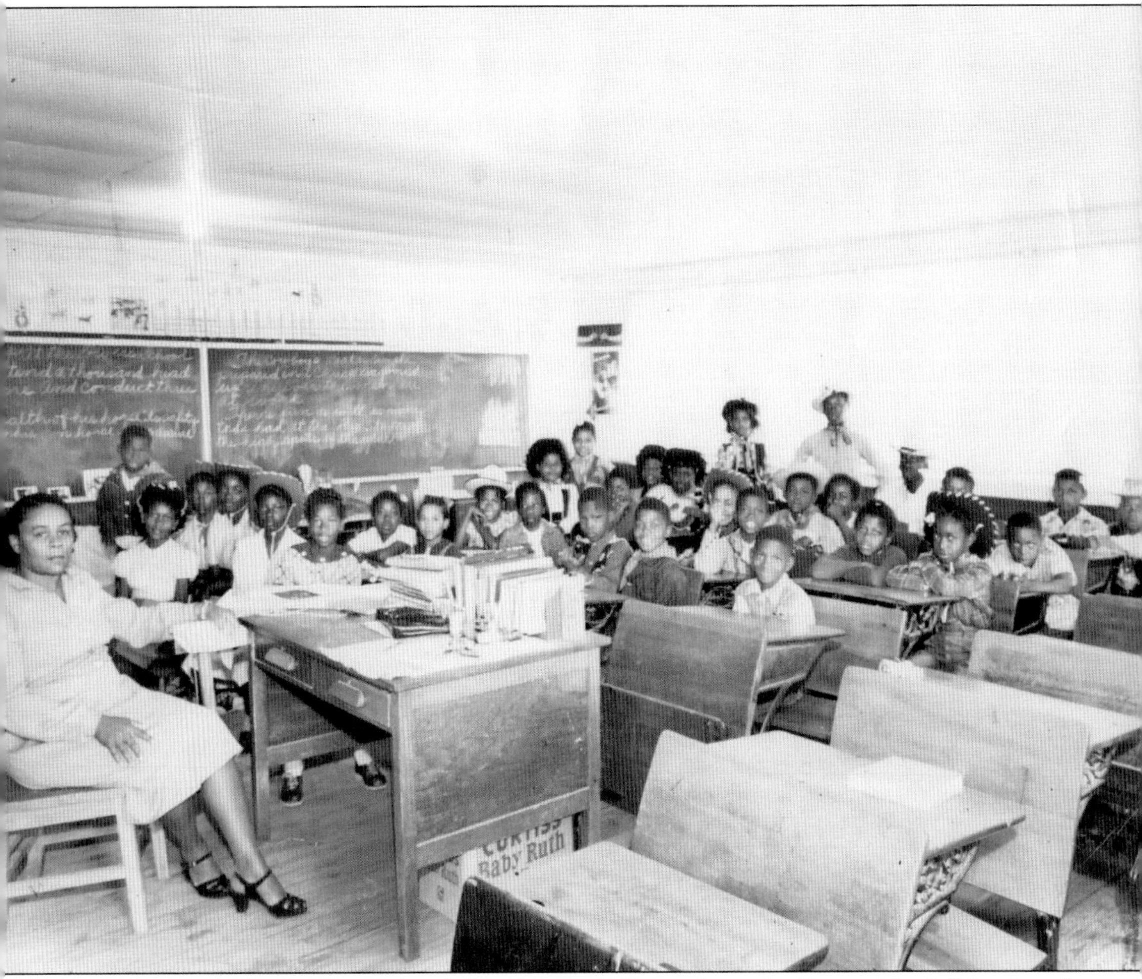

Earlie Mae Wheeler, pictured with her class in 1950, taught at the Sowers No. 2 School in the Bear Creek community. Born in Bastrop County, she was educated at Huston-Tillotson College in Austin. She began her teaching career in a segregated one-school room in 1931. Norma Stanton noted that 68 children and their parents attended school. The parents wanted to learn how to read and write, so after a long day of teaching the children, Earlie Mae found the energy to teach the parents at night.

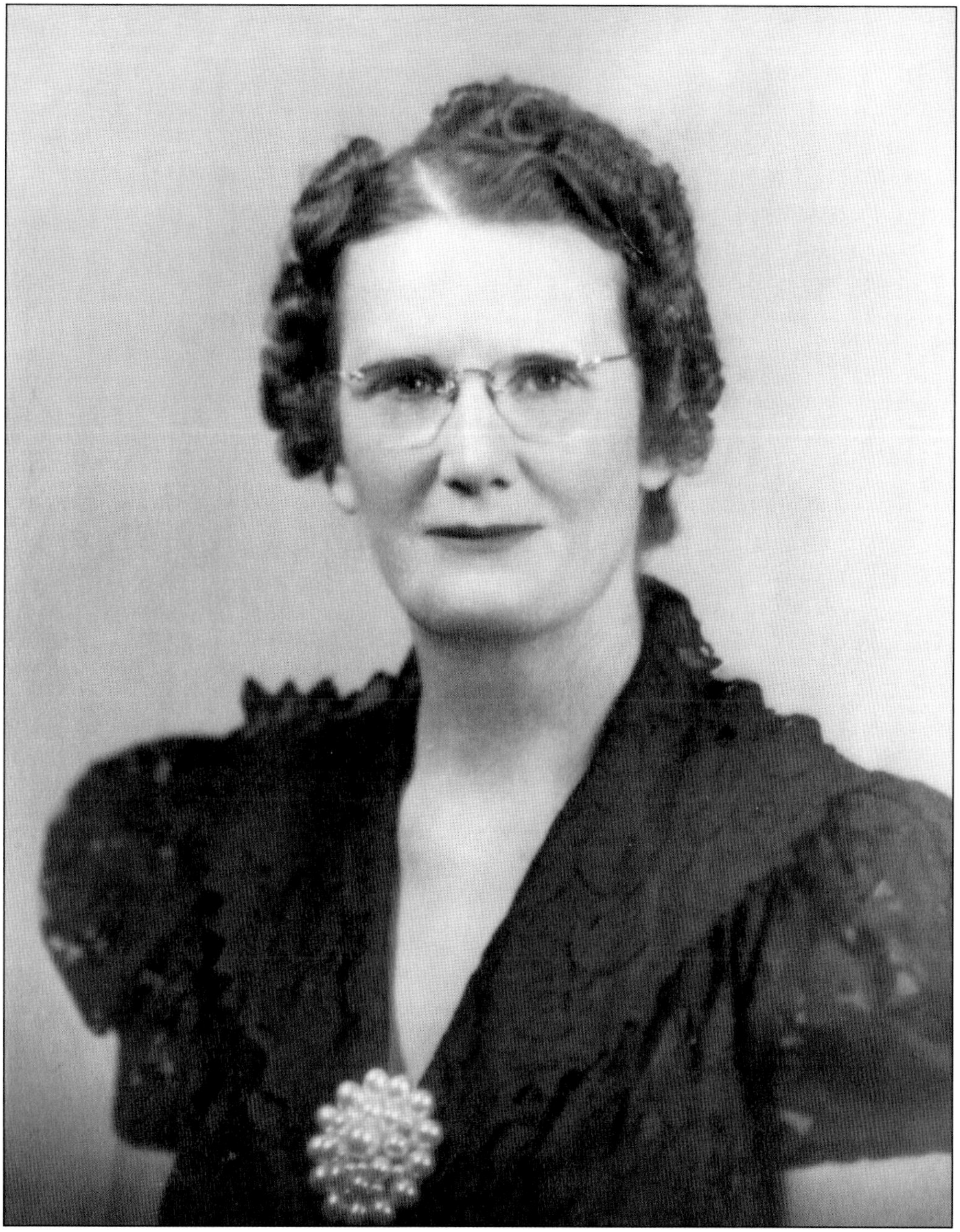

Esther Weaver was born in 1902 and moved with her family to Dallas County as a child. She attended business college while working as a secretary for a Dallas law firm. In 1919, she married Ben Hurwitz, a successful Dallas builder. She spent the next several decades serving in civic organizations while building a sense of community and improving the quality of life and beautification for Irving residents. She and her husband donated land for the improvement of roads in what is now eastern Irving. She was also instrumental in obtaining bus service for the city. In the 1930s, she cofounded the Irving Felicity Club, a women's organization for community welfare. Her other civic activities included cofounder of the Dallas County Library System, the Business and Professional Women's Club of Irving, the Irving Presidents' Council, and the Irving Improvement League.

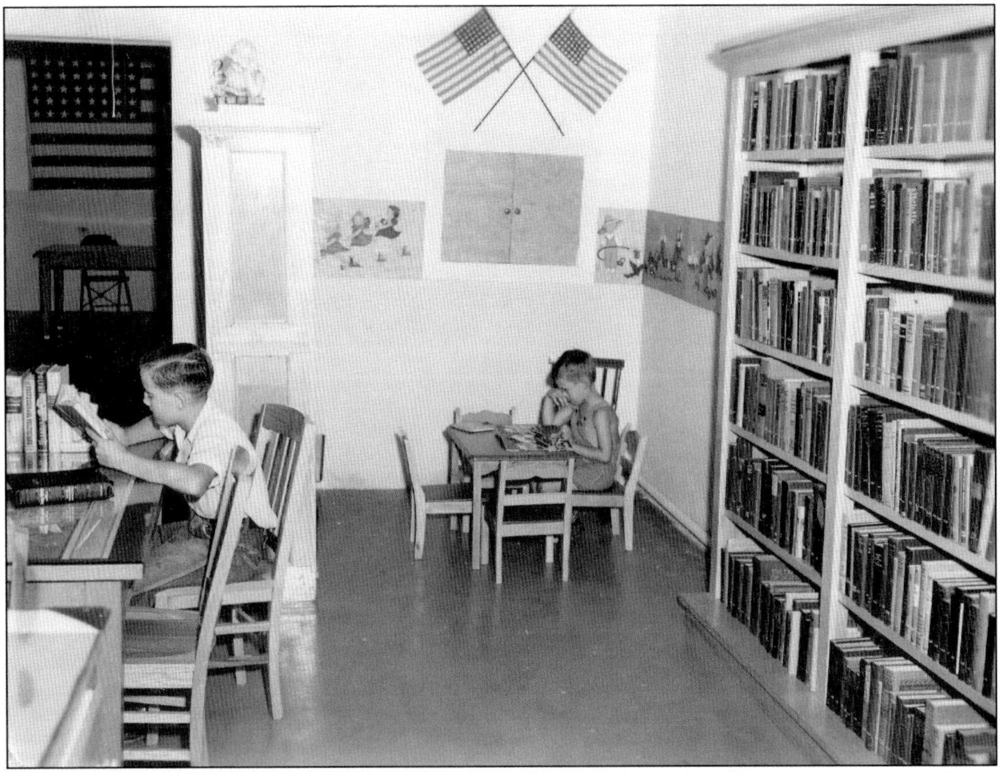

Esther (Weaverz) Hurwitz was instrumental in establishing the city of Irving's first public library on May 5, 1941. With a stipend of $25 from the county, she found a place that would host the library. The beginnings of the library were housed inside a furniture store, a corner of which was used for bookshelves where the community was invited to peruse the collection.

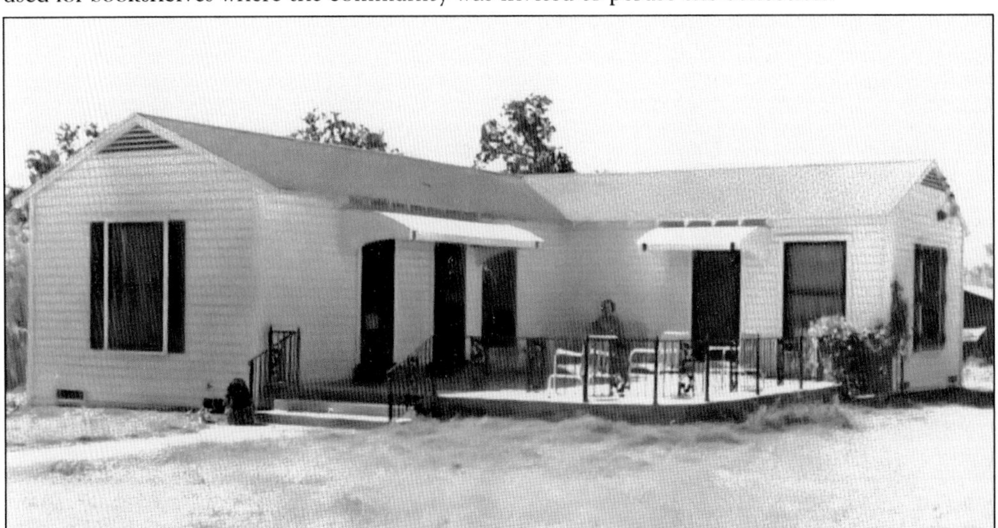

Among Esther Hurwitz's greatest accomplishments was winning the battle that allowed the Irving Public Library to become part of the Dallas County Library System in 1941. She served as librarian of the Irving Public Library for 21 years, until the city opened a municipal library in 1962. The first library is pictured here in 1951.

Josie O. Davis was a teacher of the Sowers community. Sowers Colored School No. 2 was in Bear Creek and served the black community. The J.O. Davis School was named after Davis because of her major contributions to education in the community. In the mid-1960s, she was instrumental in the establishment of the Ben Washington Baptist Church.

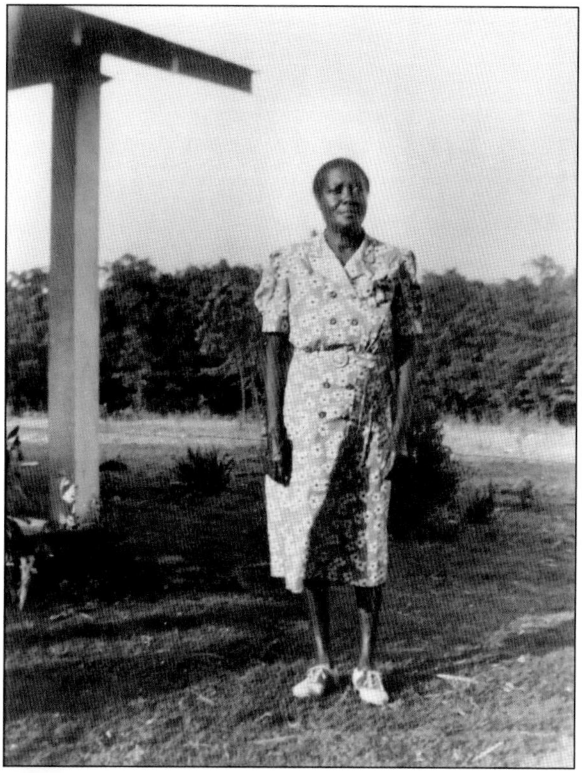

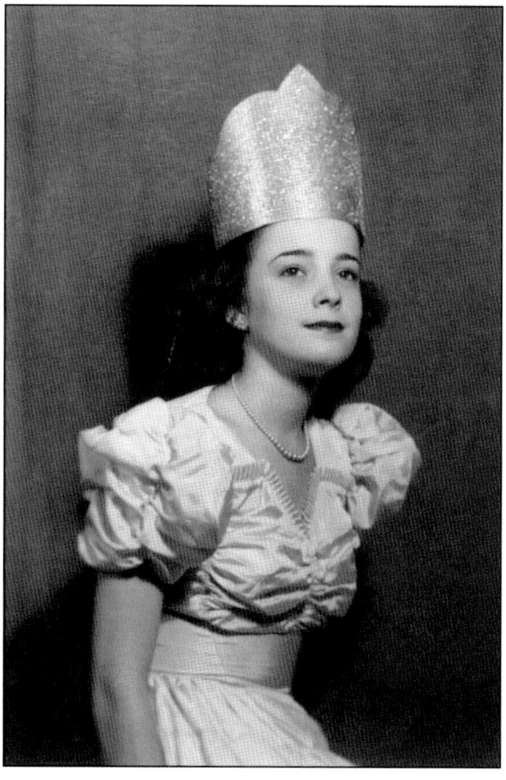

Mary Delay, Irving's first Miss Irving, is shown wearing the latest fashion in pageant gowns with a stitched waistline. Delay was not only beautiful but talented as well. She was crowned sweetheart of the Sowers School No. 2 for her volunteer activities there. This photograph was taken in 1946.

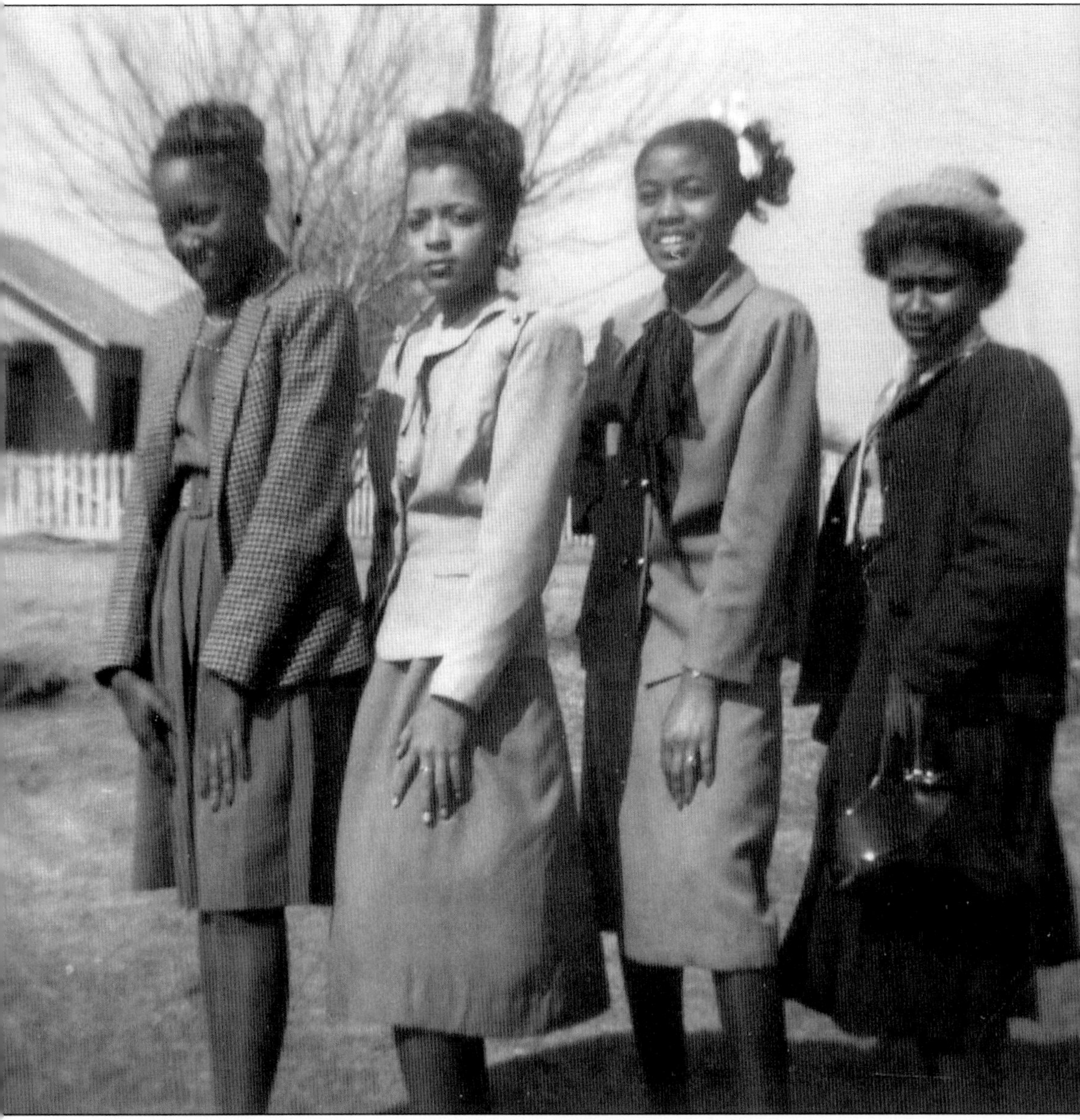

Women's fashions during the 1940s were designed with squared shoulders, small waistlines, and skirts just above or below the knee. Women were encouraged to design and create their own style. They were educated on how to conserve material or update older dresses to the latest fashions. Blouses were frequently worn with skirts and jackets. Four beautiful young women are seen in the latest fashions during Easter time.

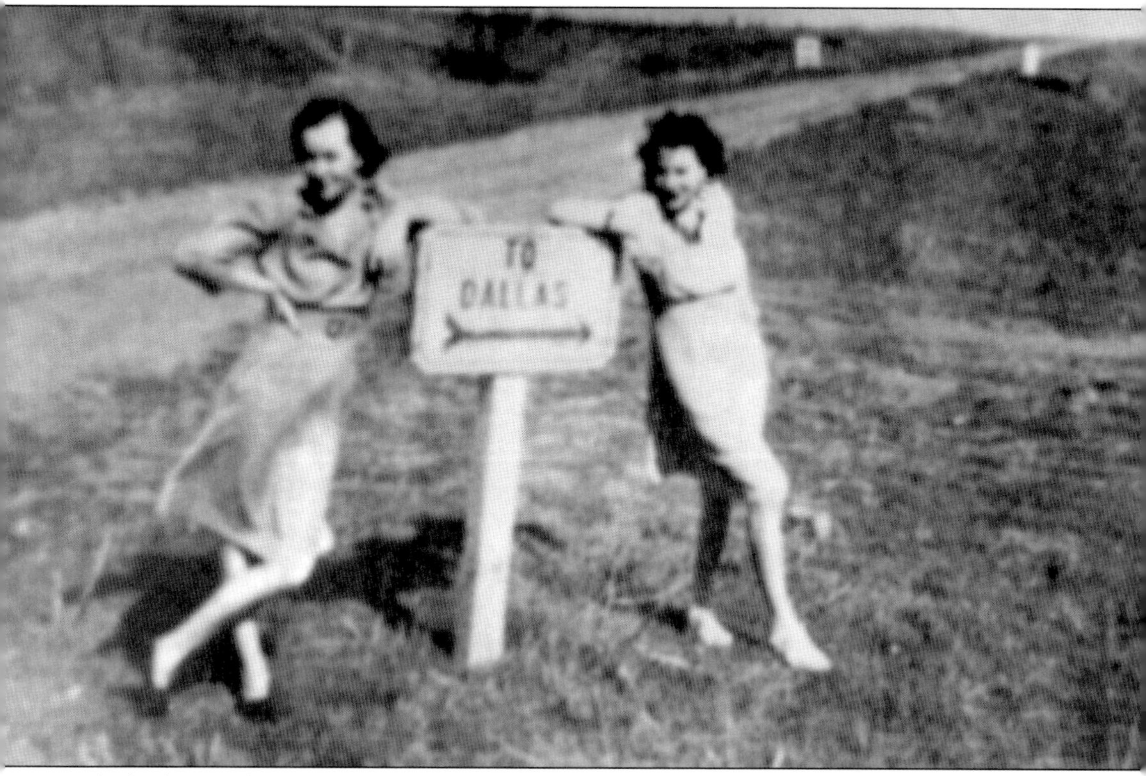

In the background is a narrow dirt road that would soon become a major thoroughfare. Highway 183 helped define the city of Irving and connect Dallas with Fort Worth. In this photograph from 1945, Etta McKinney and Betty Tyndall are shown posing in their utility-style dresses leaning on the sign.

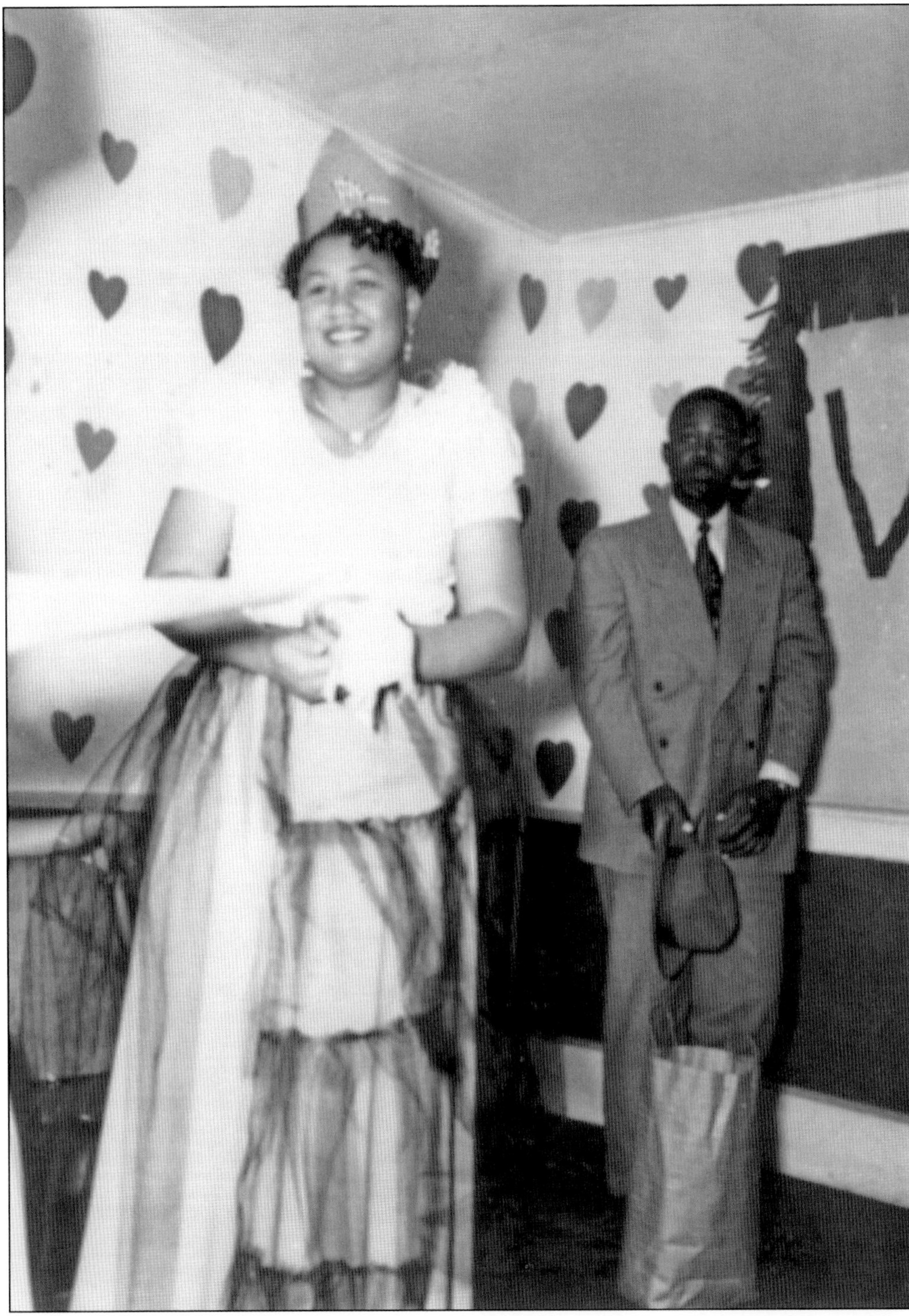

Women of the Bear Creek community were not only brave, strong, and resilient but beautiful as well. An annual beauty contest was held in Bear Creek to celebrate the women of the community. Although many women participated, only one queen would be selected. Pictured here is Mary Morton, queen of the Sowers School No. 2.

Four

From Irving's Redbrick House to the University of Dallas

Colonial Americans who settled in Irving were educated and believed that education was the responsibility of the family and church. Since worship was important to the settlers, it was important that the young learned how to read Bible verses and scripture. Settlers raised financial support from their community to build a schoolhouse referred to as an "old field school," which was usually one room that housed all grade levels. Many communities designated an old log cabin to serve as a schoolhouse. According to historian Joseph Rice, land was free or inexpensive, and most communities had enough financial resources to support doctors, lawyers, and teachers. In other communities where funds were scarce, money was raised to pay the schoolteacher. During the early years, there was one teacher who taught students of all ages regardless of their education level. All lessons were given in the same one-room school.

During the time of the abolitionists, African Americans in general were not allowed to attend school because it was believed that they would organize and rebel and leave the colony. After the Civil War, however, all African Americans were free, and they began to build separate communities and schools. The Bear Creek, Elm, Estelle, Kit, Sowers, Twin Wells, and Union Bower communities were strong educational supporters.

In 1905, a two-story, two-room wooden schoolhouse called the Lively School was built to serve the children of Irving and the surrounding farm communities. When the Irving Independent school District (IISD) was established in 1909, it took over the schoolhouse. Curriculum for elementary and high school students was defined, and education was formalized. Future student leaders would soon graduate and either go off to college or work for their family farm or business.

When the IISD was established, the school district built a high school so that the children could continue their education through 12th grade.

The concept of the old one-room wooden schoolhouse was about to change. In 1913, the IISD constructed a three-story redbrick building that housed all grade levels. A new school was constructed next to the redbrick building, which became a high school in the early 1930s. In 1936, a new high school was built, and the middle school students were moved into the old high school. The elementary school kids continued in the three-story redbrick building. In 1946, a new high school was built on Sixth Street, so the middle school students were moved to the old high school. These schools were built on the five-acre campus at what is now Second and Jefferson Streets.

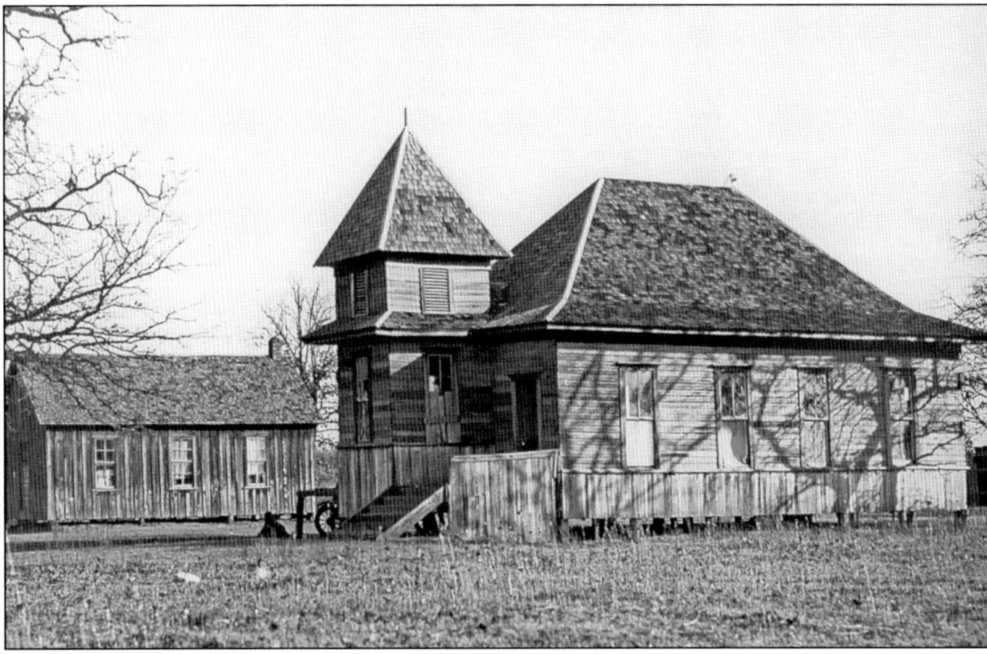

Within the Sowers community, land was earmarked for African American residents so that they could begin their community school (pictured at left). In 1884, it began as a freedom school, supported by donations from residents because church was important to them. The church served as the community's school. After the Civil War and during the era of reconstruction, segregation, and Jim Crow laws, this church played an important role in helping the residents of Bear Creek maintain their community. In 1897, the Bear Creek congregation moved to a larger church. The church is still thriving today. Pictured here at right is the second church, built in 1925.

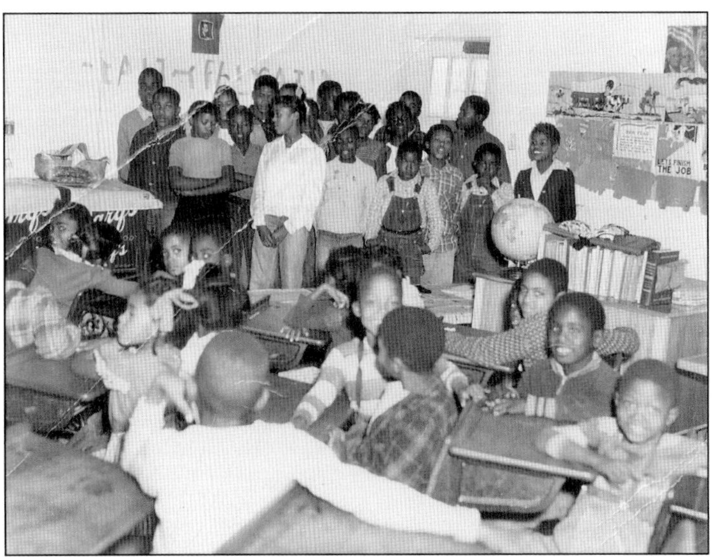

The Bear Creek community school later became part of the Dallas County Common School District as the Sowers School No. 2 on Bear Creek. The school offered only elementary grades to African American students, who then traveled to Dallas or Grand Prairie to attend black high schools. Segregation in this area did not allow black students to attend high schools in Irving.

Josie O. Davis taught in the Sowers School No. 2 from 1930 to the 1940s. Davis served not only as a teacher but also as a leader and mentor to the youth. In 1960, the Irving IISD constructed a new school building for African American students in Bear Creek and named it the J.O. Davis School in her honor. Pictured here in 1946 are, from left to right, Pat Taylor (Josie's granddaughter), unidentified, Samuel Morten, and Dixie Callaway.

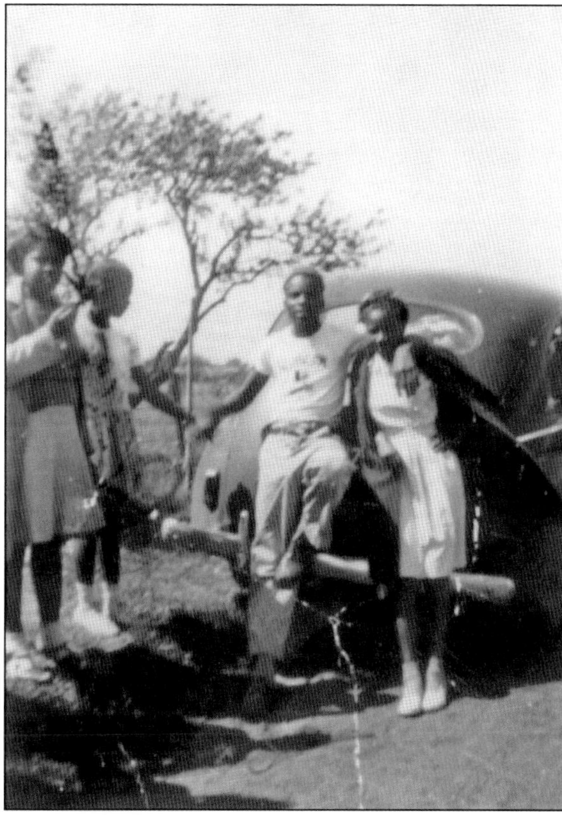

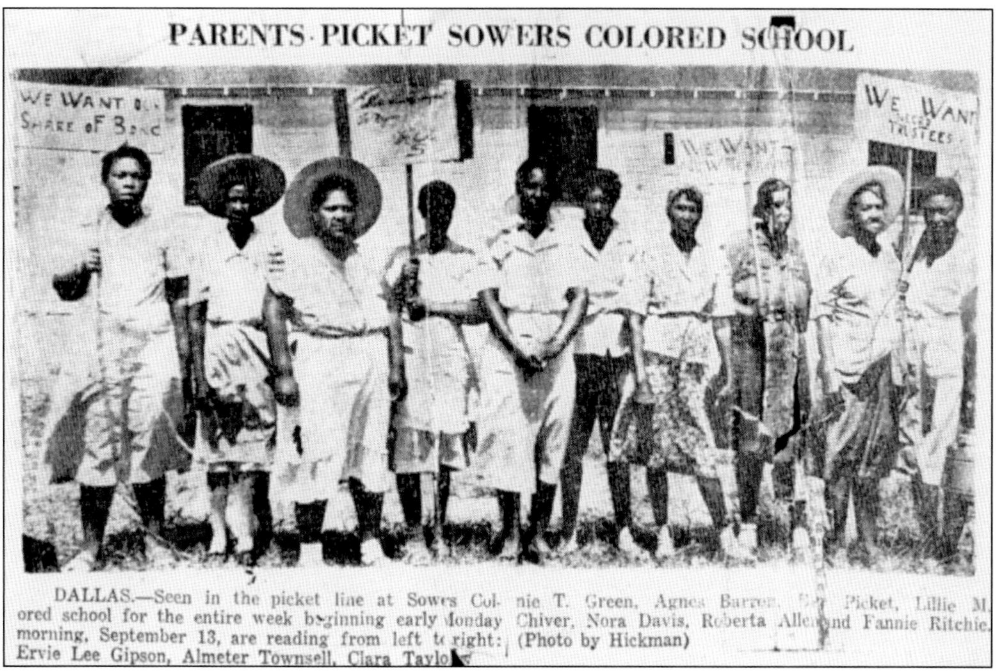

PARENTS PICKET SOWERS COLORED SCHOOL

DALLAS.—Seen in the picket line at Sowers Colored school for the entire week beginning early Monday morning, September 13, are reading from left to right: Ervie Lee Gipson, Almeter Townsell, Clara Taylo[illegible] nie T. Green, Agnes Barren, [illegible] Picket, Lillie M. Chiver, Nora Davis, Roberta Allen and Fannie Ritchie. (Photo by Hickman)

Parents of Bear Creek students are shown protesting for equal rights to bond money, as other schools within the Dallas Common School District were allotted.

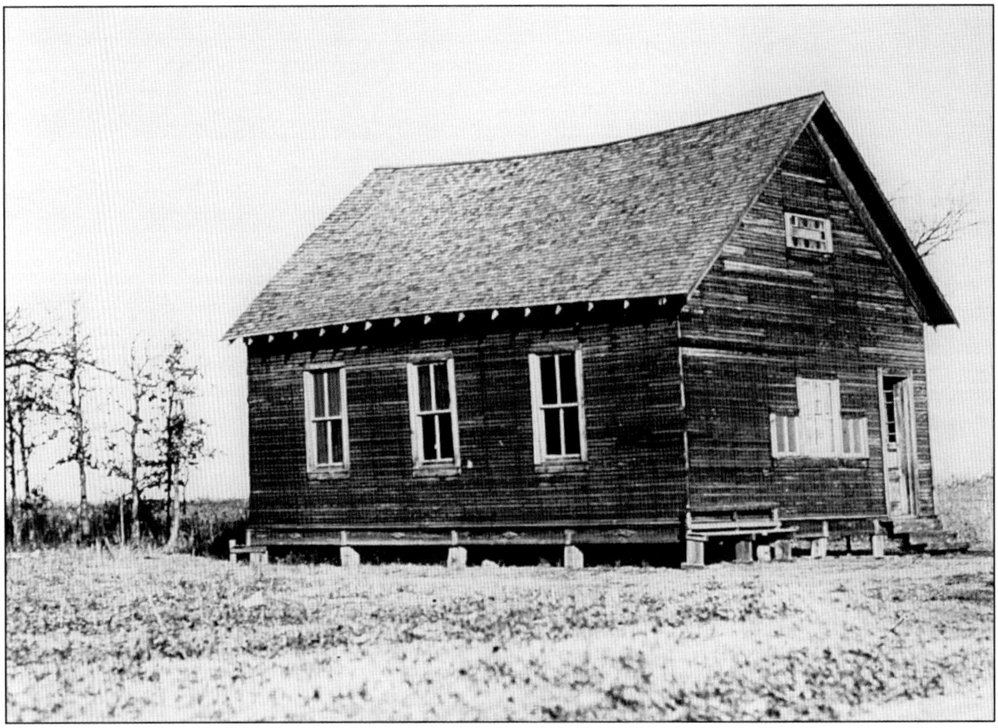

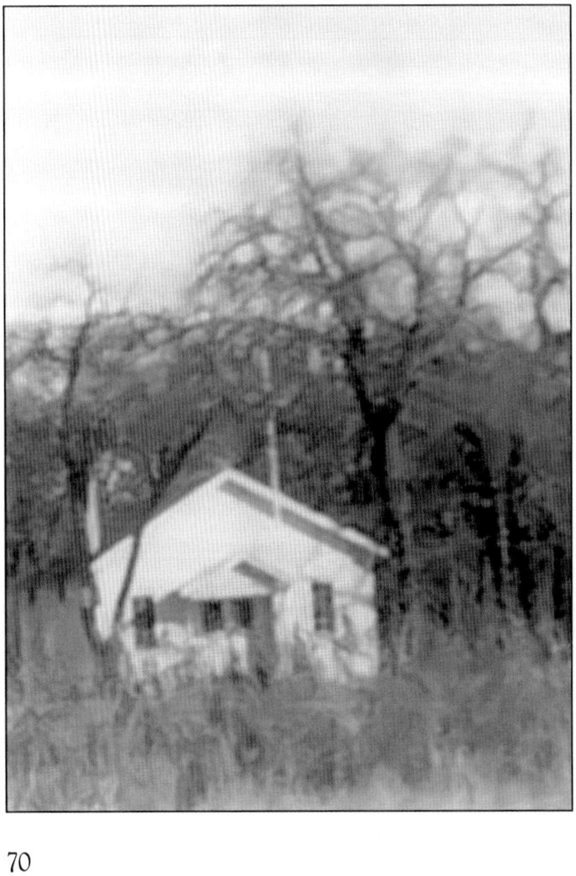

Pictured here is an African American church built by residents. This church would help the members shape their community.

In the early 1880s, the Elm community built its first school. Five individuals contributed $25 each for building materials. The school provided grades one through seven.

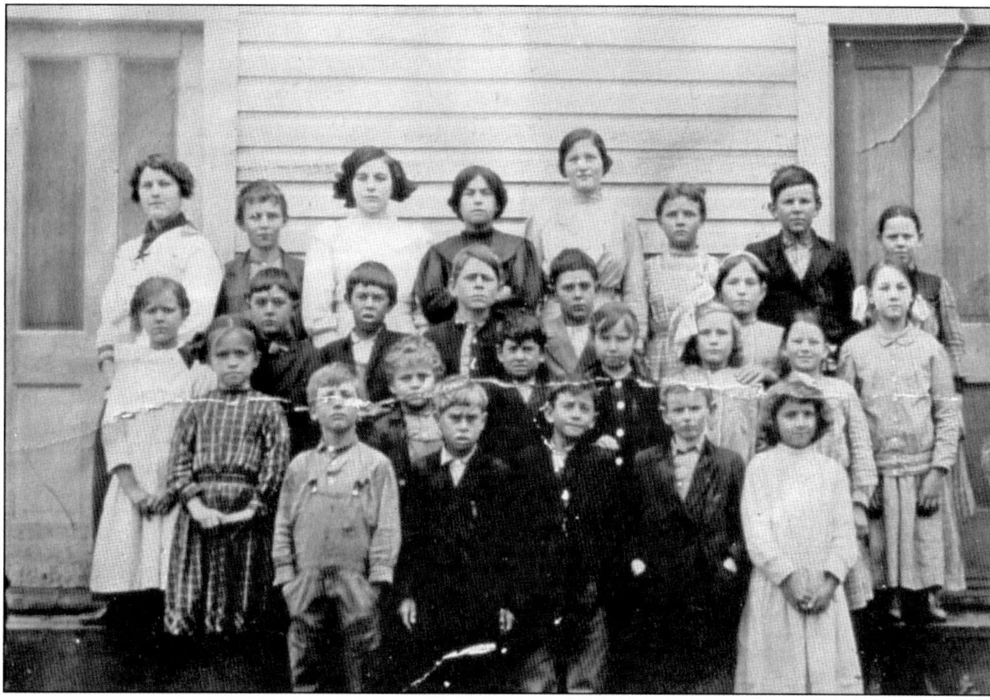

Students are pictured in front of the old Elm School in 1914.

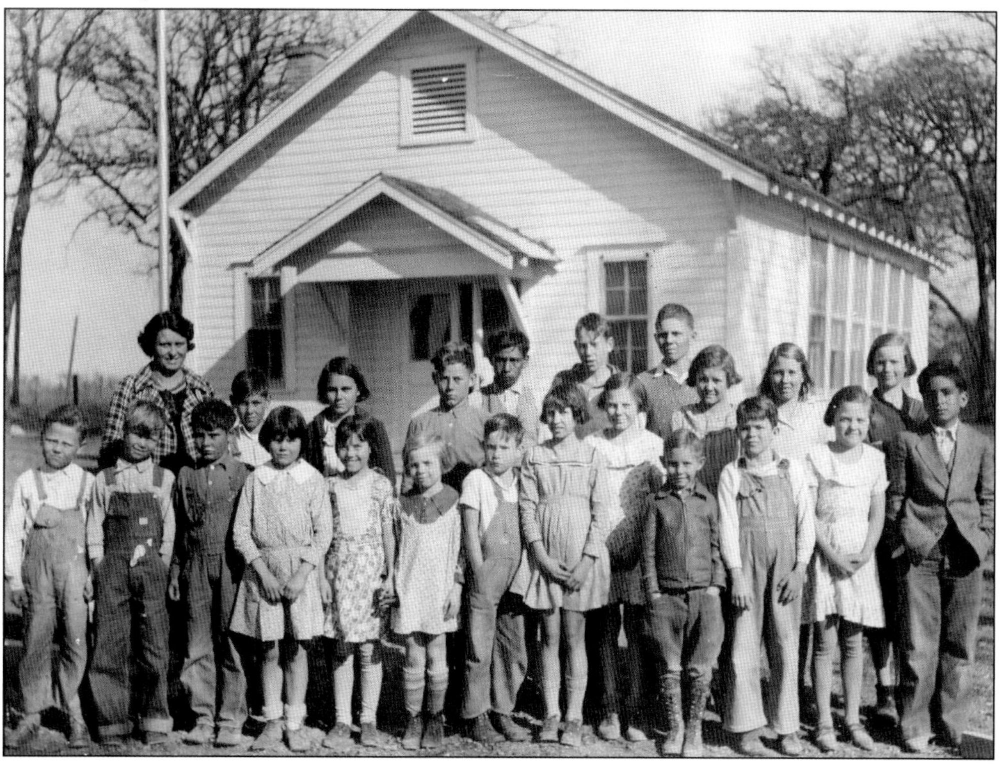

In 1934, a new school was built in the Elm community. Students are pictured in front of the new Elm School in 1935.

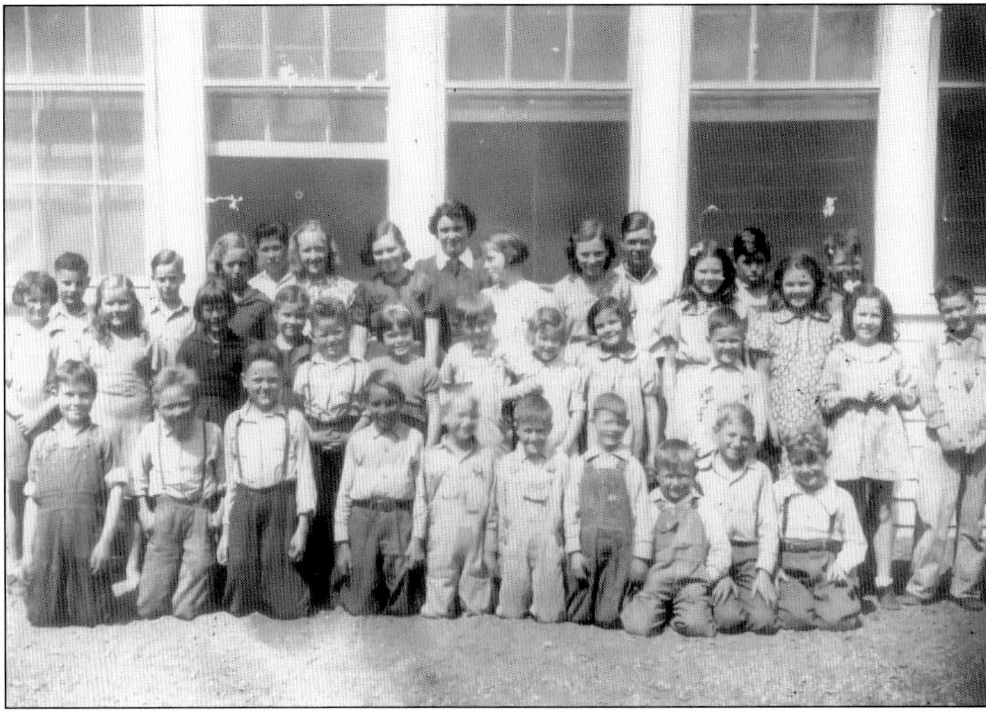

After the establishment of the IISD in 1909, the Elm community students could attend high school in Irving after seventh grade. Students are shown posing in front of the Elm School in 1939.

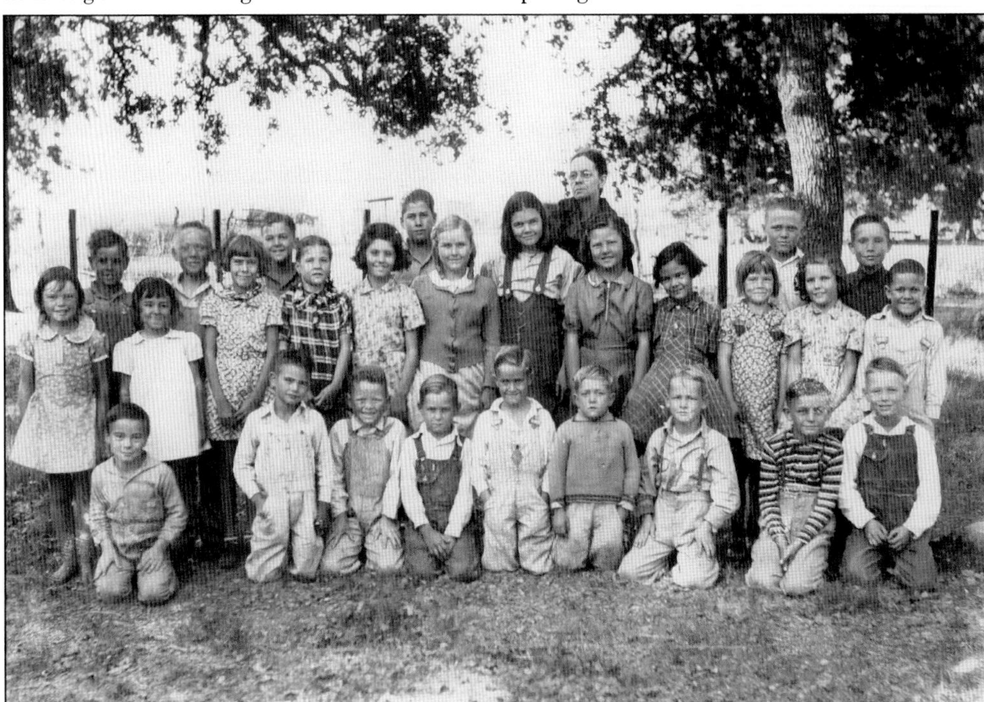

The Elm School operated from the 1880s until 1948, when it became a part of the IISD. Students are shown posing in front of the Elm School in 1940.

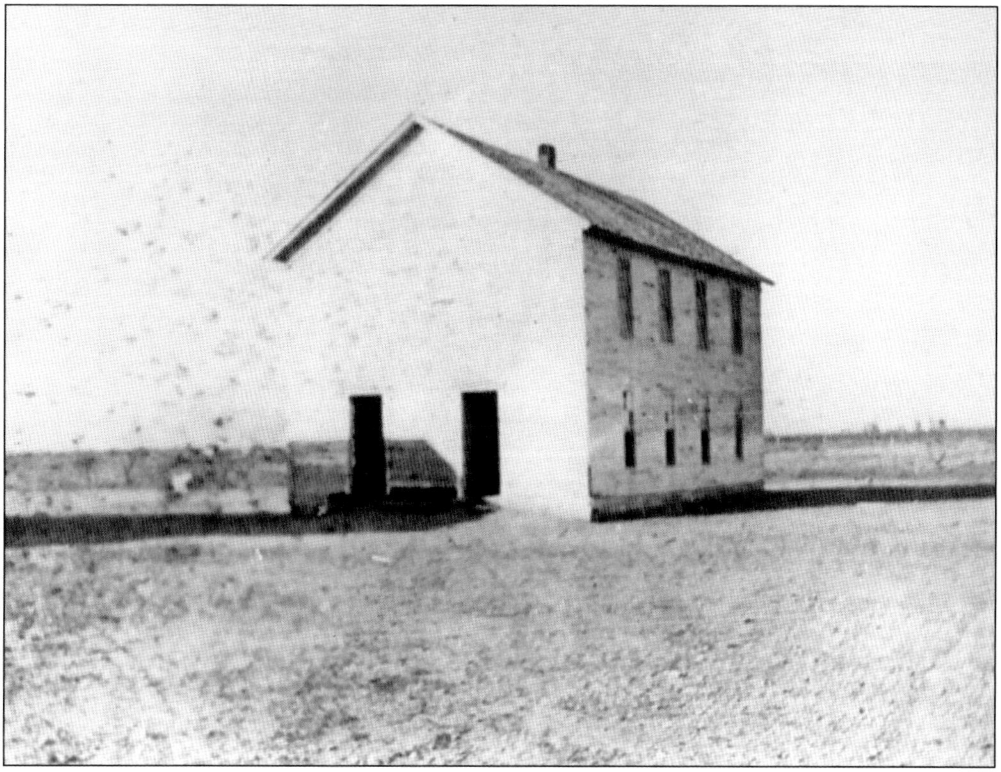

In 1884, the Harrington brothers donated land to construct this wooden building. The two-story building held the Estelle School on the first floor, and the second floor was used as the Masonic lodge.

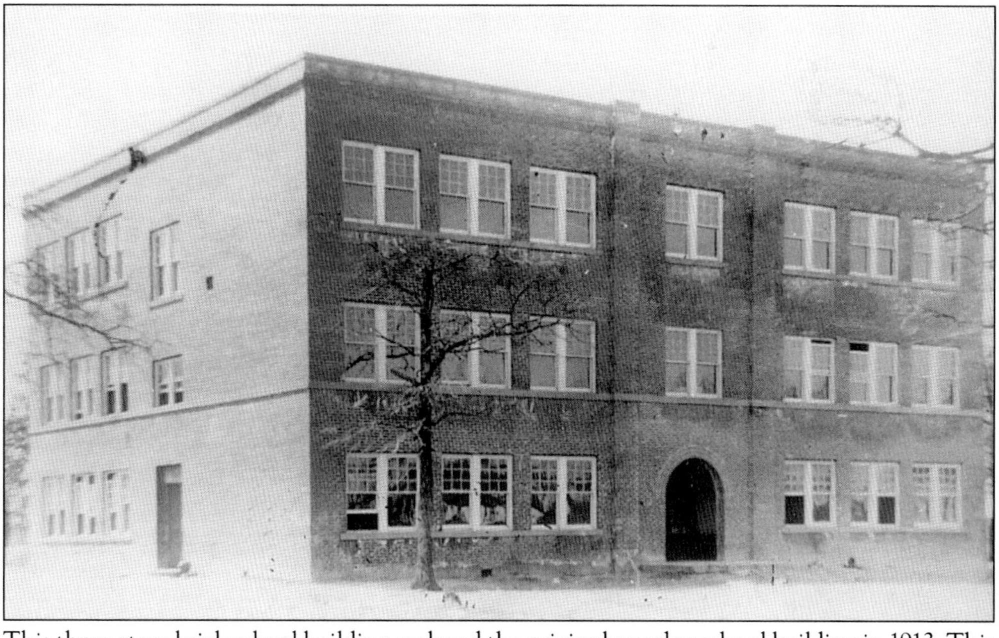

This three-story brick school building replaced the original wooden school building in 1913. This photograph was taken in the mid-1920s.

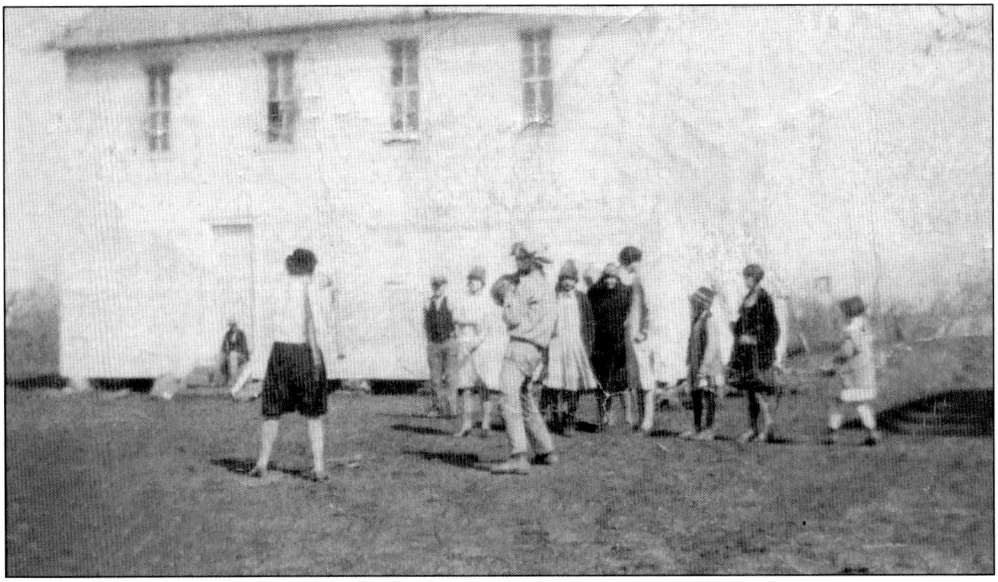

Students of the Estelle School are shown playing in the foreground. J.D. Powers is seen in catcher's gear at the center of this 1930 photograph.

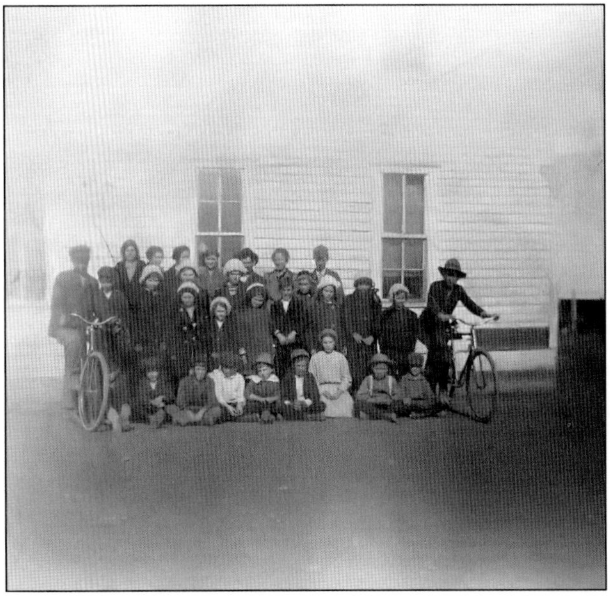

Estelle students are shown posing in front of the school in the 1930s. Buck Powers is seen next to the bike at left.

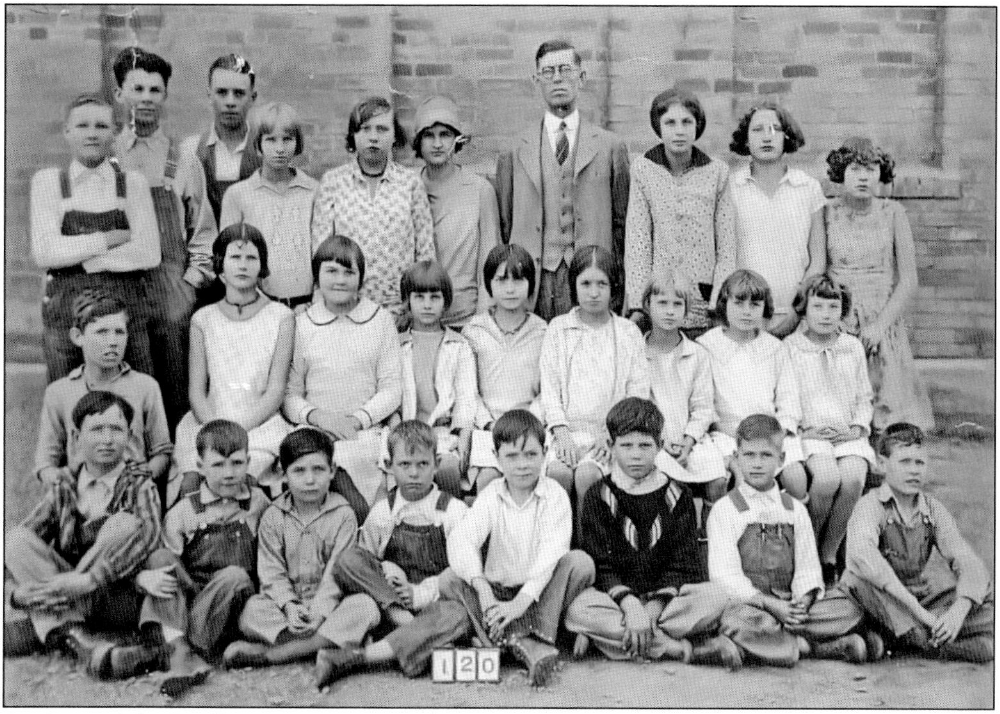

Students of the Estelle community school are pictured here. Their grade level is unknown.

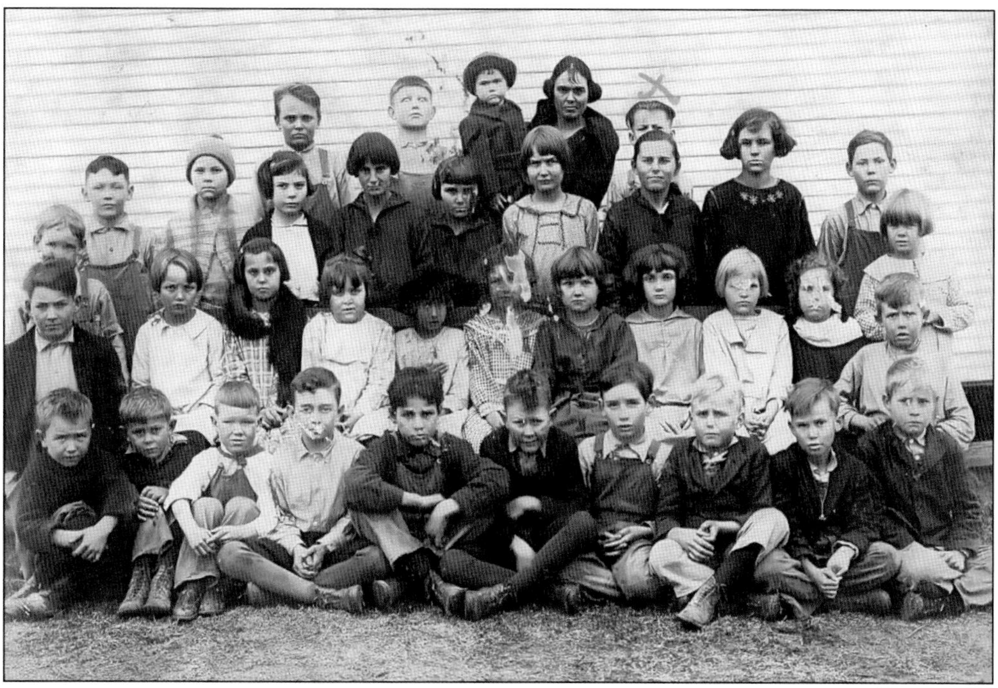

These are third grade students of the Estelle community school. Their teacher was Mrs. Boswell.

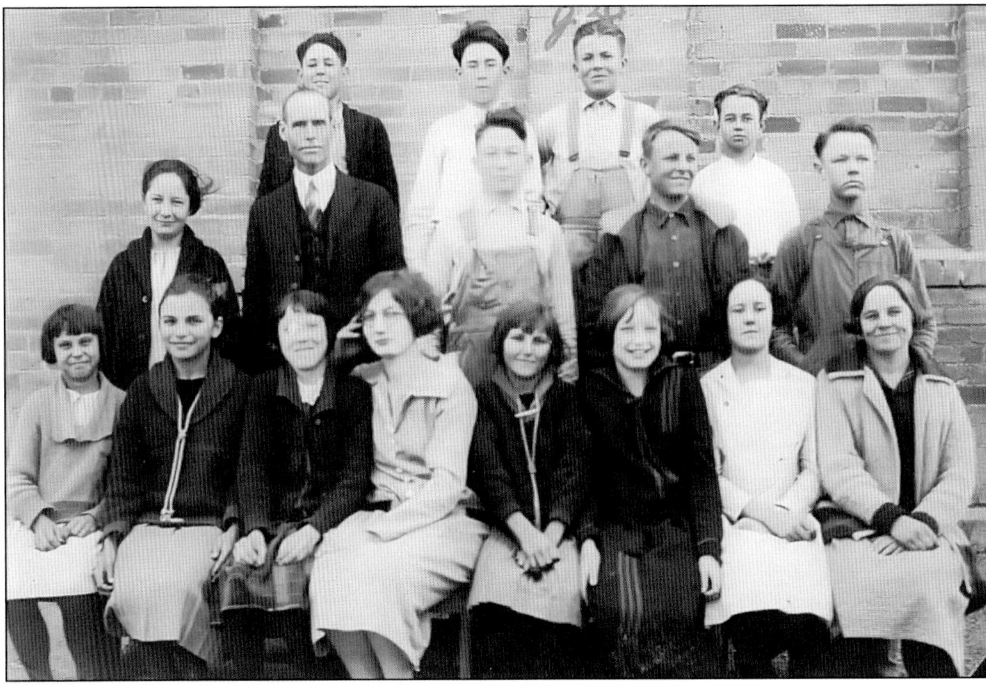

Teacher Mr. Nichols is pictured with students from the Estelle School. Their grade is unknown.

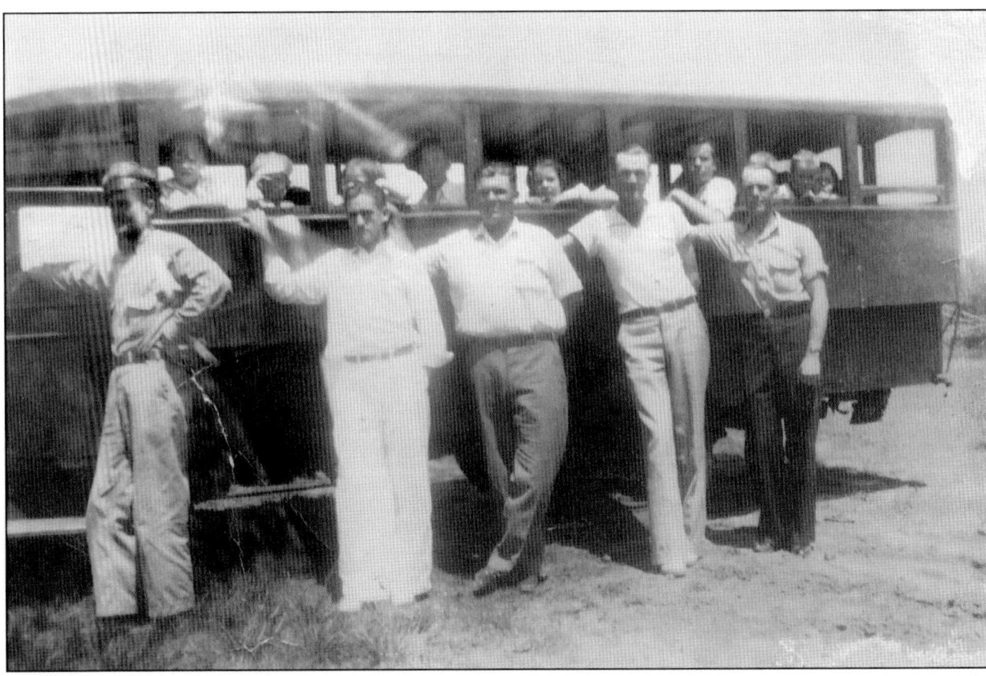

Standing in front of an Estelle school bus are, from left to right, S.H. Ramsey, Gene Ramsey, J.D. Powers, Tom Ramsey, and Morris Taylor, with unidentified children inside the bus.

The Estelle Baptist Church was founded in the Bear Creek community in 1853. Later, it was moved to the Estelle community a short distance away, where it remained until 1960 when the property was purchased for the construction of the Dallas/Fort Worth Airport. Today, the church is known as the First Baptist Church–Las Colinas.

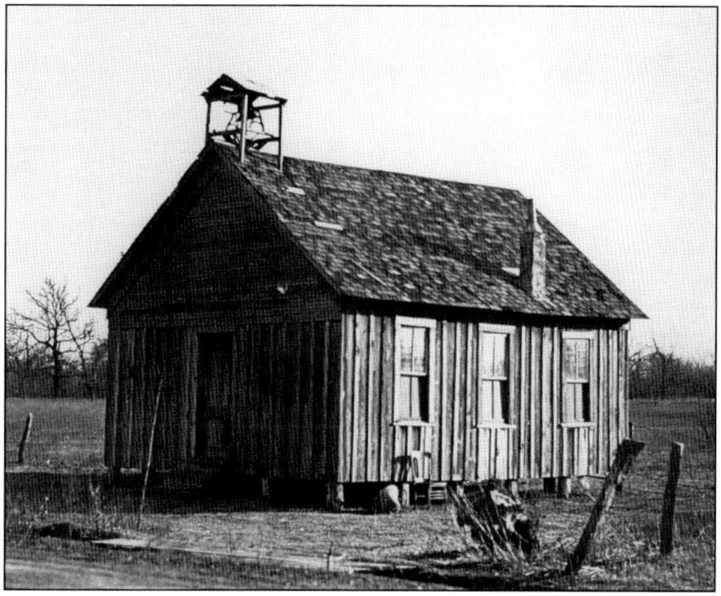

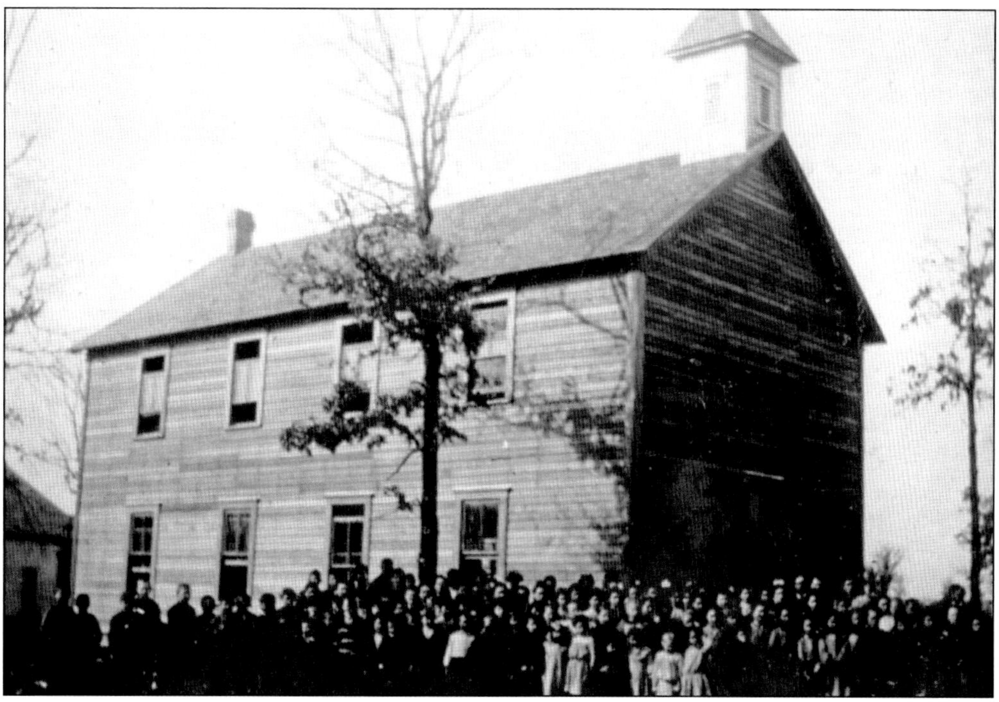

The Kit community was the first to establish a schoolhouse in the late 1800s, when Hezekiah Lucas secured a one-room log cabin for the school. Netta Bacus, soon-to-be wife of Otis Brown, was the schoolteacher. In 1904, a tornado raged through the community, and the schoolhouse was destroyed. In 1905, the school was rebuilt and called the Lively School. Students from the Kit and Irving communities were taught here. In 1909, the Texas legislature created the Irving Independent School District, and this building soon became the home of IISD.

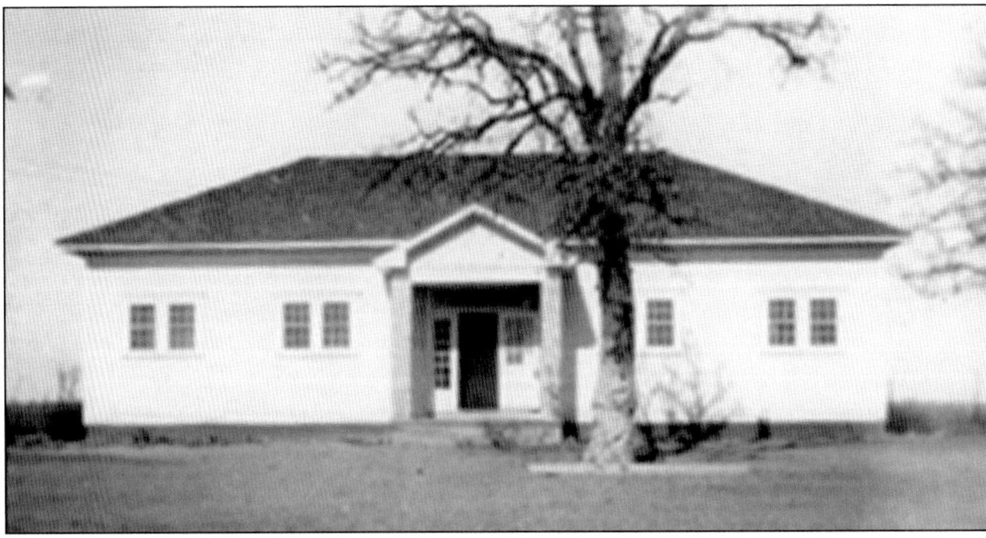

In the 1880s, residents of the Sowers community constructed a small one-story frame building to serve as a schoolhouse for the children of the area.

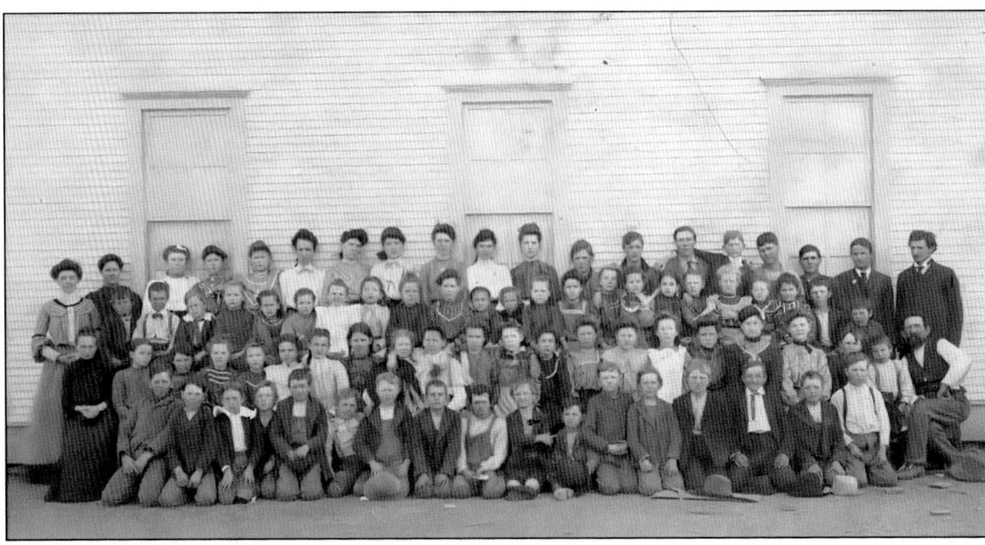

The Sowers student body is pictured with teacher John Roberts in 1910. The Sowers School served the community from the 1880s until the 1950s. By the 1930s, the school had three rooms and three teachers.

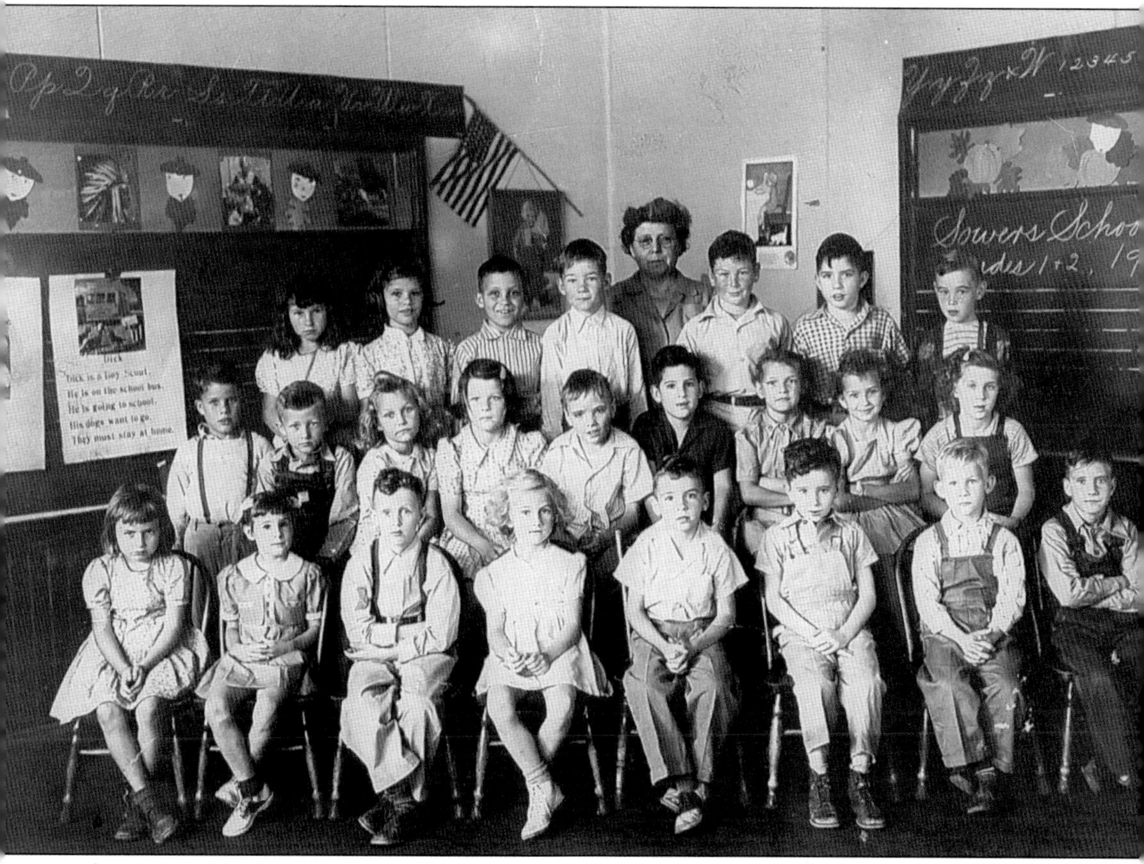

In later years, the Sowers School offered only elementary grades. Older children attended the Irving High School, which was about three miles east. The school was located on Pioneer Road when it was incorporated by the IISD in 1955. First and second grade students are pictured in the Sowers School classroom in the late 1890s.

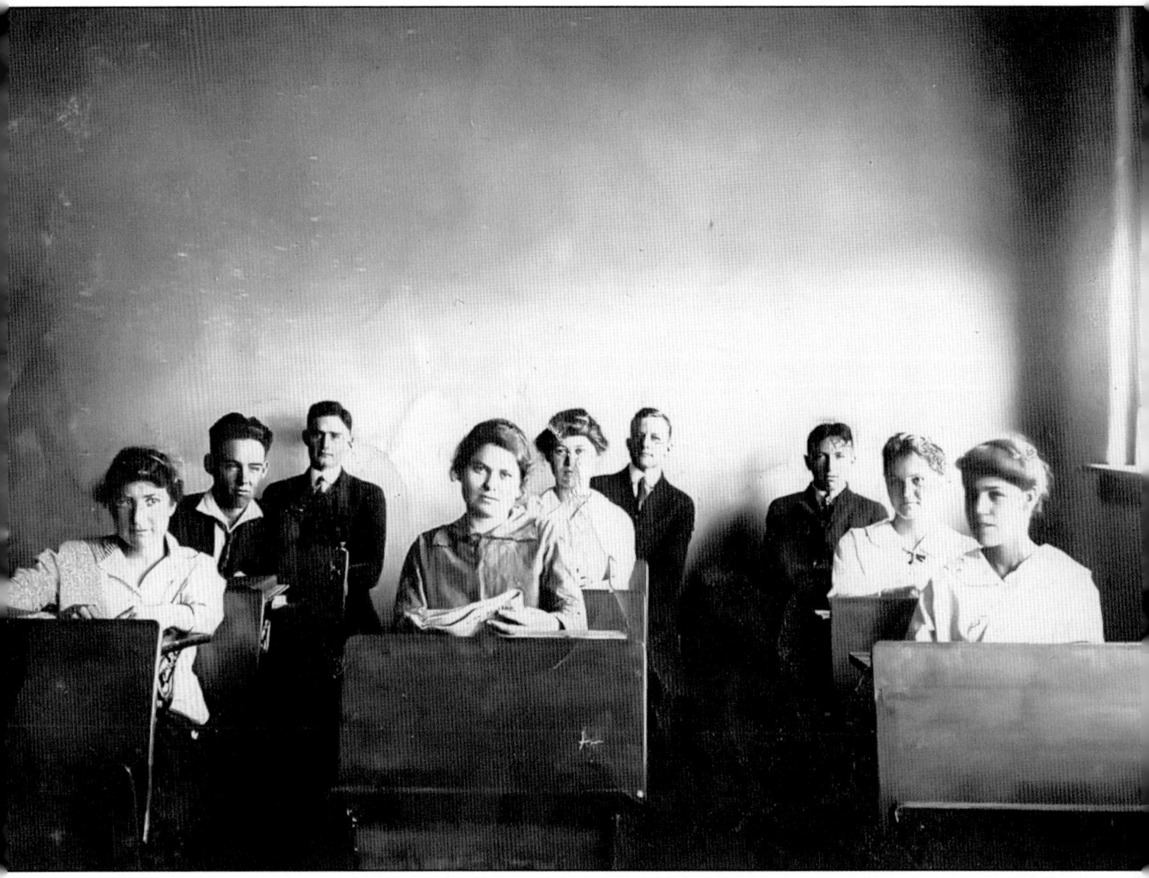

When the population of the Twin Wells area peaked at 150 in 1940, community residents sent their children to Irving schools. The senior class of Irving High School is pictured in 1916. From front to back are (left row) Osten Cushenberry, Frank Haley, and Roy Lively; (center row) Theo DeHaes, Inez Moore, and Homer Duckworth; (right row) Susie Clark, Velma Duckworth, and Roy Miller. Frank Haley would later marry classmate Velma Duckworth, who was the granddaughter of Chaney Miller. (Courtesy of the Haley-Miller Collection, Irving Archives, Irving Public Library.)

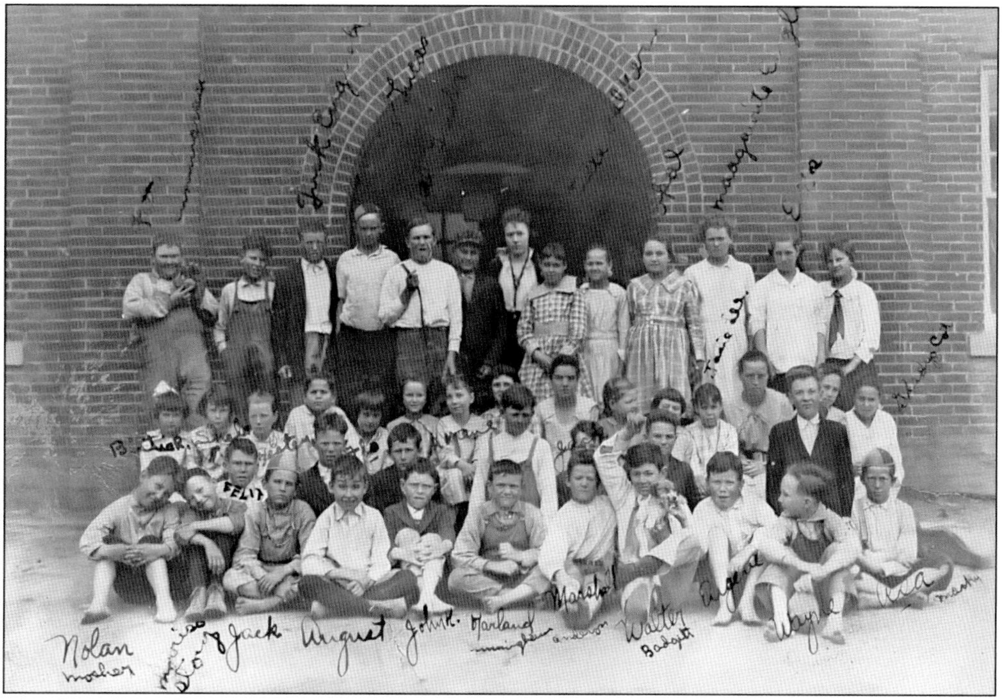

Third grade students are pictured in front of the Irving School in 1920.

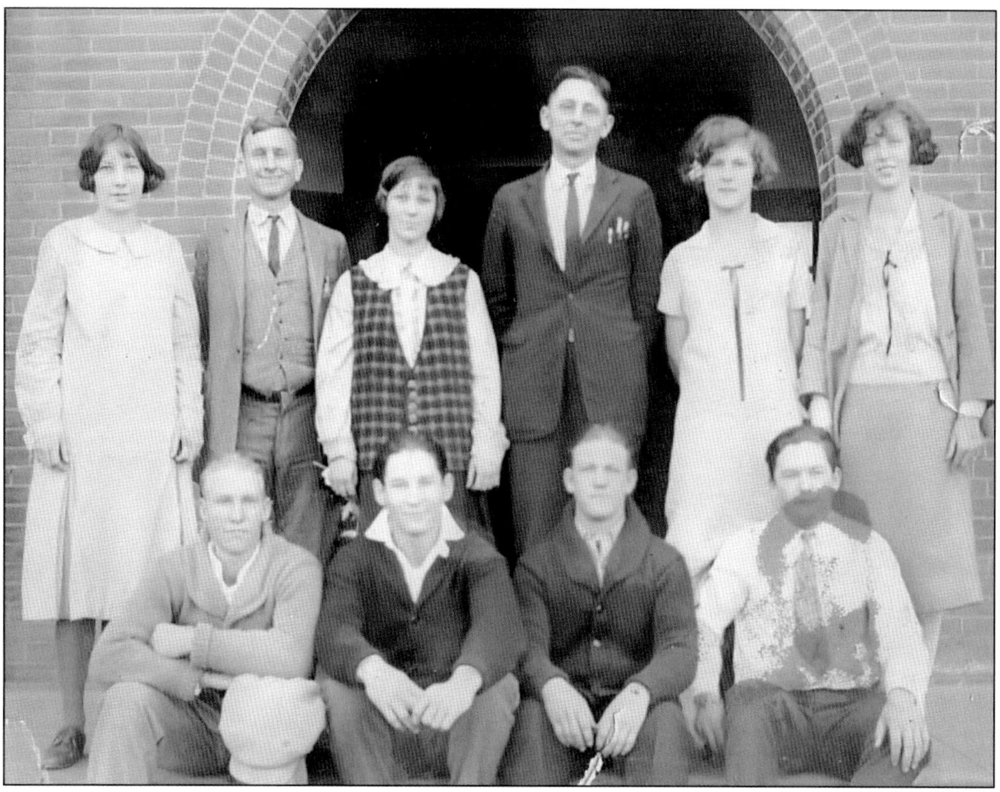

The graduating seniors of Irving High School are pictured in 1925.

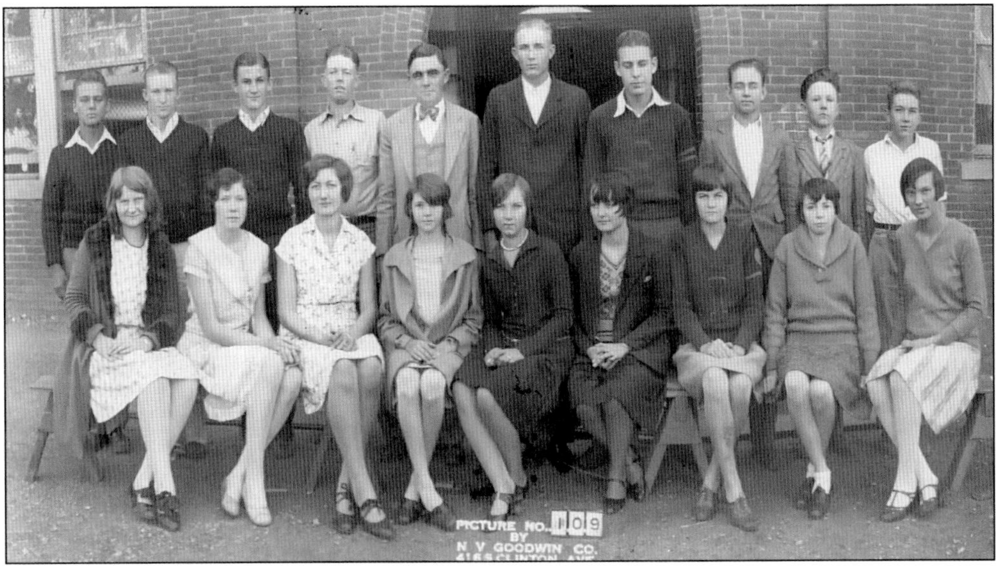

The junior class of the Irving High School is pictured in 1930.

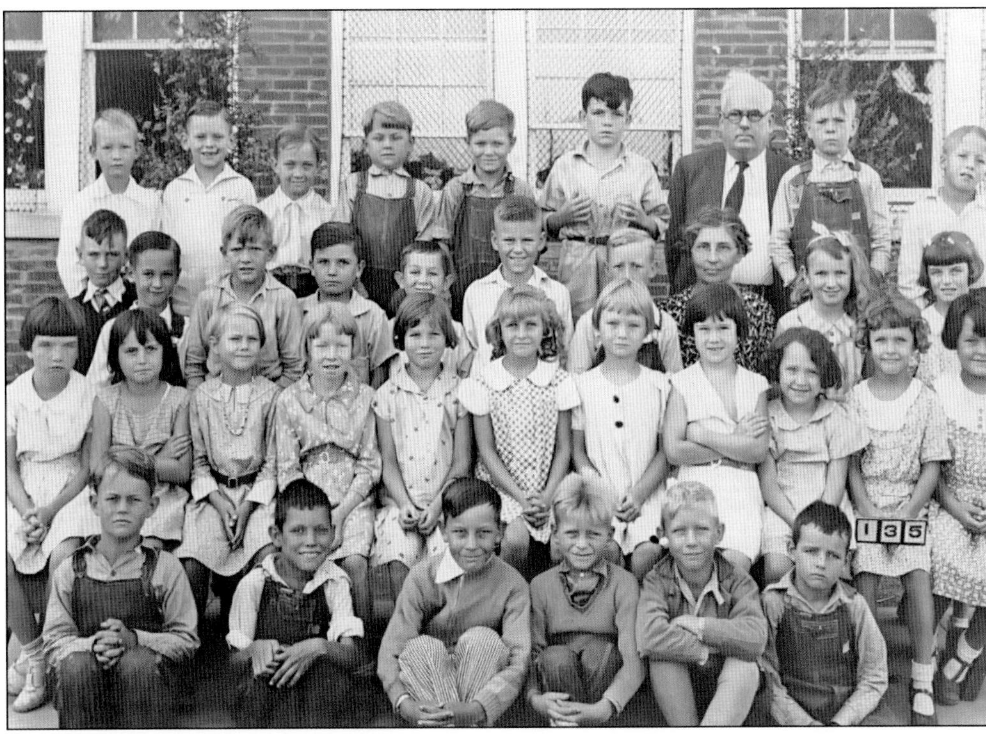

Second grade students of the Irving School pose for a class photograph in 1934. Their teacher Gela Harkey is third from right in the back row.

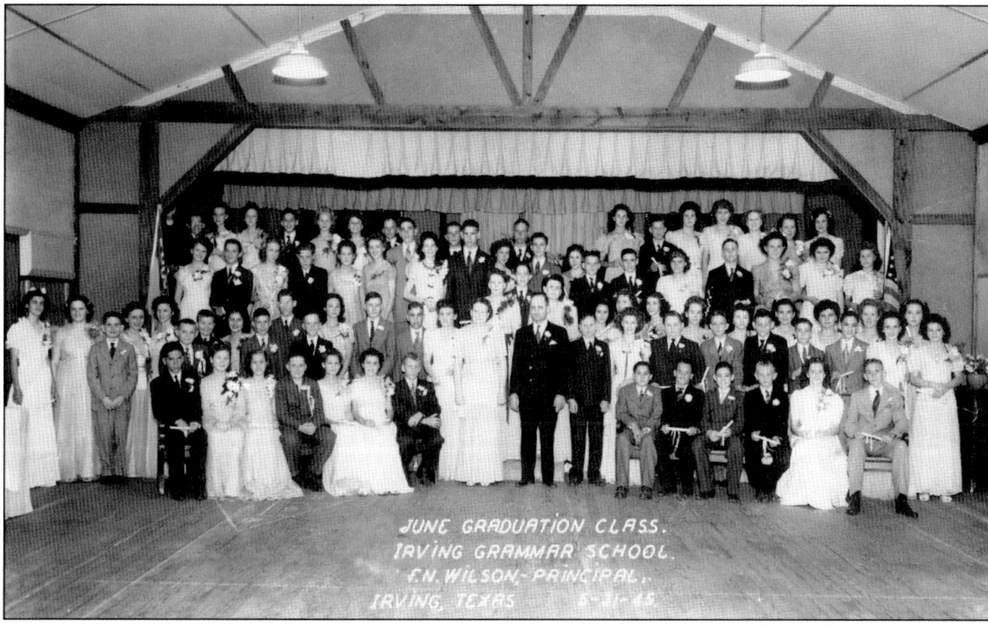

The eighth graduating class of Irving Grammar School is pictured in 1945. Teacher Gela Harkey is third from right in the third row, and Superintendent A.S. Johnston is third from right in the back row.

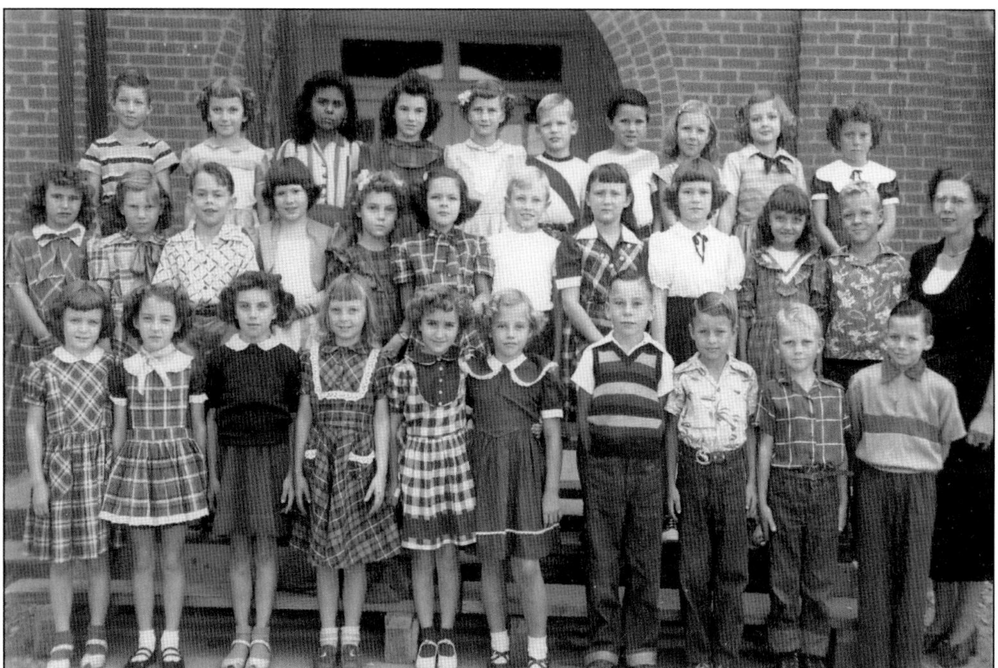
Third grade students of the Irving School pose for a class photograph during the 1950–1951 school year.

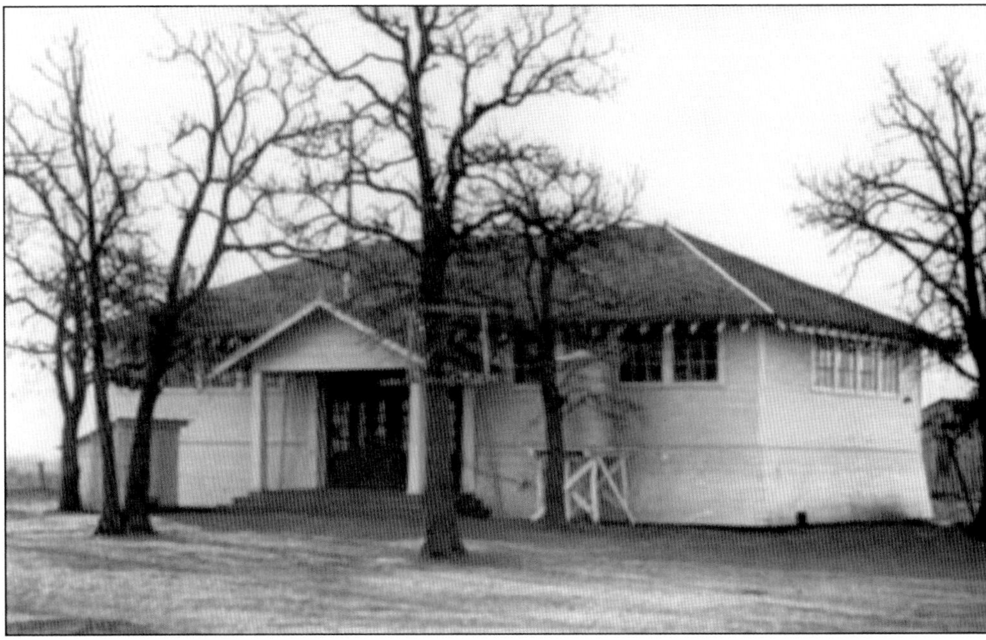

The Union Bower community provided a one-room community school for the children during the 1880s. The Union Bower School is pictured above in 1925. The one-story wooden building served the community until 1940, when a new brick building was constructed. In 1963, the Union Bower School became part of the IISD. Students are pictured below in front of the brick Union Bower School.

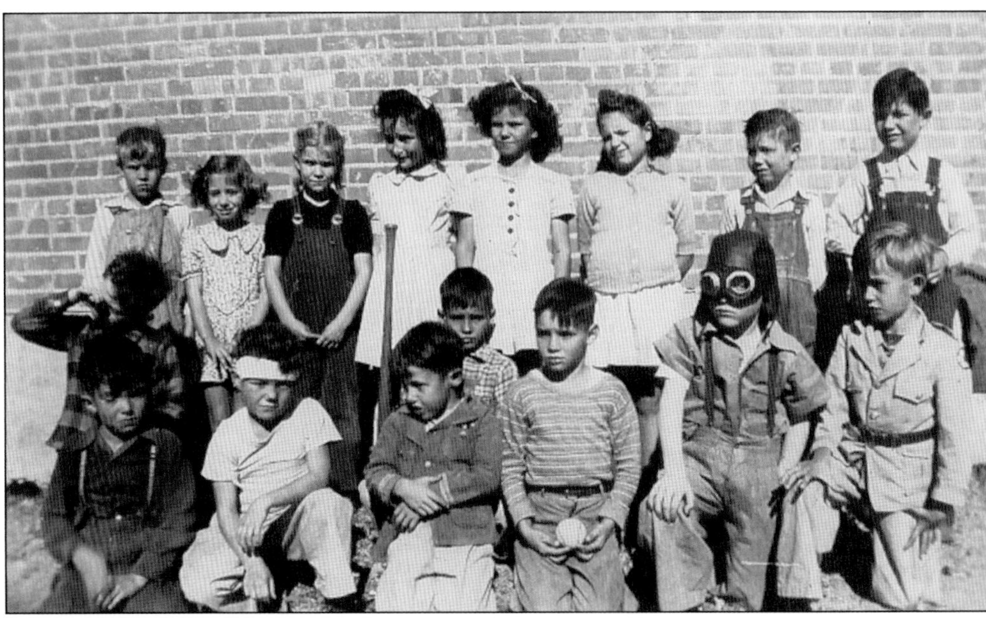

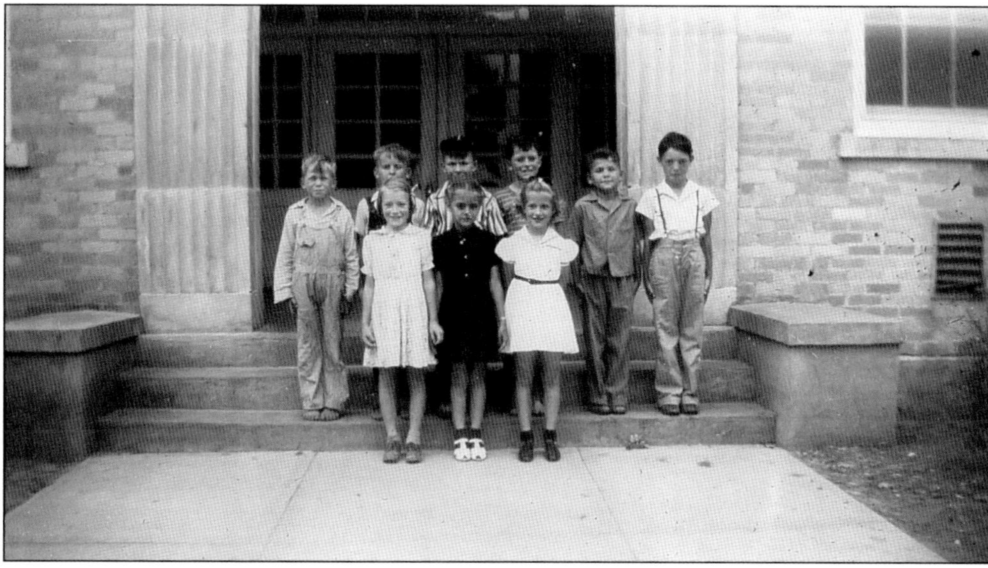

Above, second grade students are pictured in front of the Union Bower School in 1942. Below, Union Bower School students pose for a class photograph in 1948.

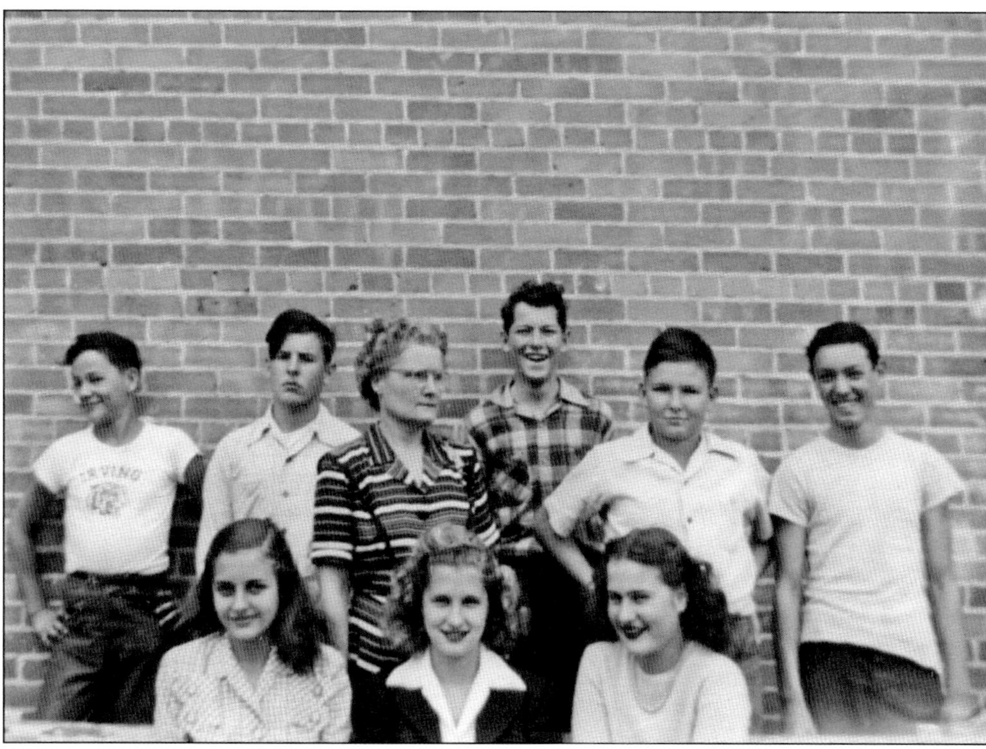

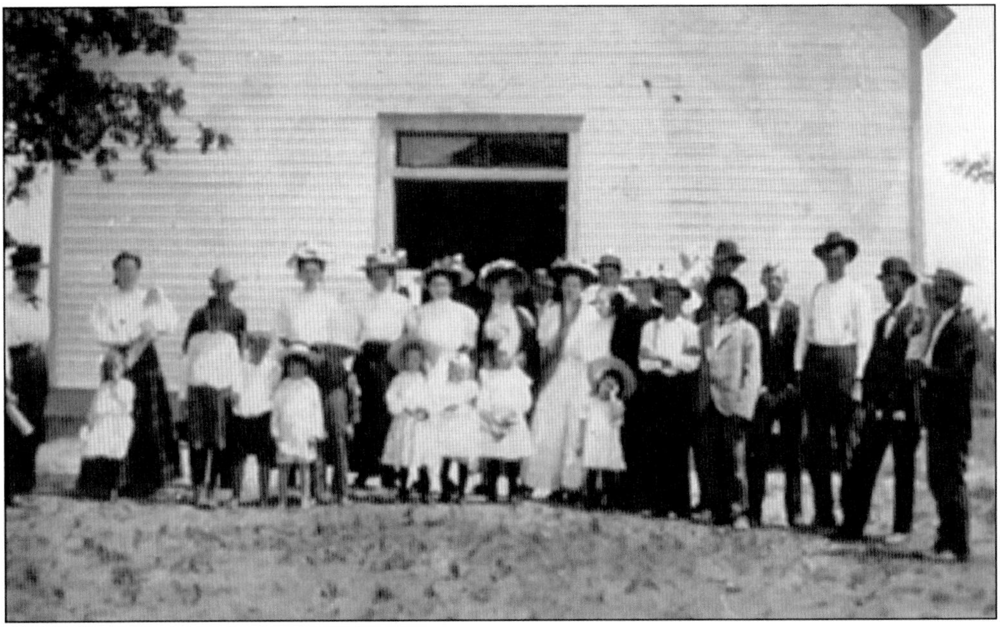

In 1885, a group of Union Bower residents from different denominations joined together to hold Sunday school classes. When word of this program reached minister W.E. Hawks in 1905, he found his way from Dallas to Union Bower to assist with the classes, as well as to become the community preacher. After being welcomed to the community, Hawks oversaw the construction of a small church, dedicated as Hawks Chapel Methodist Church in 1907. Students from the Union Bower School are pictured here.

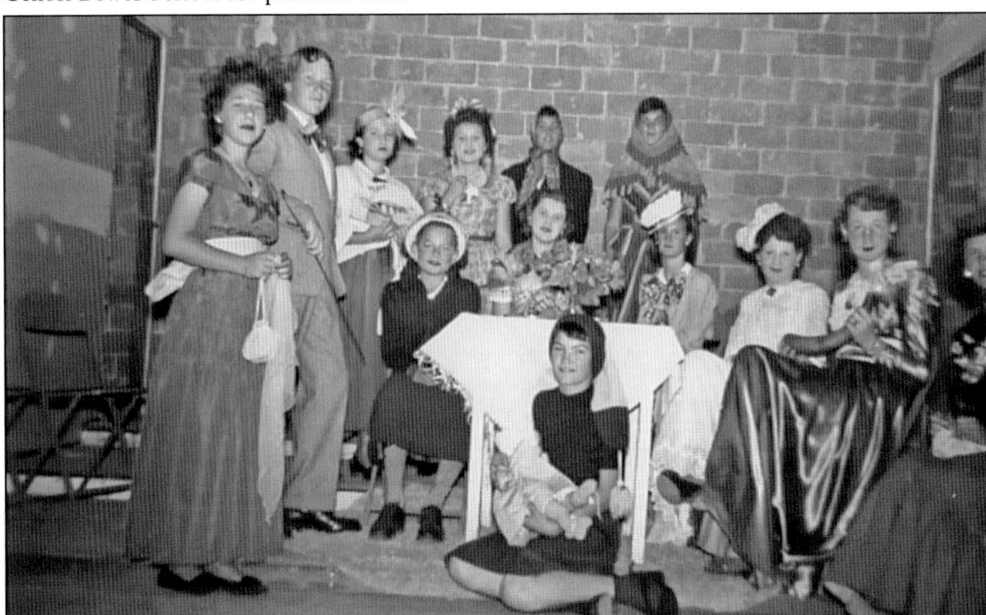

The Hawks Chapel Methodist Church became the Union Bower Methodist Church in the 1930s. Later in the decade, the building was damaged by fire, but a concrete block church was quickly built, and in 1959, the church was sold to the Oak Haven Methodist Church congregation. These eighth grade students of Union Bower participated in a play held at the church.

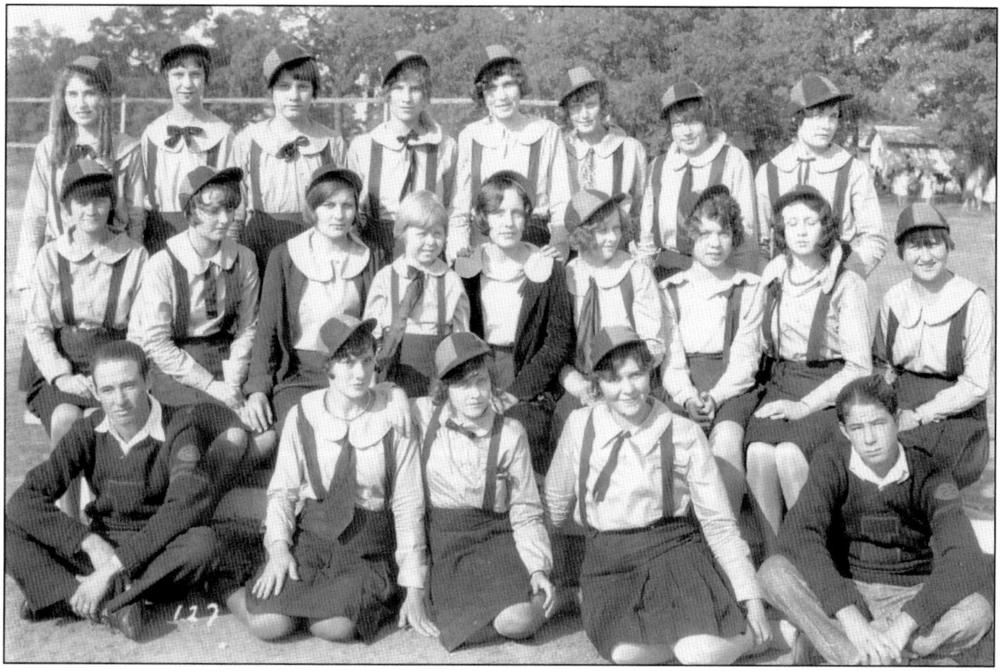

The Irving High School Pep Squad is pictured in 1929. From left to right are (first row) Alfred Graham, Dally Toney, Jenette Ricker, Neva Williams, and Louis Walk; (second row) Evelyn Anderson, Theresa Miller, Doris Harkey, Billy Gilbert (mascot), Frances Hillman, Amy Kate Jenkins (teacher), Gail Lucas, Maidie Hart, and Dorothy Lee; (third row) Jewell Mae Lytle, Lily Helen Clark, Josephine Clark, Mary Britain, Ruth Caster, Mary Lively, Marjorie Gleghorn, and Sybil Coulte.

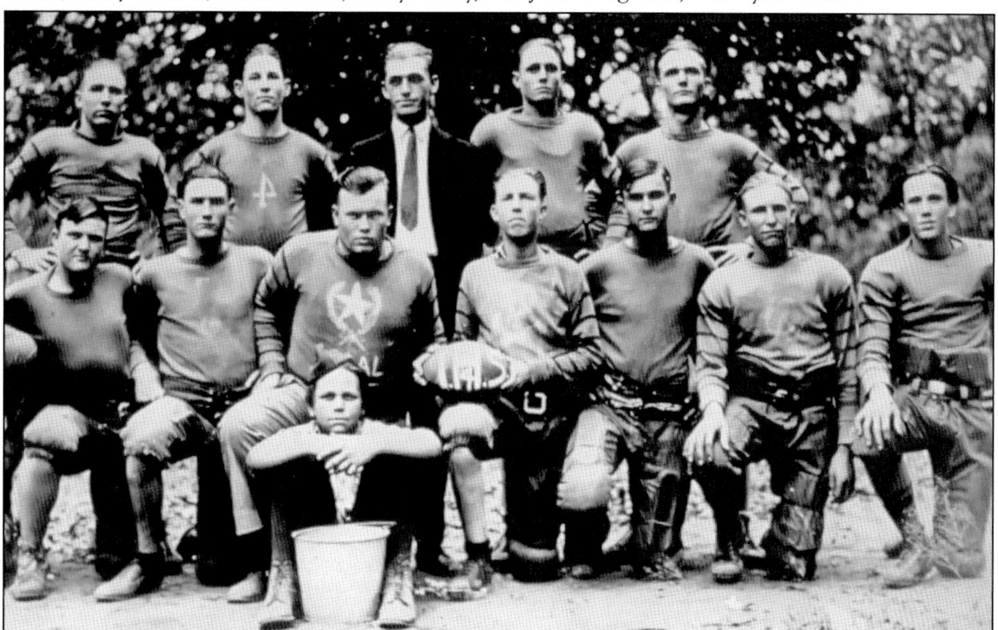

Football originated in Europe in the mid-19th century and was brought over by early settlers. The rules and regulations were perfected in the 20th century, making it one of the most popular national sports in America. One of the first Irving High School football teams is pictured in 1924.

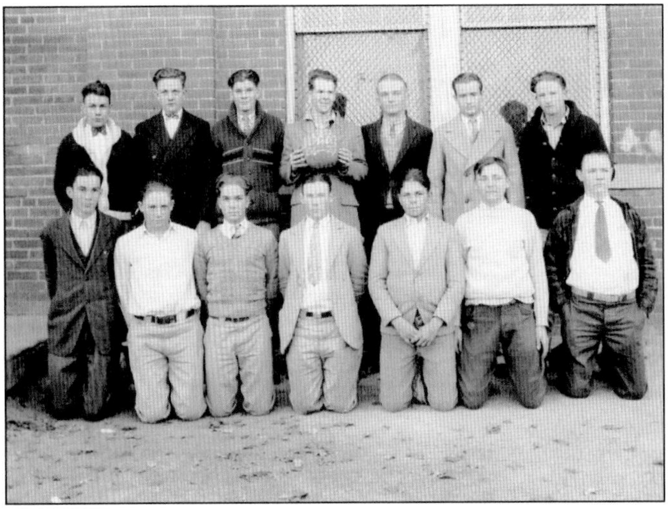

Basketball began in the late 1800s. The Irving High School basketball team is pictured during the 1927–1928 school year. From left to right are (first row) Woodrow Nabors, Marvin Story, John Roberts, Gaddis McFarland, Adolph Walker, Frank Hamm, and Dorris Harrington; (second row) Earl Brown, C. Lucas, John "Jack" Wilson, Floyd Huffstuttler, Edwin Eckert, ? Roberson, and Morris Story.

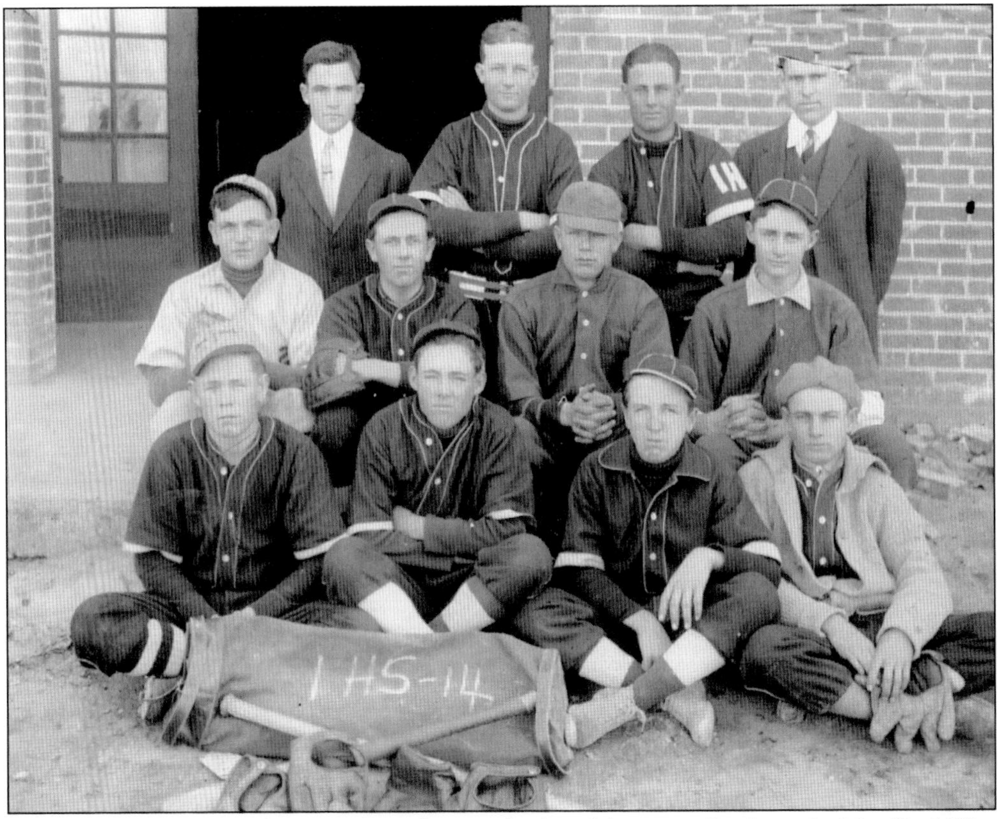

Baseball had been around since 1838 with no real rules of the game. By the end of the Civil War, however, the rules and regulations of baseball had been established. High school teams began to compete for city and state recognition. The first Irving High School baseball team is pictured in 1914.

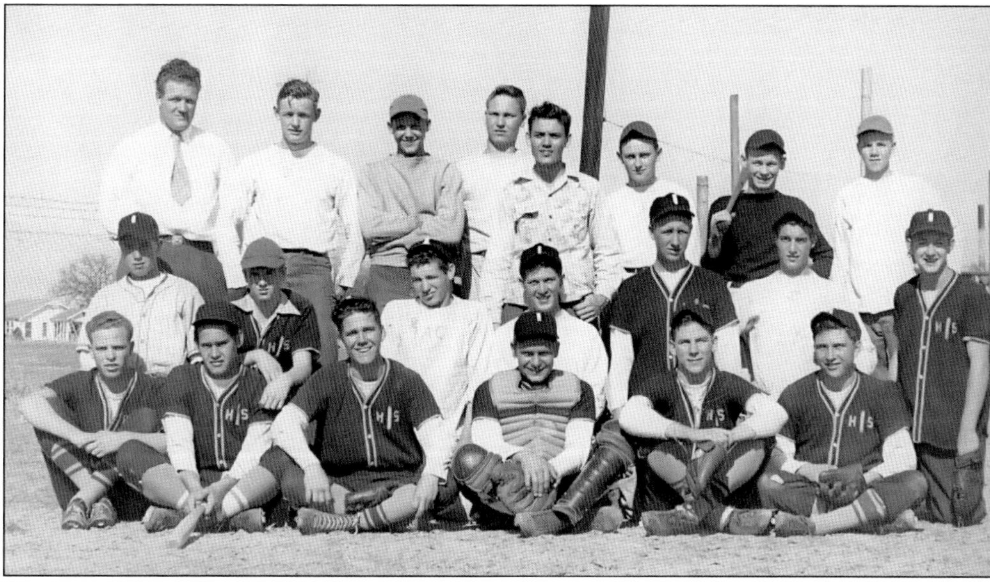

The Irving High School baseball team is pictured in 1947. These are the smiles of young men who were happy to play on the high school team. Not every young man who tried out for the Irving High School baseball team made it to the roster. Those who did were agile, fast, and strong.

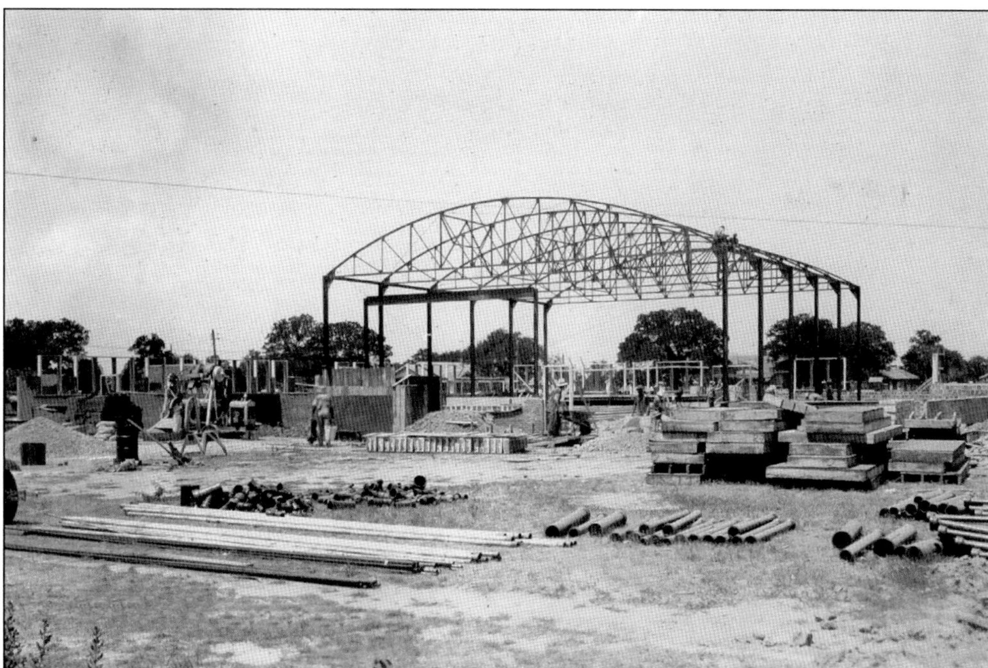

Pictured here is Irving High School under construction. This modern brick schoolhouse with multiple classrooms served various grade levels. The Irving school has come a long way from the former little one-room wooden schoolhouse to a sophisticated, modern schoolhouse of the 20th century.

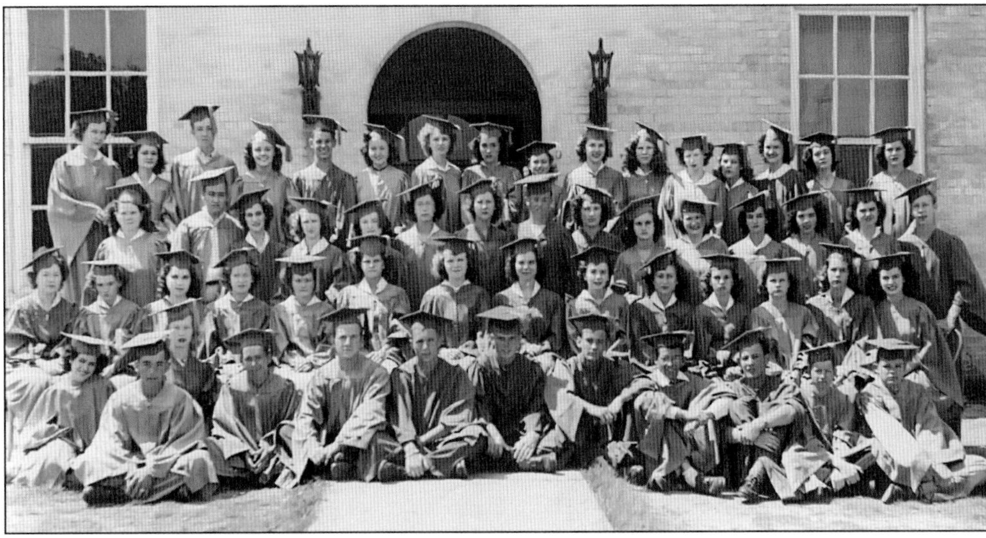

Pictured here is the Irving High School graduating class of 1945. Soon, these students would go on to college, start their own families, or establish careers.

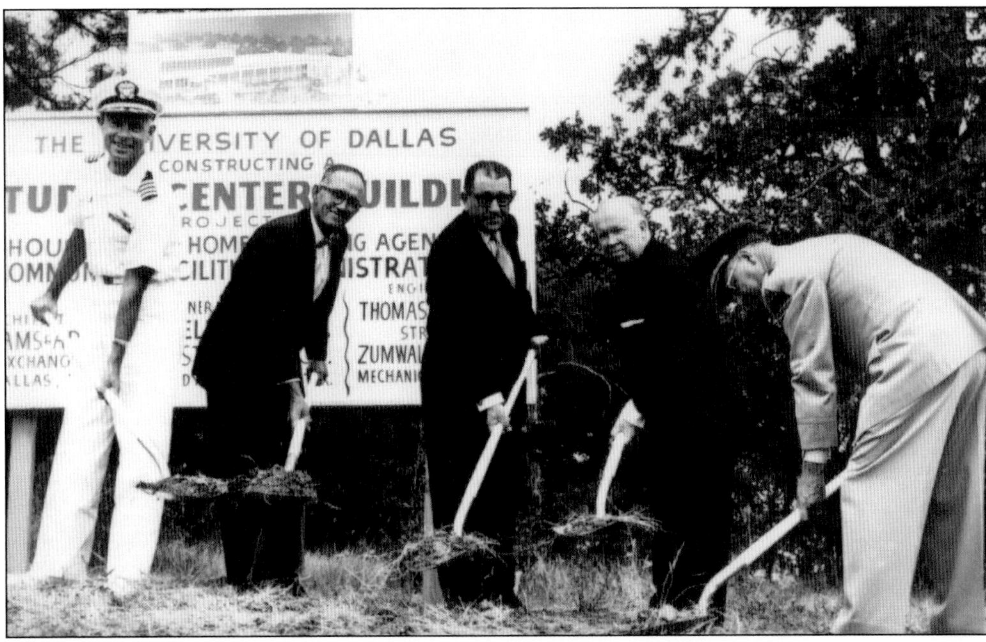

The University of Dallas in Irving dates to 1910, when the Vincentian Fathers took the name for the Holy Trinity College that they had founded five years earlier. Holy Trinity College closed in 1928, and the property was transferred to the Catholic Diocese of Dallas. In 1955, the Sisters of St. Mary of Namur were given the property to establish a new institution of higher education that would integrate Our Lady of Victory, a junior college in Fort Worth. In 1956, the sisters, together with founding members Eugene Constantin Jr. and Edward R. Maher Sr., convinced Bishop Thomas K. Gorman to establish the only university in Irving. The University of Dallas is a four-year coeducational institution, welcoming students of all faiths and races and offering academic programs at the undergraduate and graduate levels. Pictured is the ground breaking for the university.

Five

Entering the Modern Era

After its founding in 1903, the town of Irving evolved into a center of commerce and social life for local residents and farmers and those of the surrounding communities. The downtown community established a drugstore and a bank. Dairy farming grew into a major business for Irving. Many of the communities that predated Irving, such as Bear Creek, Estelle, Elm, Kit, Sowers, Union Bower, and Twin Wells, soon became part of Irving proper when the city annexed these areas.

Over time, the self-sufficient and self-governing communities became one, and the City of Irving established and maintained the role of local government. Politics and business reshaped the farmland and communities by introducing modern machinery and automated processes, thus creating a contemporary city.

In 1910, phone service connected Irving to the rest of the United States. The cost of the service was $1 a month for a party line and $1.50 for a private line, and citizens paid to be connected.

In 1911, Lone Star Gas brought a line through Irving. This gas distribution system was not a big hit, as the expense of distributing the gas throughout homes and businesses was a problem. Citizens were not in a hurry to utilize the modern service. Gas was not essential to cooking. The women continued to use their wood- and coal-burning stoves because their families claimed that food just tasted better that way.

On October 25, 1952, voters accepted the proposal to make Irving a charter city, which allowed it to annex adjoining land. This charter also gave the city additional governmental powers to expand the size of the city council.

During this decade, Irving welcomed the University of Dallas and hired its first paid firefighter. Businesses continued to move into the city. When Plymouth Park opened in 1955, it was one of the largest shopping centers between Dallas and Fort Worth.

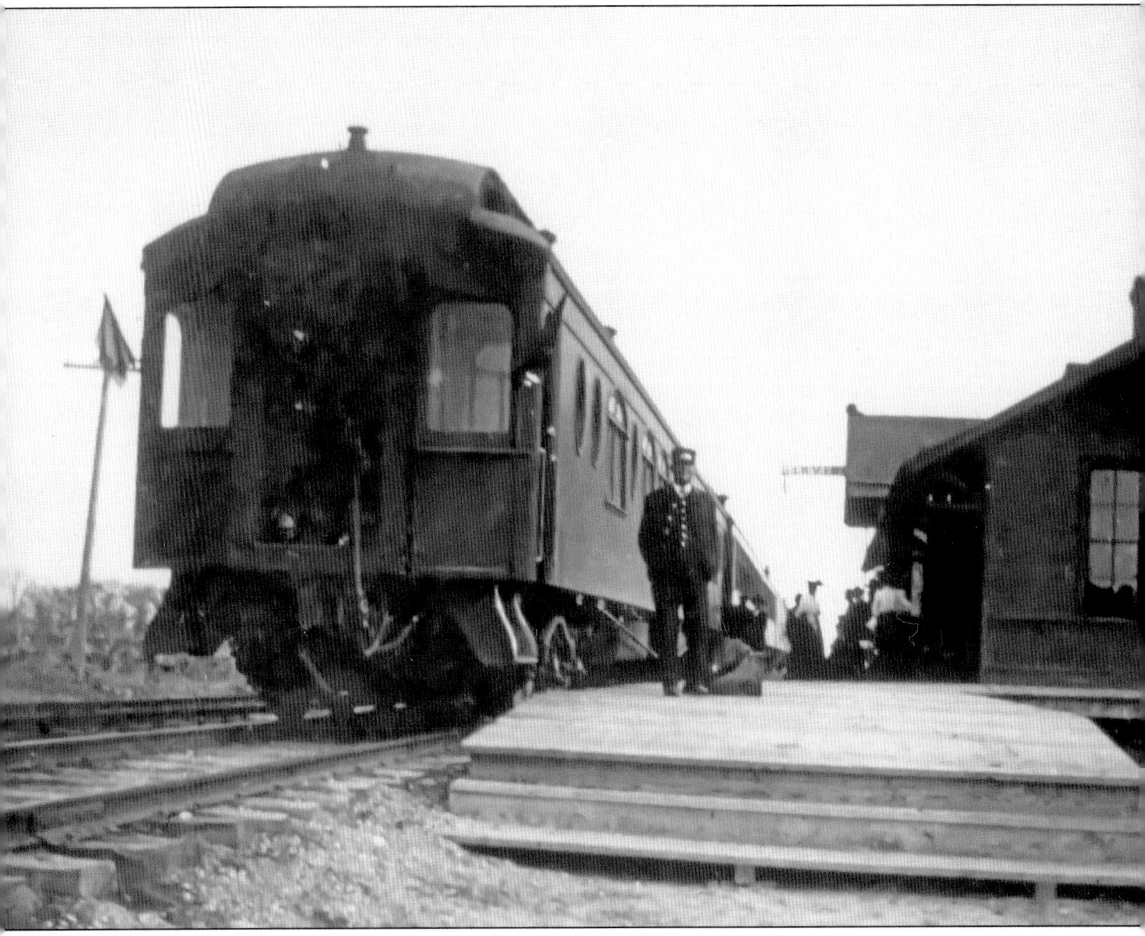

The Irving train station was completed in 1903. In fact, the Chicago, Rock Island & Gulf depot was one of only two buildings standing on the day the town of Irving was established on December 19, 1903. (Courtesy of the Estelle Bates Collection, Irving Archives, Irving Public Library.)

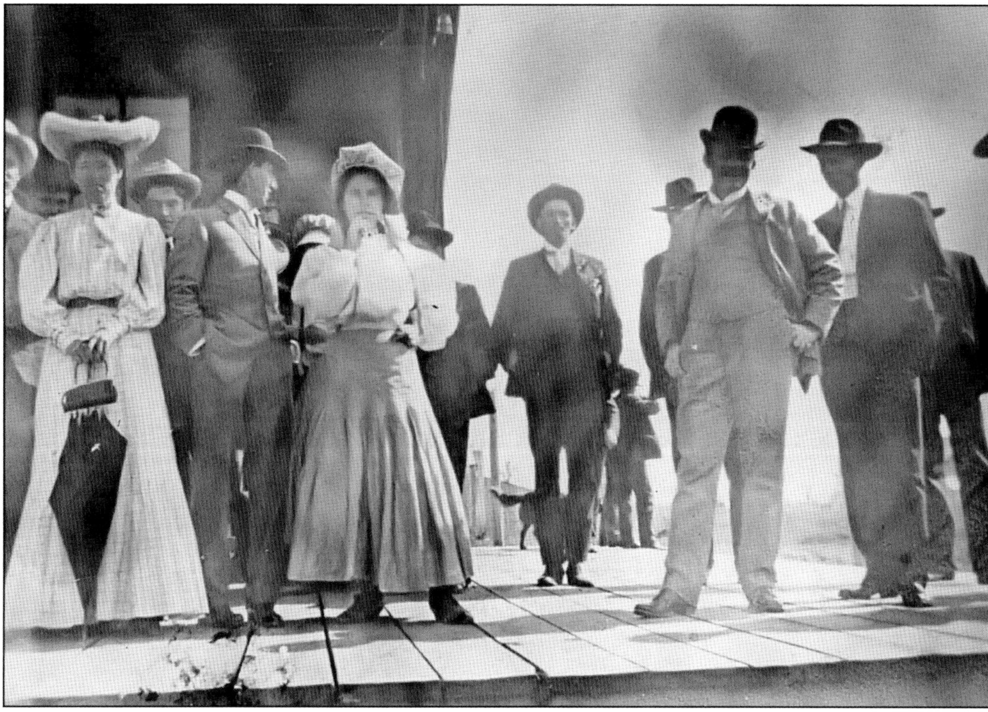

Once Irving was established as a railway stop on the Rock Island line, frequent riders took advantage of this means of transportation. They rode to and from their homes in Dallas, Fort Worth, and Irving for recreation and business. Residents of Dallas County are shown waiting at the depot.

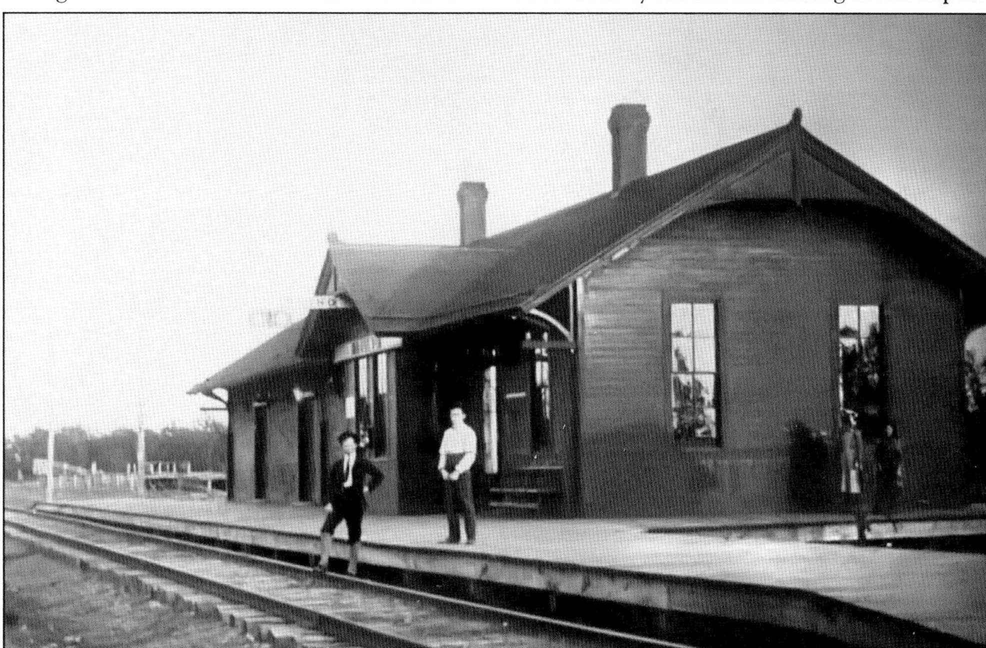

John Alexander Murphy is pictured on the railroad tracks of the Irving depot in 1904. Locals sometimes referred to the Irving depot as Murphy's Mansion because Murphy was the manager.

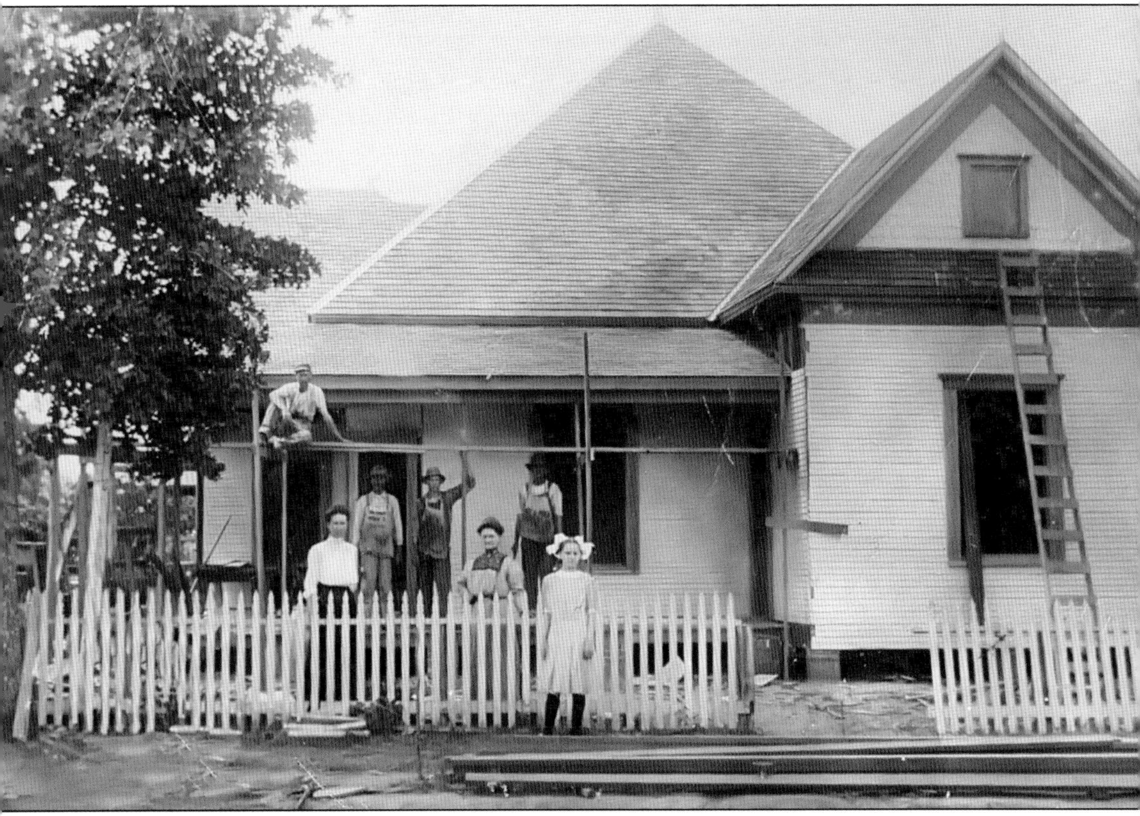

Pictured here is the home of Otis and Netta Brown. In 1903, the first house was built in Irving. The Browns sold their house in 1905 after the birth of their first child to build a larger house. The Browns lived in this house until 1919 while raising their five sons. Through the decades, the house was the home of several mayors of Irving.

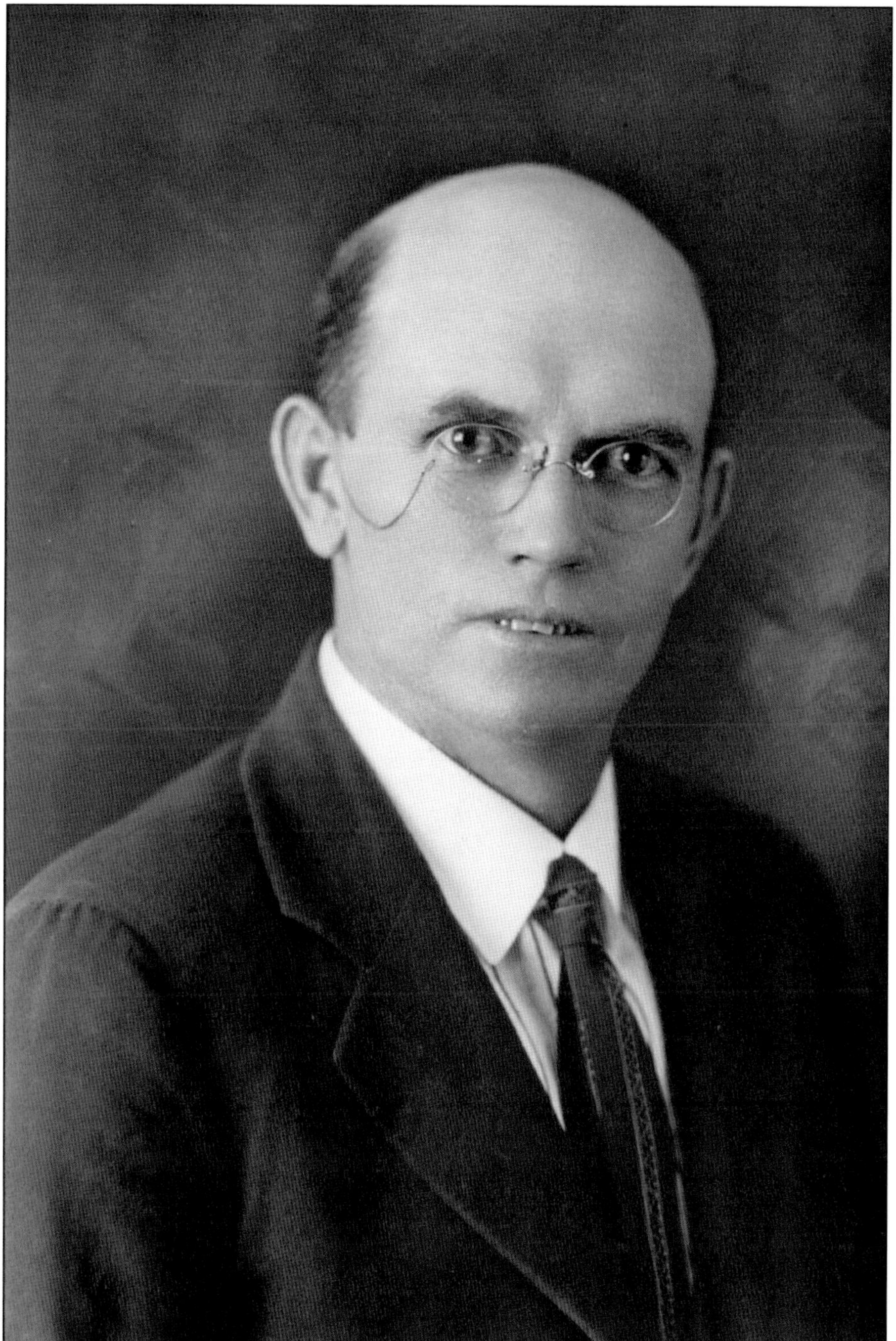

Otis Brown governed the modern city of Irving as mayor from 1914 to 1917. As Irving's cofounder, he had the town's best interests at heart. Mayor Brown, pictured here in 1914, knew the planning and zoning of the city and was the visionary for the future success of Irving. Successive mayors were C.G. Miller (1917–1919), P.H. Lively (1919–1921), W.F. Miller (1921–1923), M.R. Price (1923–1925), C.G. Miller (1925–1927), John Haley (1927–1933), F.M. Gilbert (1933–1937), C.P. Caldwell (1937–1943), E.J. Johnson (1943–1947), and Hans Smith (1947–1951).

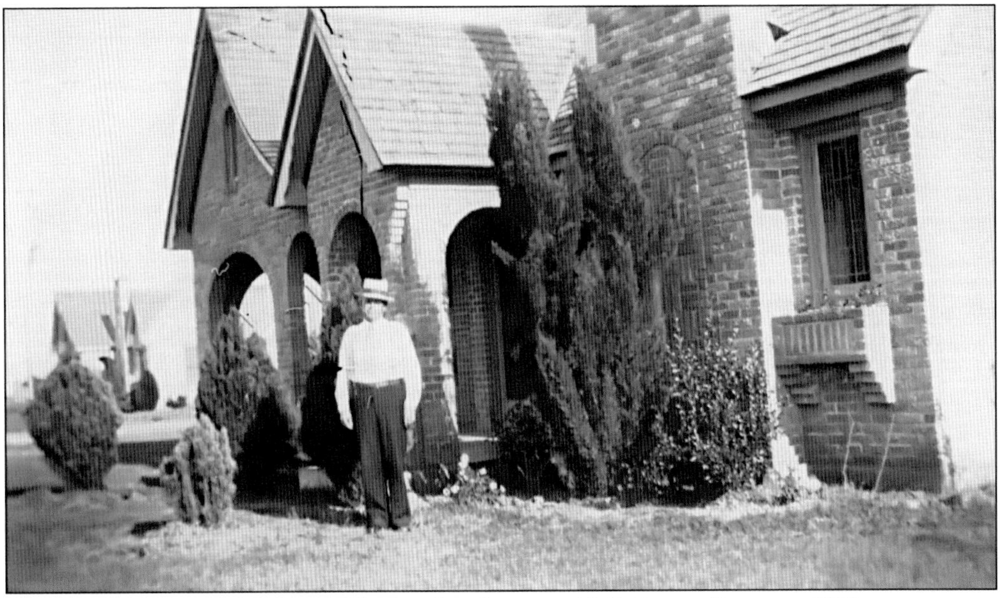

Otis Brown is pictured in front of his modern home at 1300 Sowers Street in 1933.

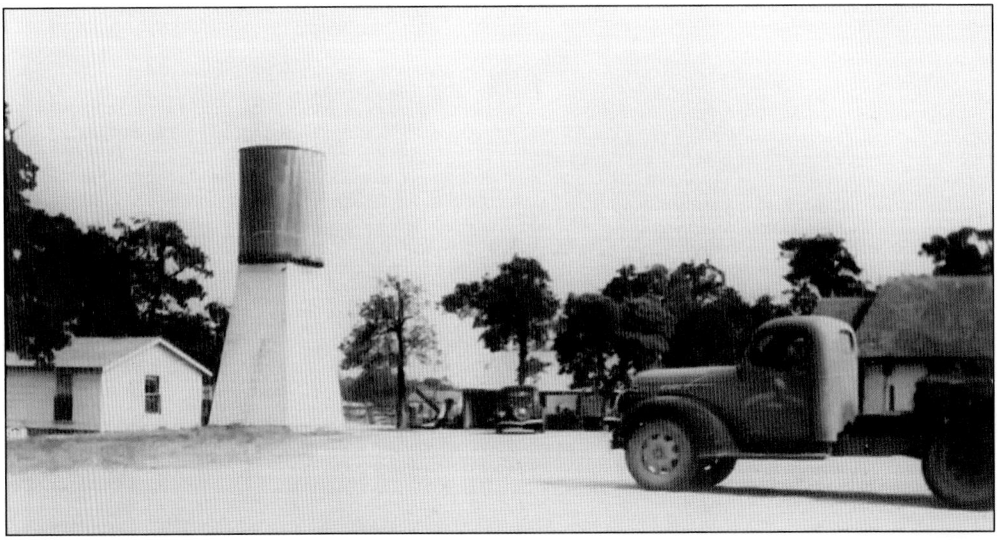

The O'Connor Dairy Farm, owned by Charlie O'Connor, is pictured here in 1930. The farm was built on 2,500 acres in the Elm community in 1917. According to historian Norma Stanton, O'Connor employed Clarence Cobb to operate the dairy farm, paying him a salary of $20 a month. The milk was processed and delivered to the community market and to the Borden Dairy Company in Dallas. The dairy operated until 1953. Ben Carpenter eventually bought the O'Connor Dairy Farm.

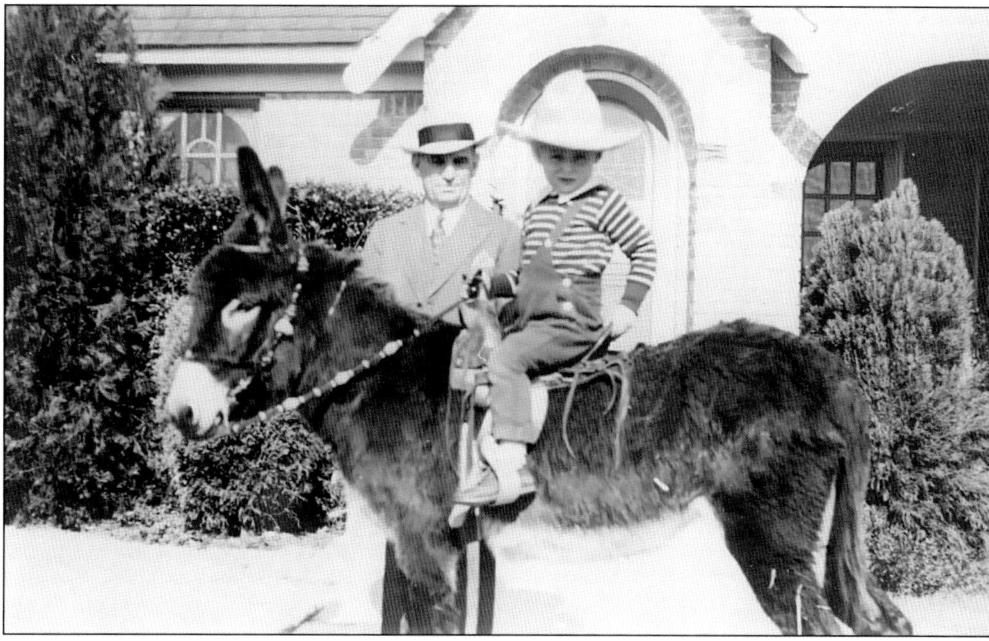

Charles O'Connor is pictured with his grandson Charles O'Connor II, riding on a donkey. Charles O'Connor is the owner of one of the largest modern dairy companies in Irving. A major street in Irving was named O'Connor after the successful dairyman.

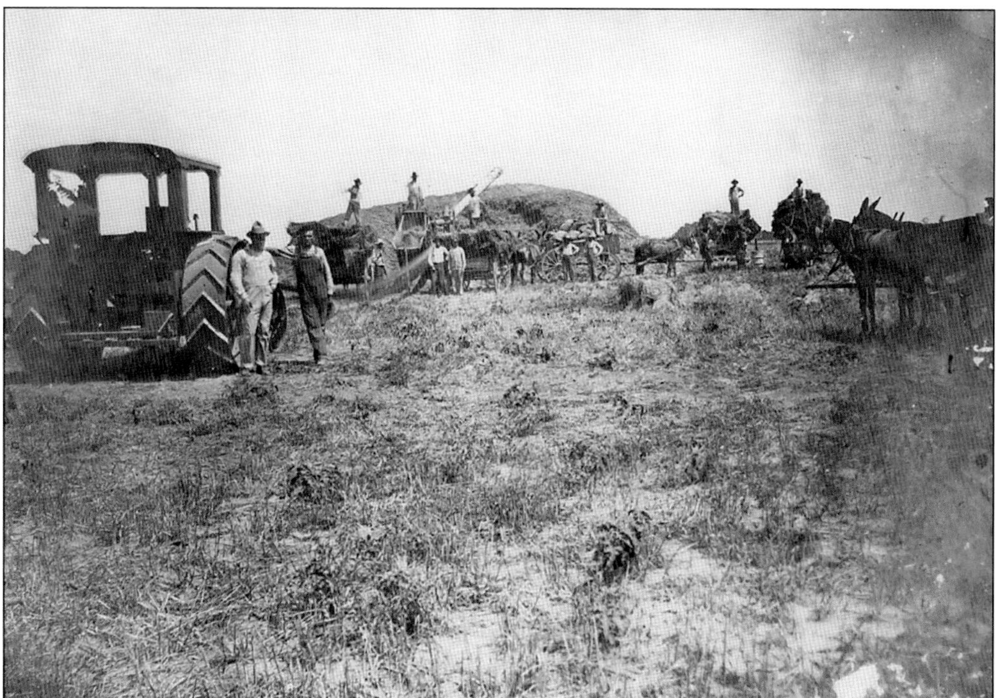

Many of the Irving farmers worked around the clock to plant and harvest crops, tend to their poultry and livestock, and cut wood to sell to neighboring markets. Pictured here is the harvesting of hay on an Irving farm.

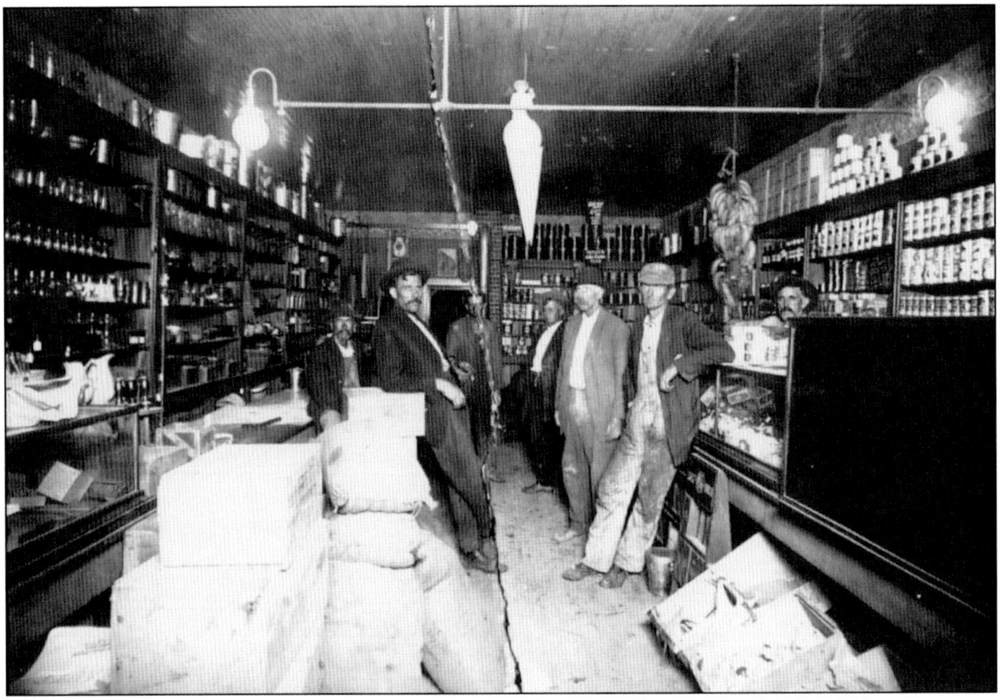

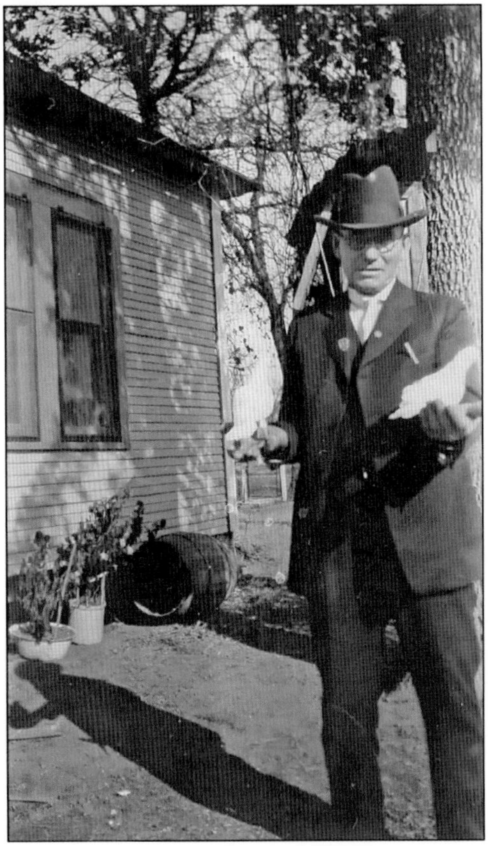

Chaney Miller, pictured behind the counter, operated Irving State Bank and a general store on Main Street. He served three terms as Irving's mayor during the late 1910s and mid-1920s.

Dr. John Haley was the son of William Haley, who came to this area in 1857. He attended school in the Sowers community, then went on to Galveston Medical School, where he received his medical degree. He returned to the Sowers community to begin his medical practice. Dr. Haley served as mayor of Irving from 1927 to 1931. Although the Great Depression fell during his term, Dr. Haley refused to allow the economics of this time to ruin Irving. Historian Joseph Rice reveals that Dr. Haley bought 1.85 acres that were to be used as parkland. He also began a cannery in 1930. In addition to his mayoral duties, Dr. Haley loved raising pigeons. He died of cancer in 1932.

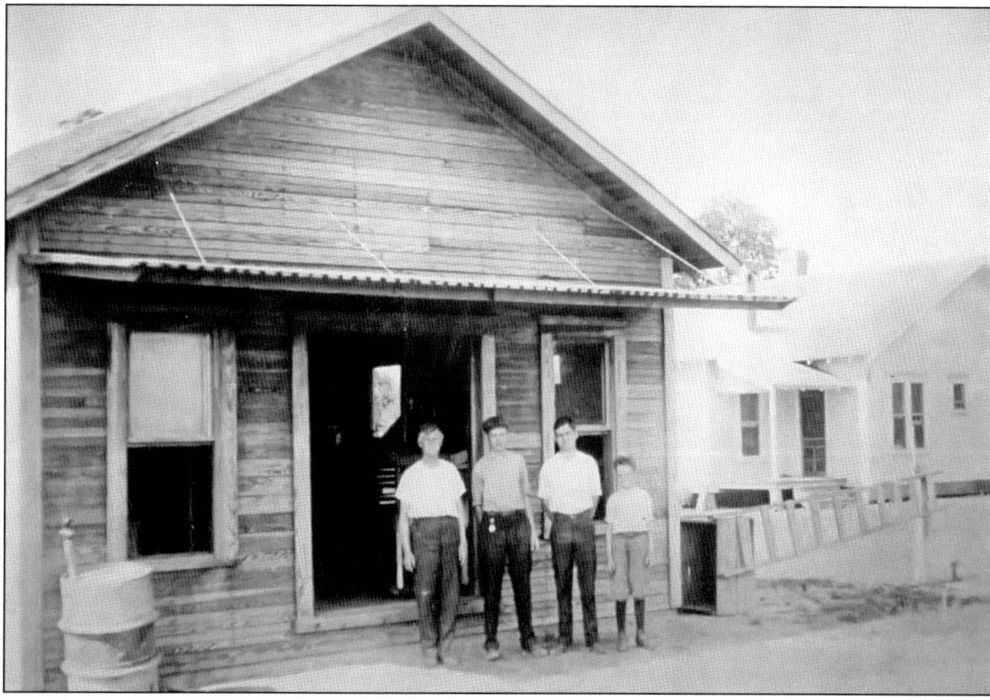

Members of the Hudson family are pictured here outside the *Irving Index* newspaper workshop. R.M. Hudson is at far left. The first edition of the paper was published in 1903. In this edition, the town of Irving was described as "The New Rock Island Town in the forks of the Trinity River," "The fruit belt of Dallas County; Trade area 52 square miles," "Irving, the choicest nook in the Garden of the Lord," and sometimes, "stump city." (Courtesy of the Estelle Bates Collection, Irving Archives, Irving Public Library.)

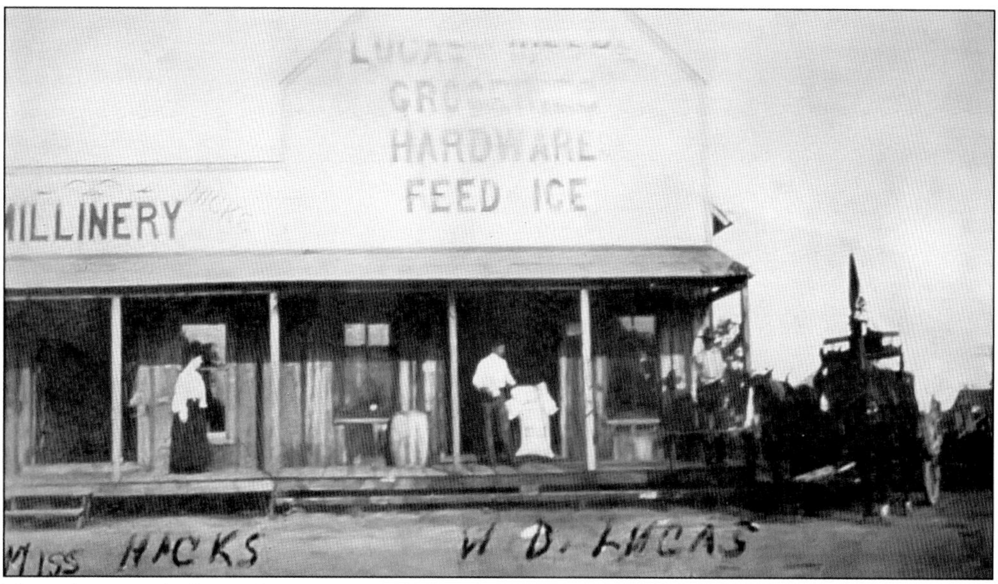

This photograph shows the exteriors of the Miss Hicks Millinery and the Lucas & Joffre store in 1905. These two early Irving businesses were in the 100 block of South Main Street. (Courtesy of the Estelle Bates Collection, Irving Archives, Irving Public Library.)

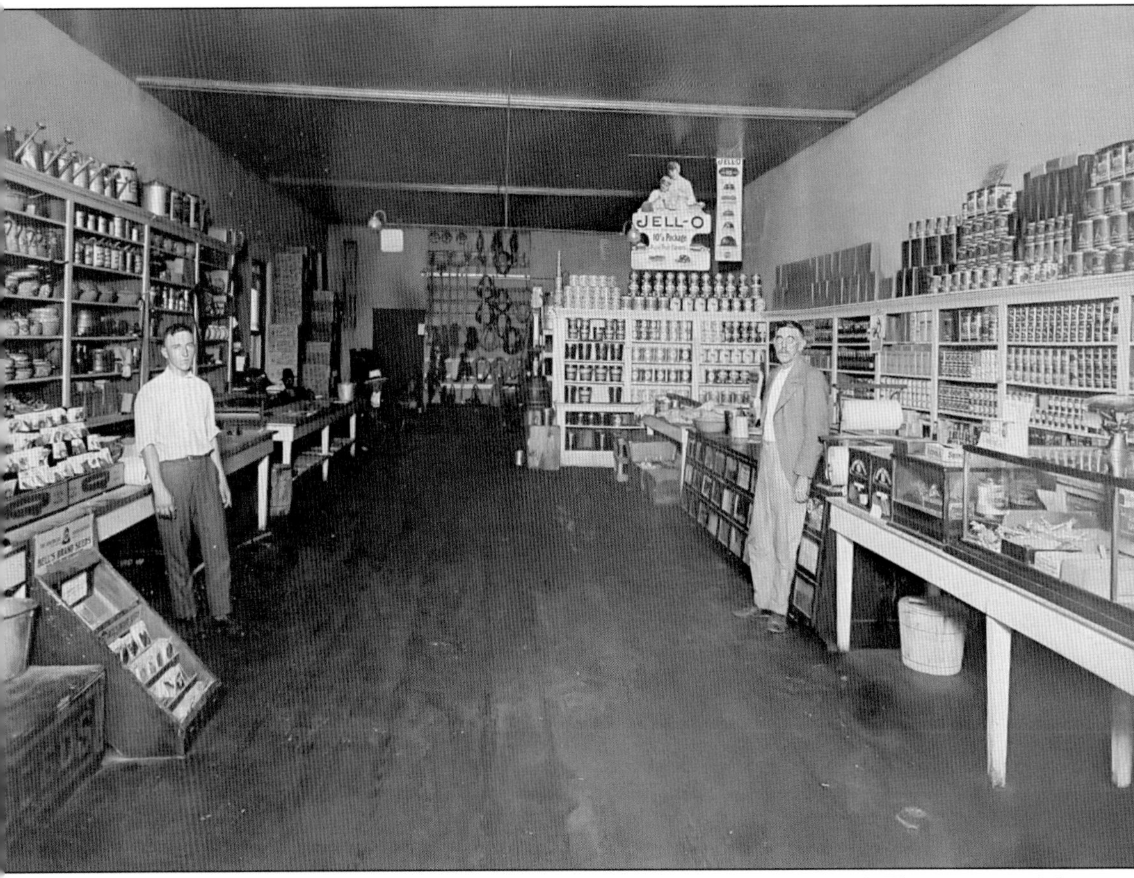

Chaney and Fletcher Miller established the Miller Brothers store in 1905. The interior of this all-purpose store appears well stocked in 1915. Chaney Miller is at right, and Roy Miller, son of Fletcher Miller, is at left. (Courtesy of the Haley-Miller Collection, Irving Archives, Irving Public Library.)

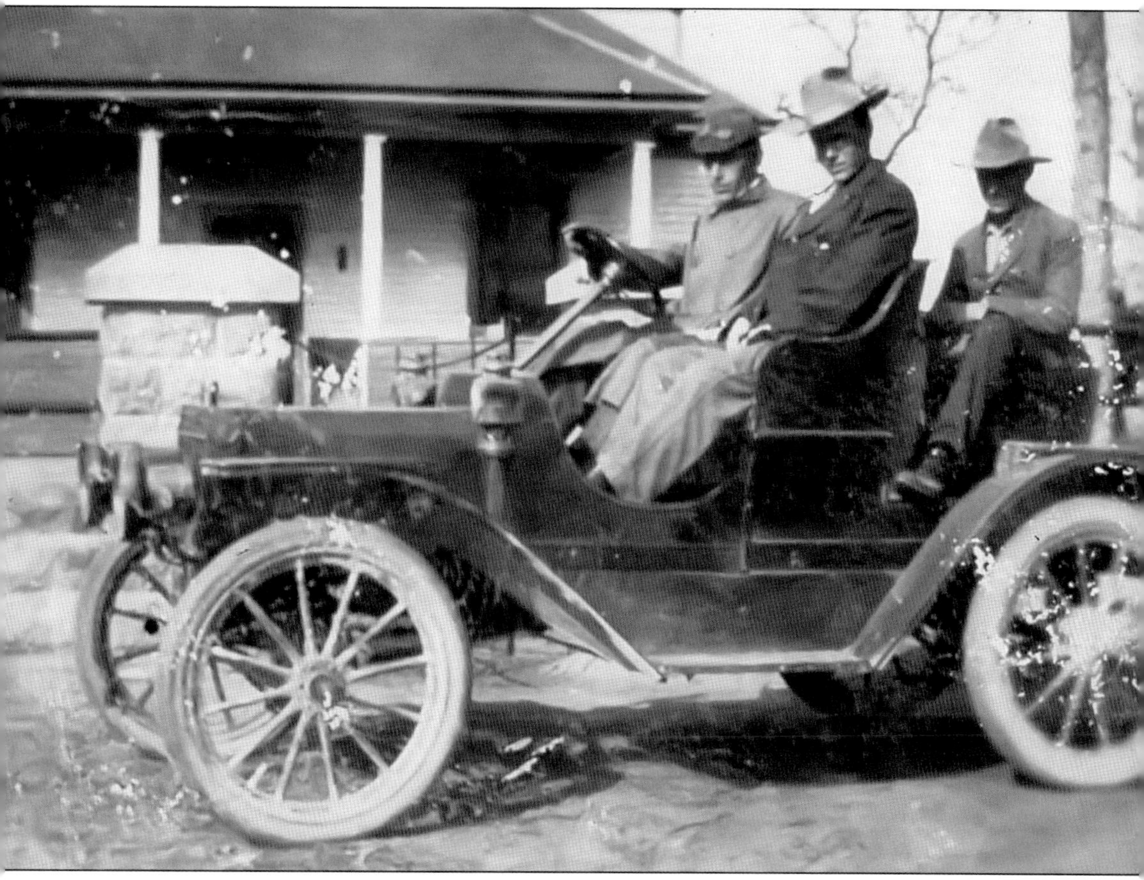

In 1909, the automobile was introduced, and Percy Schulze was the first to own one in Irving. This first car was known as "the little red Hupmobile." It had no top and no seat on the back platform. Because it was built for only two passengers, the hump on the back was called the "mother-in-law seat" to discourage her from riding with the couple because the backseat would not be comfortable. Percy Schulze (behind steering wheel) and Otis Brown are seated in the front seat, with Fred Joffre in the mother-in-law seat.

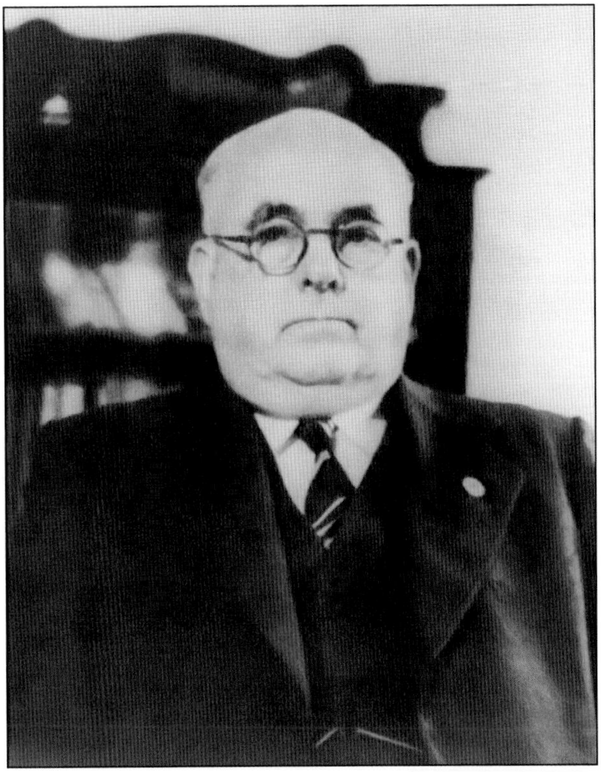

In 1927, the first Irving Independent School District superintendent was hired. Before that time, the school was operated and managed by its local community. IISD superintendents standardized the student curriculum at various levels. Management of education would change from the community to a formal method of operation. At left is Superintendent A.S. Johnston (1927–1946), and below is Frank Morgan (1946–1947).

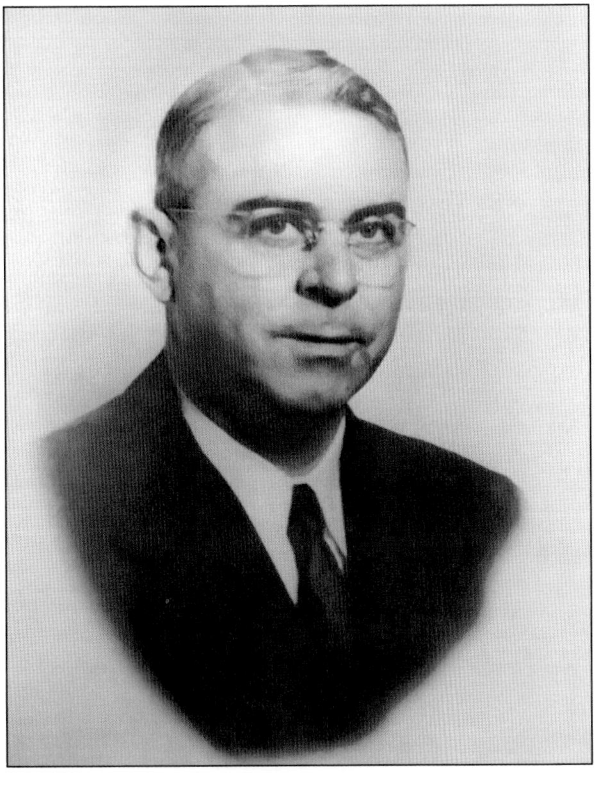

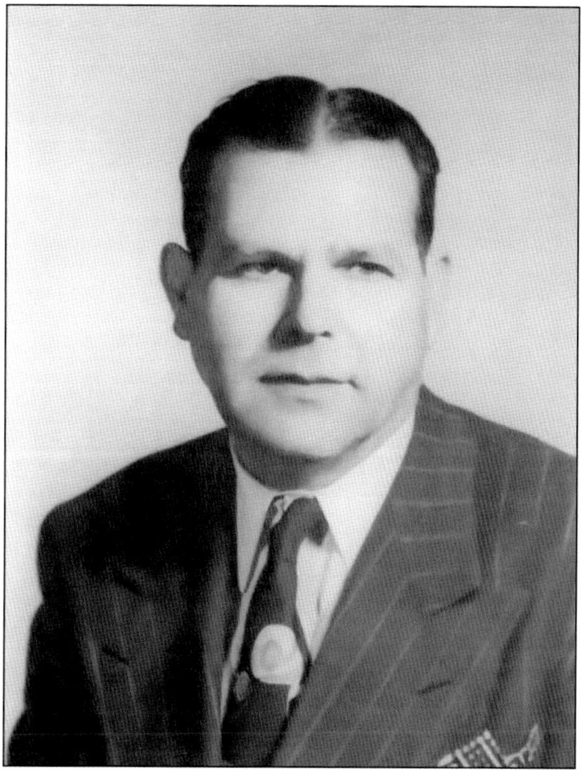

At right is Superintendent B.E. Dunagan (1947–1949), and below is Superintendent John Beard (1949–1956). Other superintendents would continue to serve the future generations.

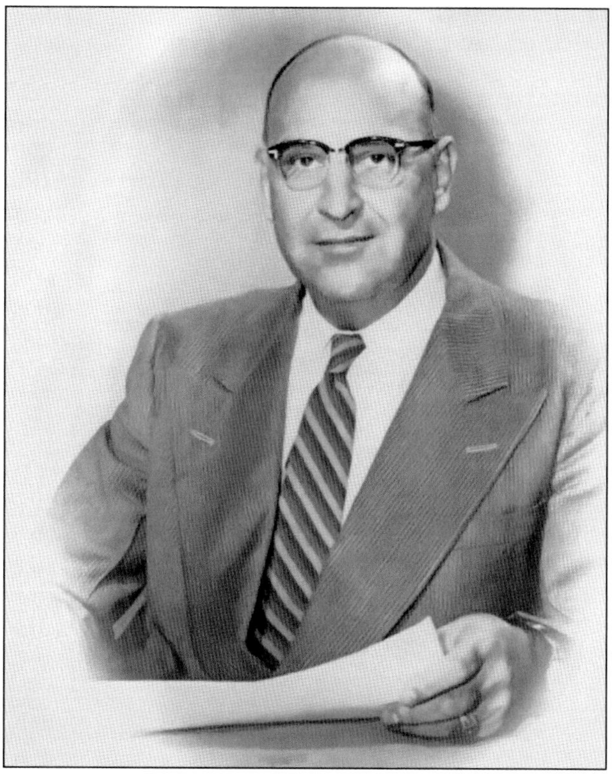

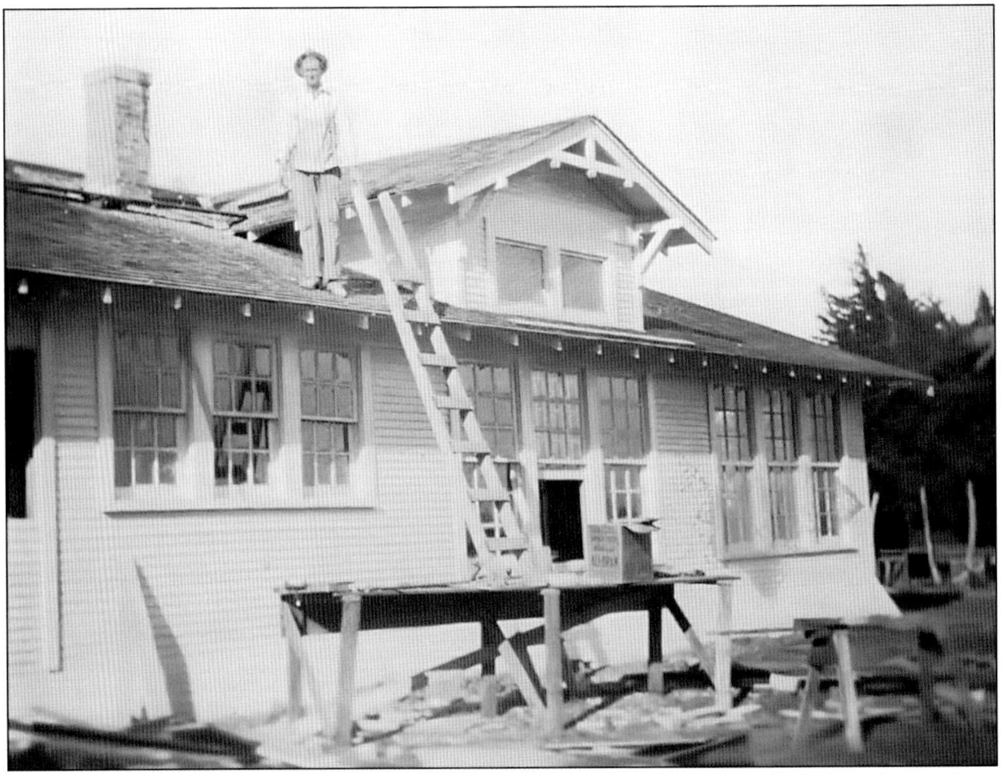

In 1925, the Texas Power & Light Company outfitted the city of Irving with its first electric line. The first water system was also established during this time. Irving soon became known as a modern city. Here, a Twin Wells home with all the modern amenities begins to take form in 1930.

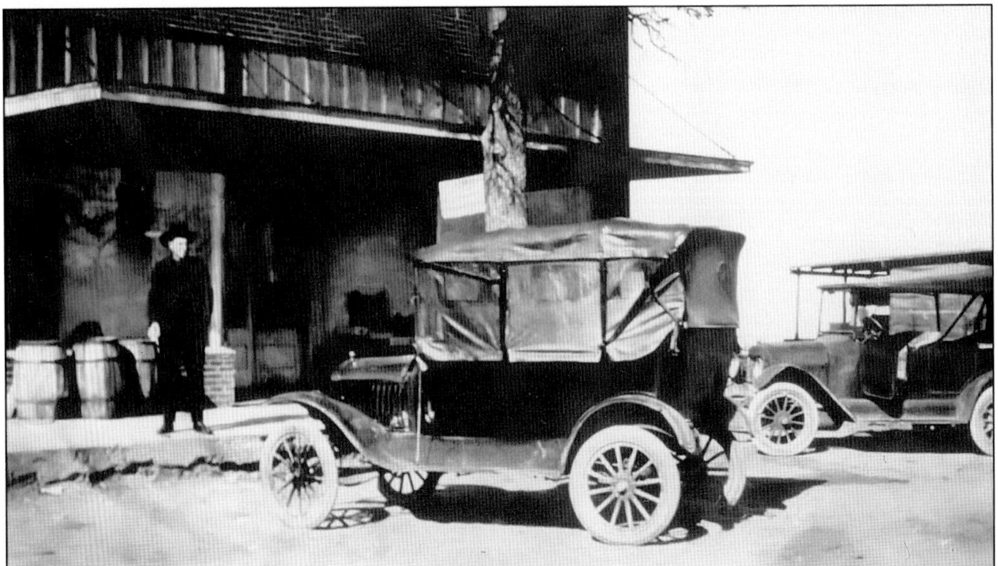

Early pioneer Doug Lucas is pictured in front of his grocery store in 1929. During the 1930s and 1940s, several grocery stores existed on First and Main Streets, including this one. With such a tight market, each store had to create a competitive advantage, even if it meant lowering prices.

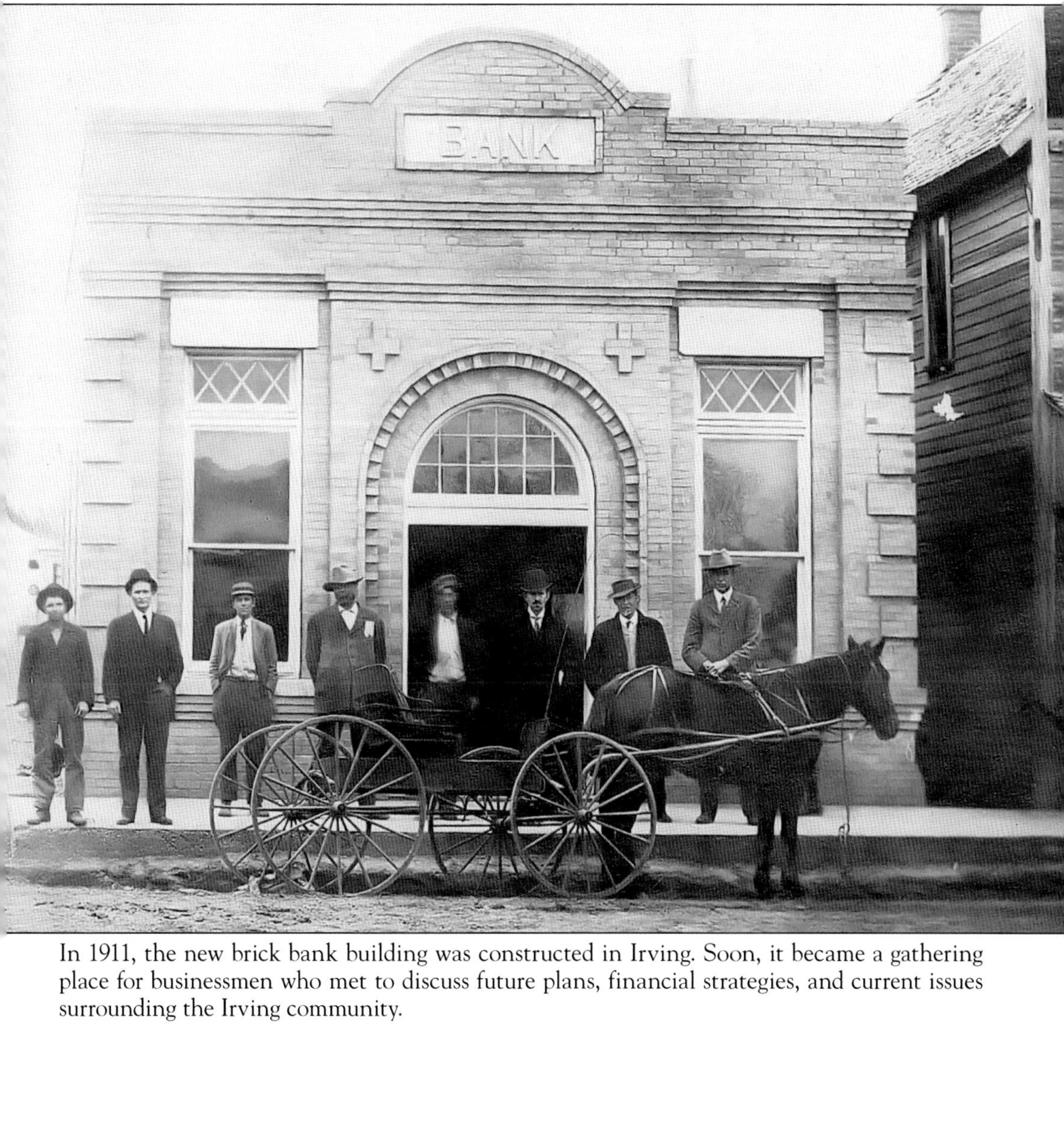

In 1911, the new brick bank building was constructed in Irving. Soon, it became a gathering place for businessmen who met to discuss future plans, financial strategies, and current issues surrounding the Irving community.

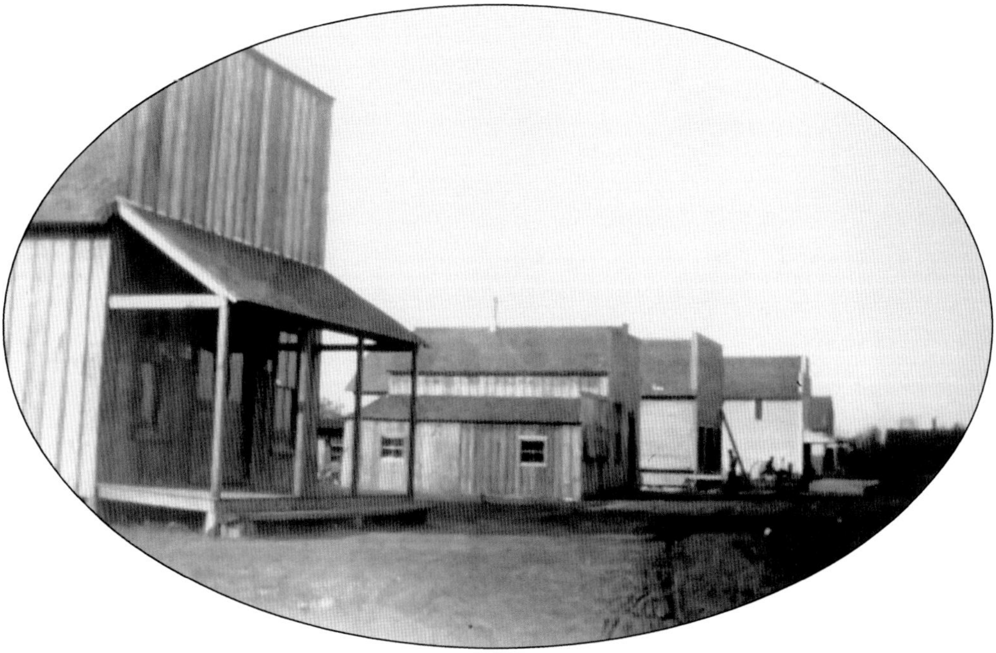

As the first streets of Irving, Main and First were designed as wider thoroughfares to accommodate future growth. The hope was that the area would become an urban center where shops and businesses would develop, attracting not only local residents but also those from the surrounding communities.

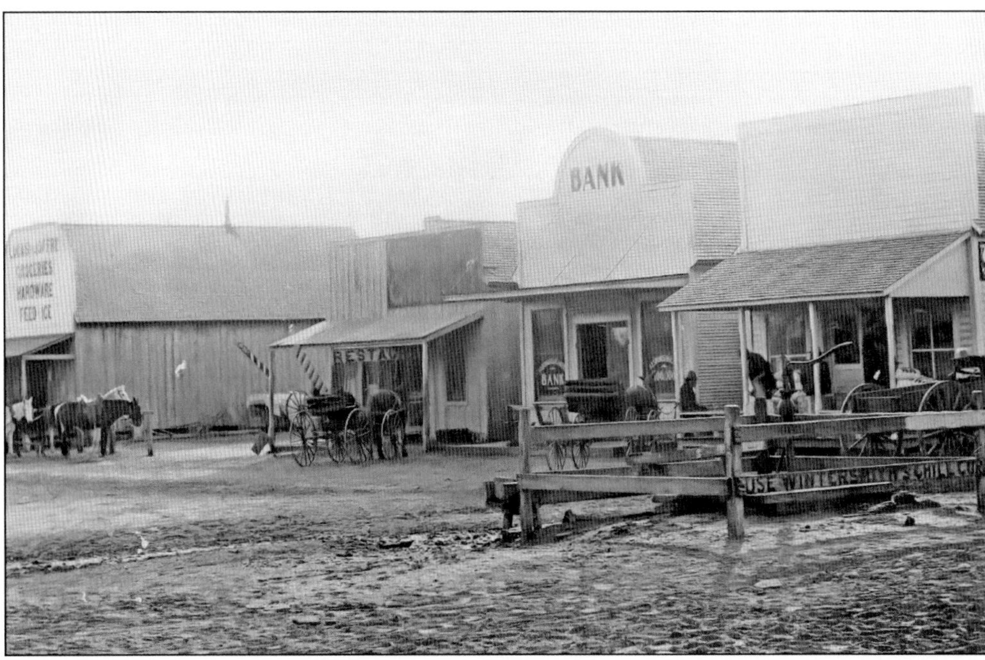

This view of downtown Irving shows the second block of Main Street in 1906. A few years after its founding, Irving boasted a bustling banking business. Patrons were able to ride into town via horse and buggy to conduct their banking business. Located on Main Street in downtown Irving, the original Merchant and Planters Bank, seen here in 1906, was created as a private enterprise.

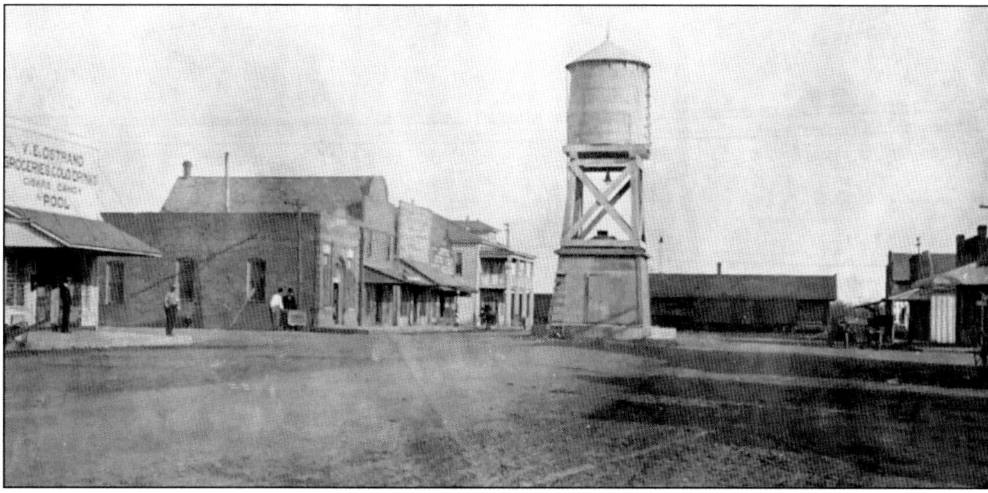

Taking pride in their cities, Texans were known for identifying the town name on the water tank. Water towers were built on flat terrain so that they could use the pull of gravity to keep the mains full and the pressure high. Every town, including Irving, had periods of peak demand for water; the extra thousands of gallons in a water tower ensured that no one was left without water. This photograph of Main Street and the water tower of Irving was taken in 1913.

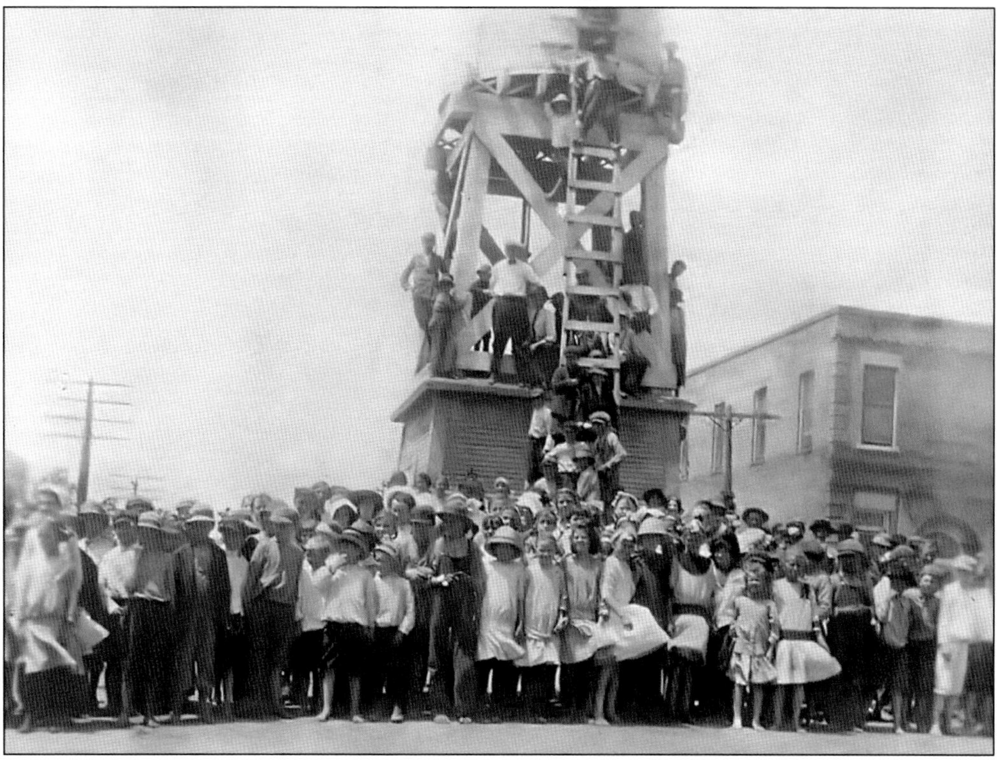

Generally, the water tower is placed either in the middle of the peak demand area or opposite the municipal pumping station. When the demand lessens, the station pumps the tower full again in preparation for the next drought. Water towers are 100 to 300 feet tall and hold 15,000 to 3,000,000 gallons. Towers can withstand northers, dust storms, and even tornadoes. Early Texas water towers resembled the "Tin Woodman's head" that is cylindrical with a "jaunty conical hat."

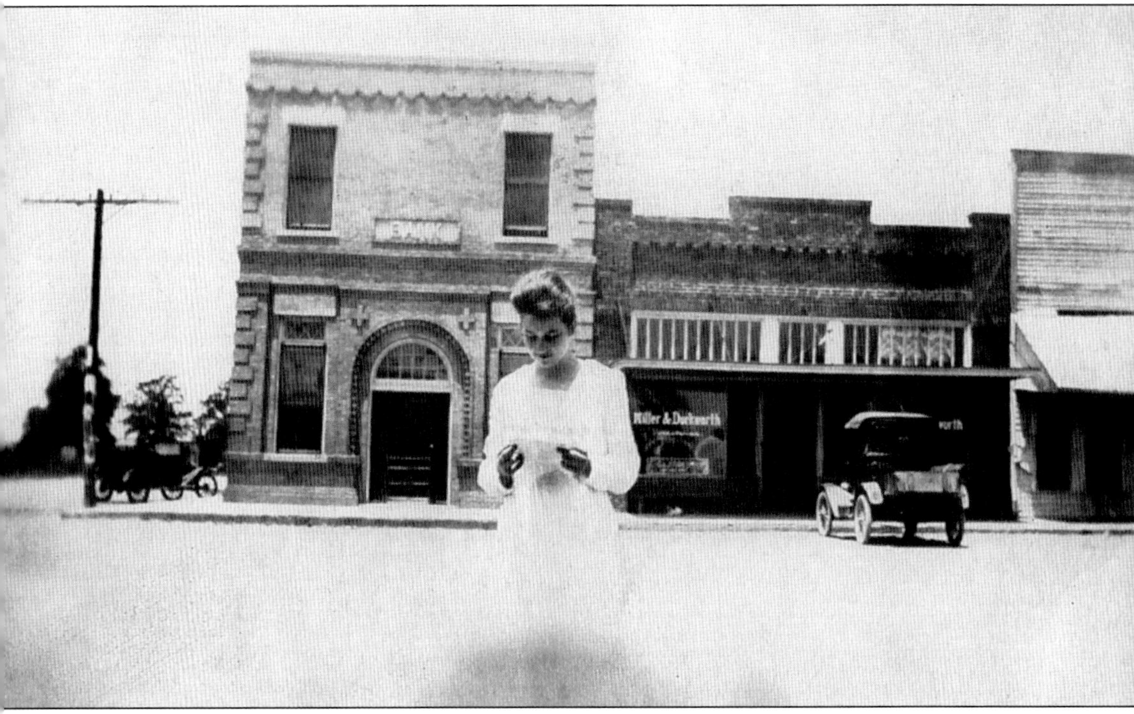

This photograph shows Main Street in Irving. On the left is the Irving State Bank, and on the right is the Miller and Duckworth store, formerly the Miller Brothers store. In addition to establishing their store in 1904, Chaney and Fletcher Miller bought the Merchants and Planters Bank and had it chartered as the Irving State Bank in 1908. (Courtesy of the Haley-Miller Collection, Irving Archives, Irving Public Library.)

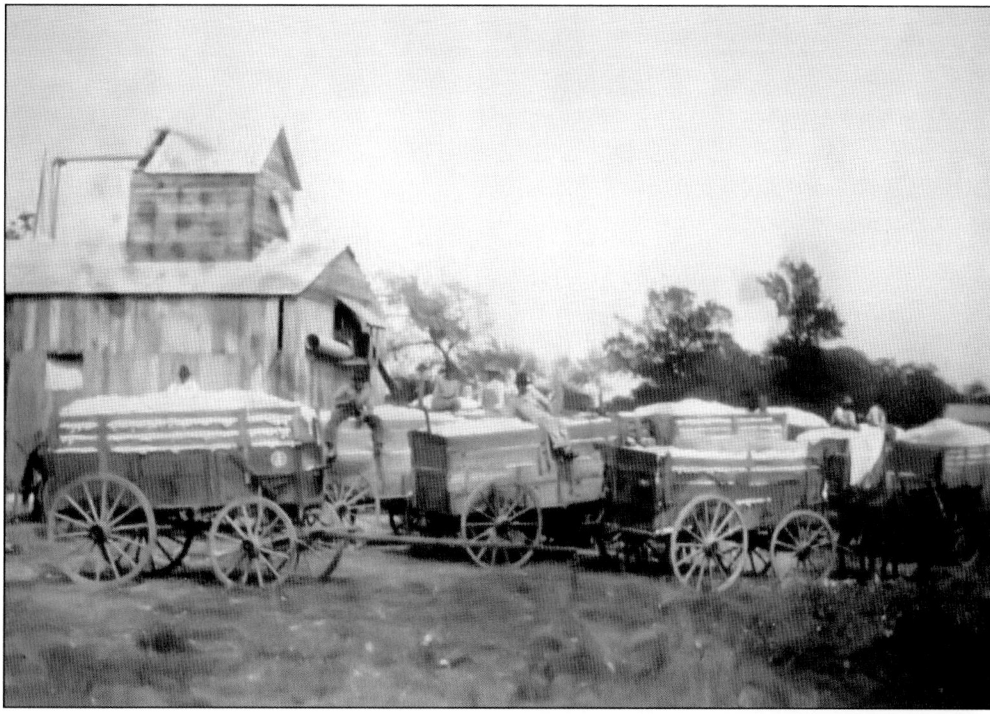

In 1918, Dallas was known as the largest cotton market, which led to the creation of cotton gin manufacturing. There were two cotton gins in the area, called Davis and Lively. Both gins transported bales of cotton to the market in Dallas.

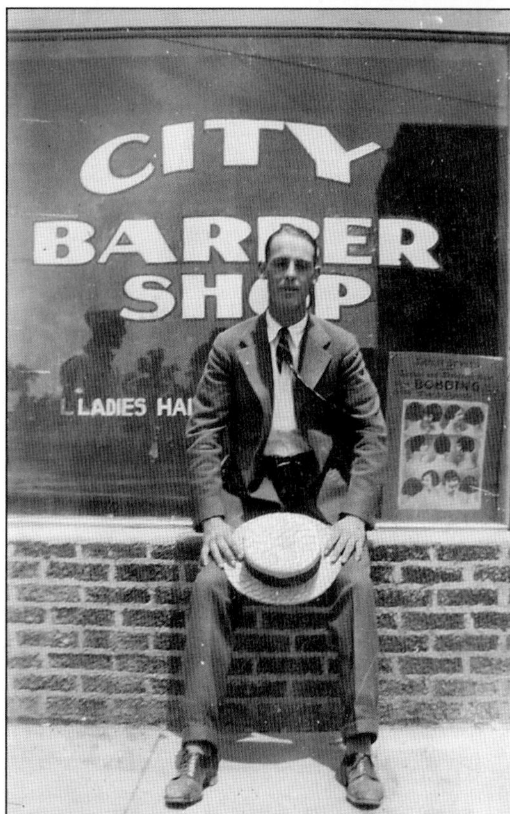

The city of Irving opened the City Barber Shop. Men frequented the shop not only for haircuts but also to hear the latest gossip or visit with their male comrades. This was a place for social interactions and discussions of local, state, and national politics. Men often debated social issues with the barber and others in the shop, where fragrant oils filled the air. This photograph was taken in 1927.

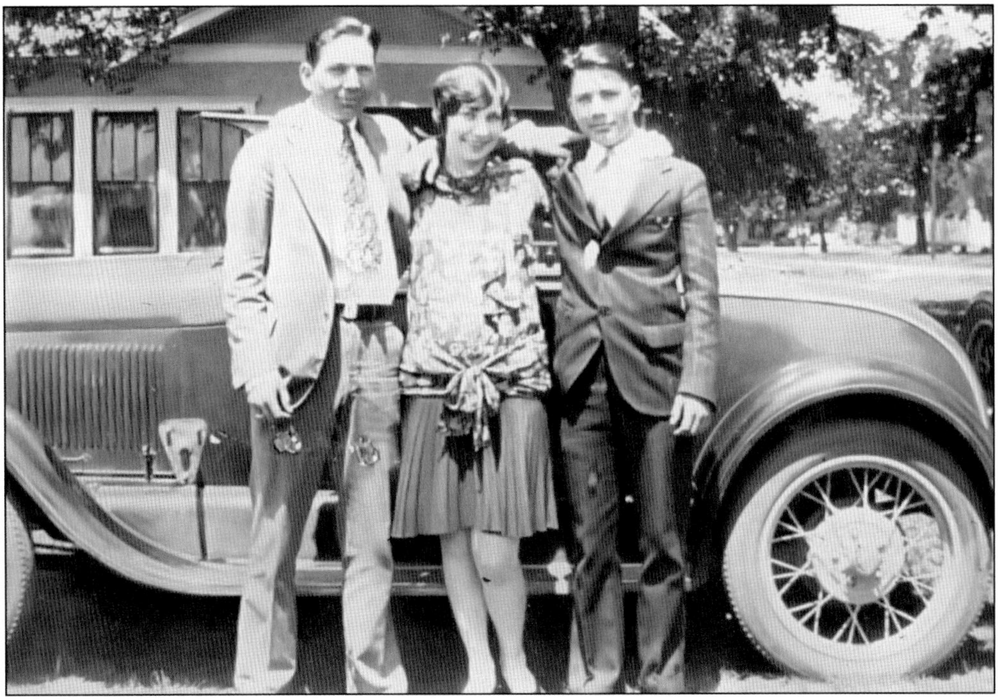

Lorene Lucas Looper is pictured with her brothers Howard and Ray. Seen behind them is a new Model A Ford from 1929. Lorene is dressed in the exact color to match her baby blue car with yellow trim. During this time, Lorene worked for a stockbroker in Dallas and recalls memories of the stock market crash: "We worked almost all night." Lorene and her brothers are the children of W.D. Lucas, the owner of a general store on the northwest corner of Main and Second Streets. As the trends of the Roaring Twenties were coming to a close, the industrial revolution was beginning to gain momentum, and the farming industry was lagging behind. Children of farmers had to leave their farms for jobs to help support their families.

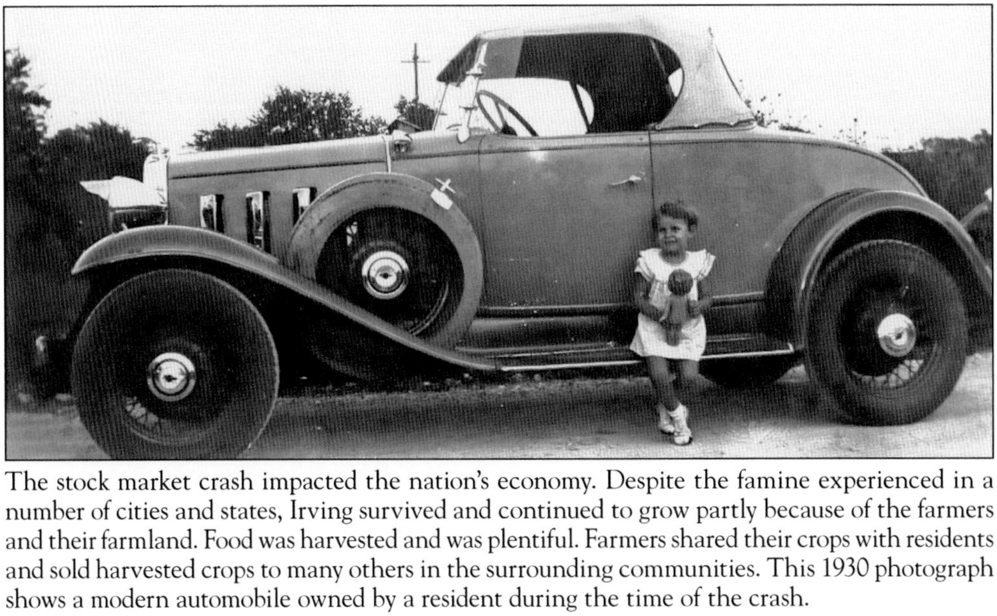

The stock market crash impacted the nation's economy. Despite the famine experienced in a number of cities and states, Irving survived and continued to grow partly because of the farmers and their farmland. Food was harvested and was plentiful. Farmers shared their crops with residents and sold harvested crops to many others in the surrounding communities. This 1930 photograph shows a modern automobile owned by a resident during the time of the crash.

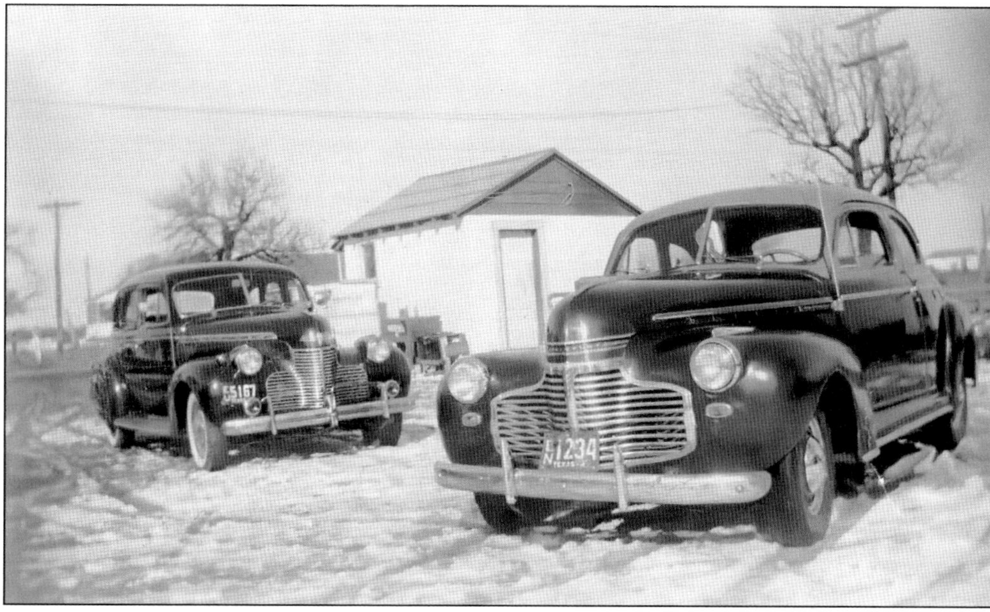

The modern auto had changed the transportation industry from buggy and carriage to that of a more efficient mode of travel. Fords and Chevys were both popular in Irving. Anyone who was anyone owned an automobile. The city of Irving had its own Chevrolet dealership, owned and operated by Smokey Vandergriff, who sold both new and used cars in a lot on First Street. Pictured here are a 1940 Chevy and a 1941 Chevy.

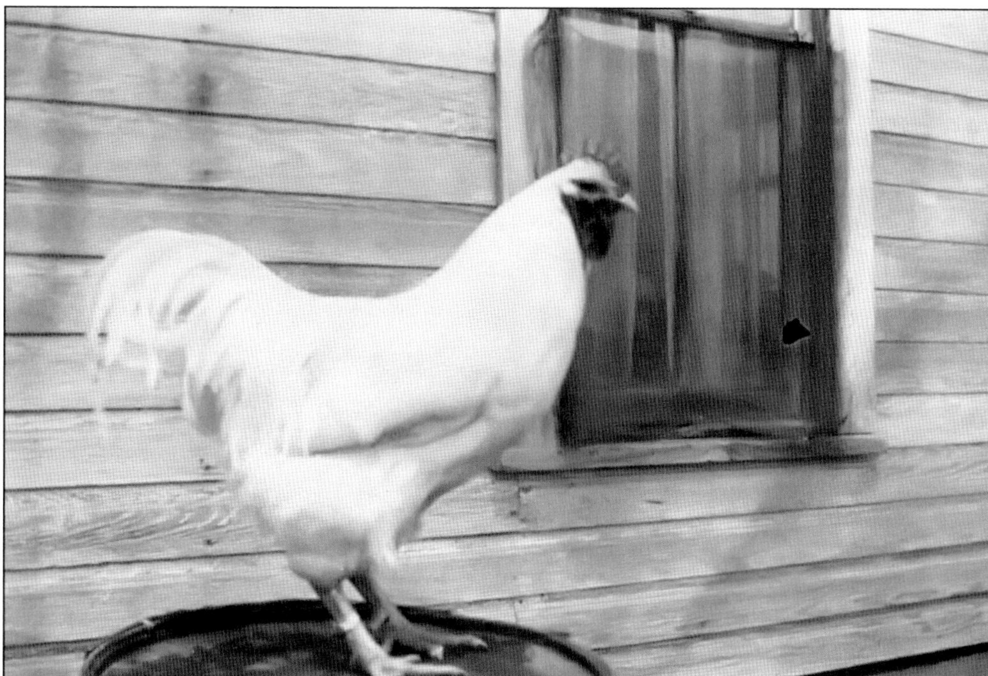

In the late 1930s, livestock and poultry shows became popular in Irving. Farmers took pride in raising their animals and enjoyed competing for the best prize. Here, Tommy Evans shows off his prize-winning chicken.

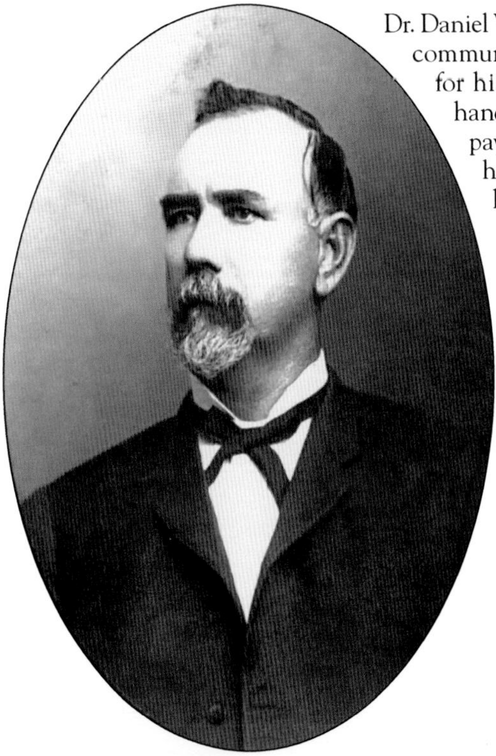

Dr. Daniel Webster Gilbert practiced medicine in the Sowers community. He traveled via horse and buggy to care for his homebound patients. If his buggy could not handle the trails, he would ride his horse. In lieu of payment for his services, Dr. Gilbert bartered with his patients, often accepting chicken, dairy, and homemade food. He soon gave up his traditional mode of transportation for an automobile, making it more efficient to travel to patients' homes. Dr. Gilbert died in 1930.

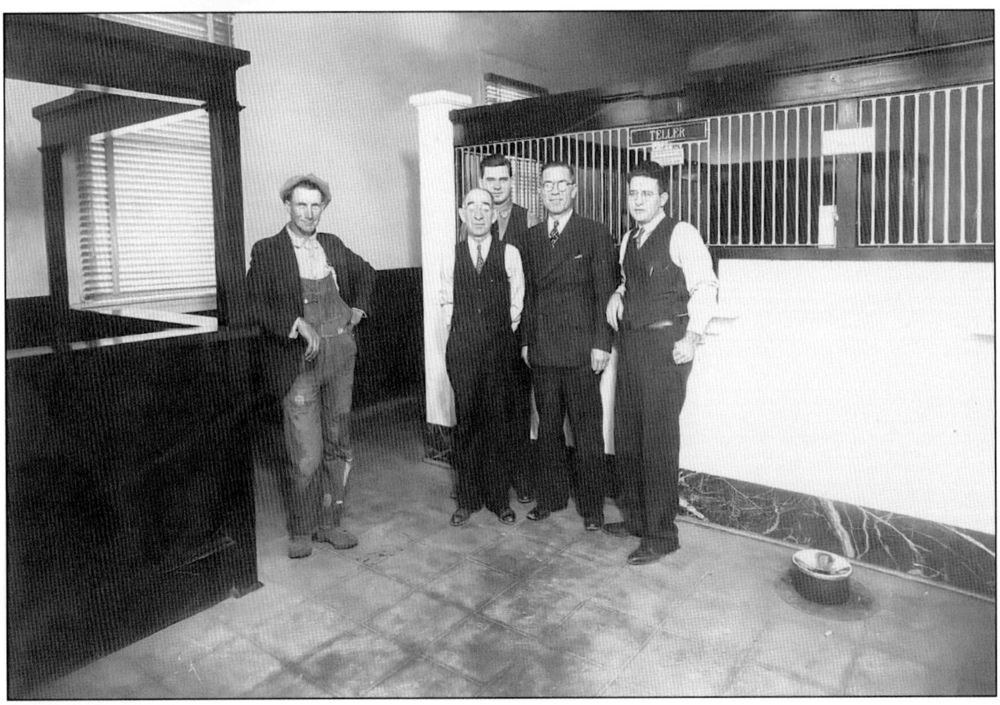

Dr. Frank Monroe Gilbert (second from right) and bank manager A.P. Mauk (left, in front of the teller's window) are pictured inside the Irving State Bank. Dr. Gilbert was president of the bank at the time of this photograph.

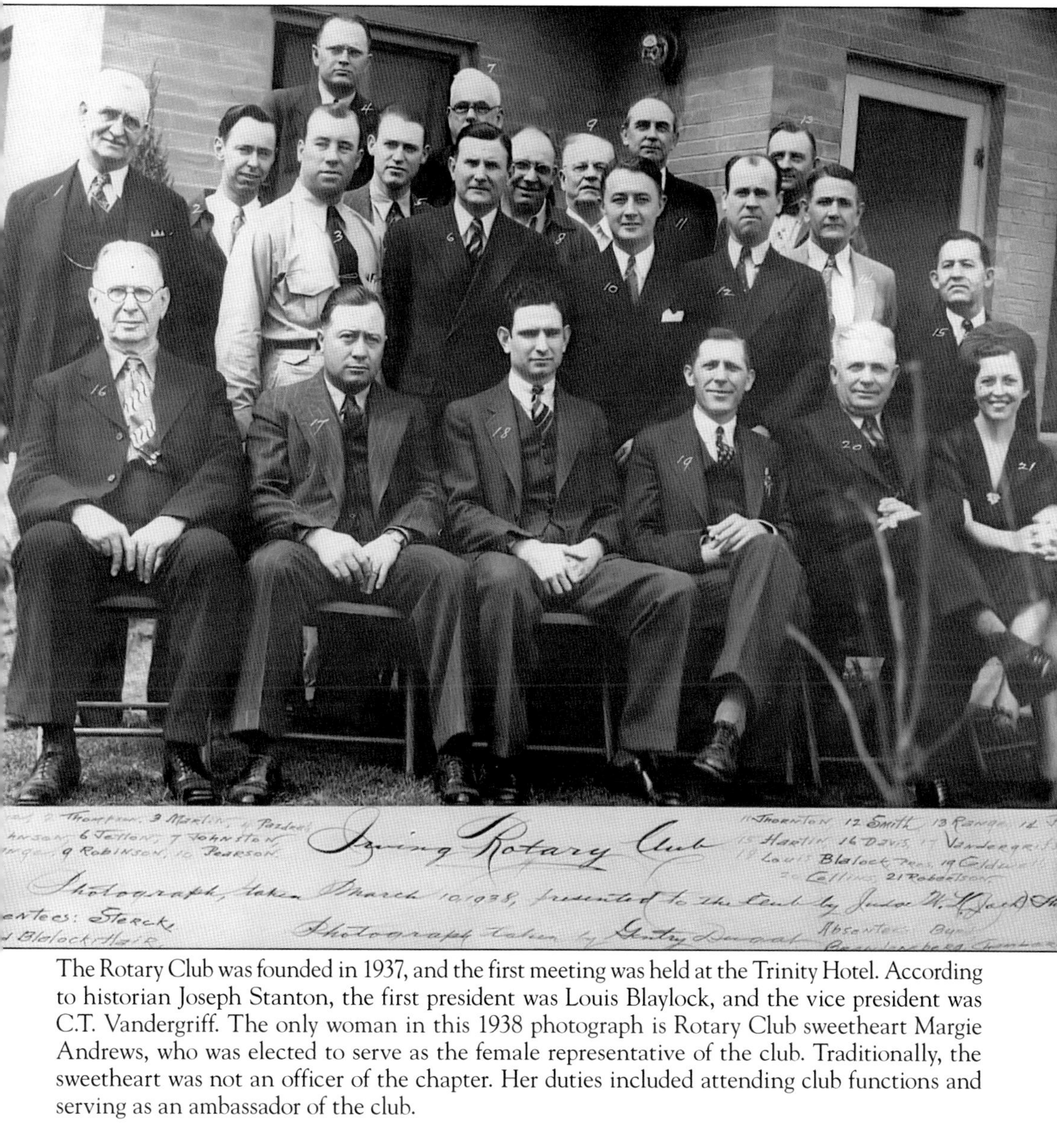

The Rotary Club was founded in 1937, and the first meeting was held at the Trinity Hotel. According to historian Joseph Stanton, the first president was Louis Blaylock, and the vice president was C.T. Vandergriff. The only woman in this 1938 photograph is Rotary Club sweetheart Margie Andrews, who was elected to serve as the female representative of the club. Traditionally, the sweetheart was not an officer of the chapter. Her duties included attending club functions and serving as an ambassador of the club.

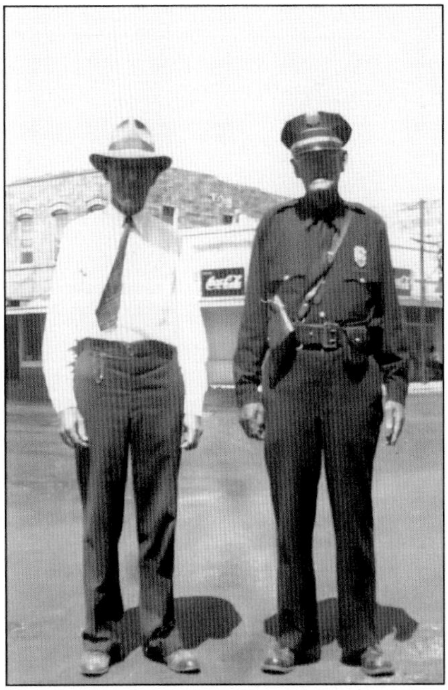

In 1940, Mayor C.P. Caldwell (left) hired George Smith (right) as the first Irving patrolman. Officer Smith patrolled the city on foot without an automobile or a two-way radio. In the event of an emergency, the telephone operator would send a signal to Smith by turning on the water tower light. When he saw the light, Smith would call the operator to receive further information. Mayor Caldwell collected contributions from local businesses to pay for Smith's salary. Before Smith, Caldwell had appointed Frank Pate as the city's marshal to keep the peace. Committed to providing the necessary public services for citizens, Caldwell was elected mayor in 1937 and reelected to three consecutive two-year terms. During his time in office, he received WPA funding to pave many of the streets and sidewalks. In addition, Caldwell hired the city's first full-time employee in 1939. He also improved the city's sewer system and water storage system. In the late 1930s, he assisted in establishing the Irving Rotary Club and the Irving Chamber of Commerce. Caldwell died in 1942.

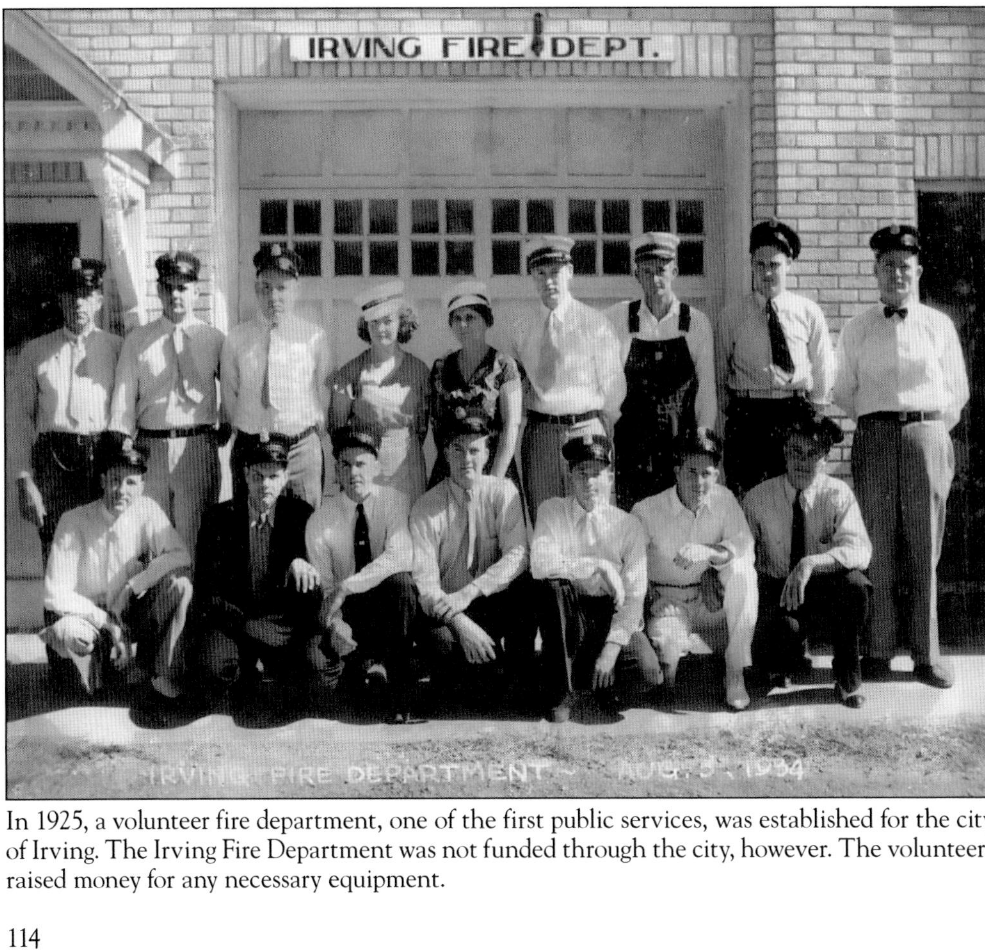

In 1925, a volunteer fire department, one of the first public services, was established for the city of Irving. The Irving Fire Department was not funded through the city, however. The volunteers raised money for any necessary equipment.

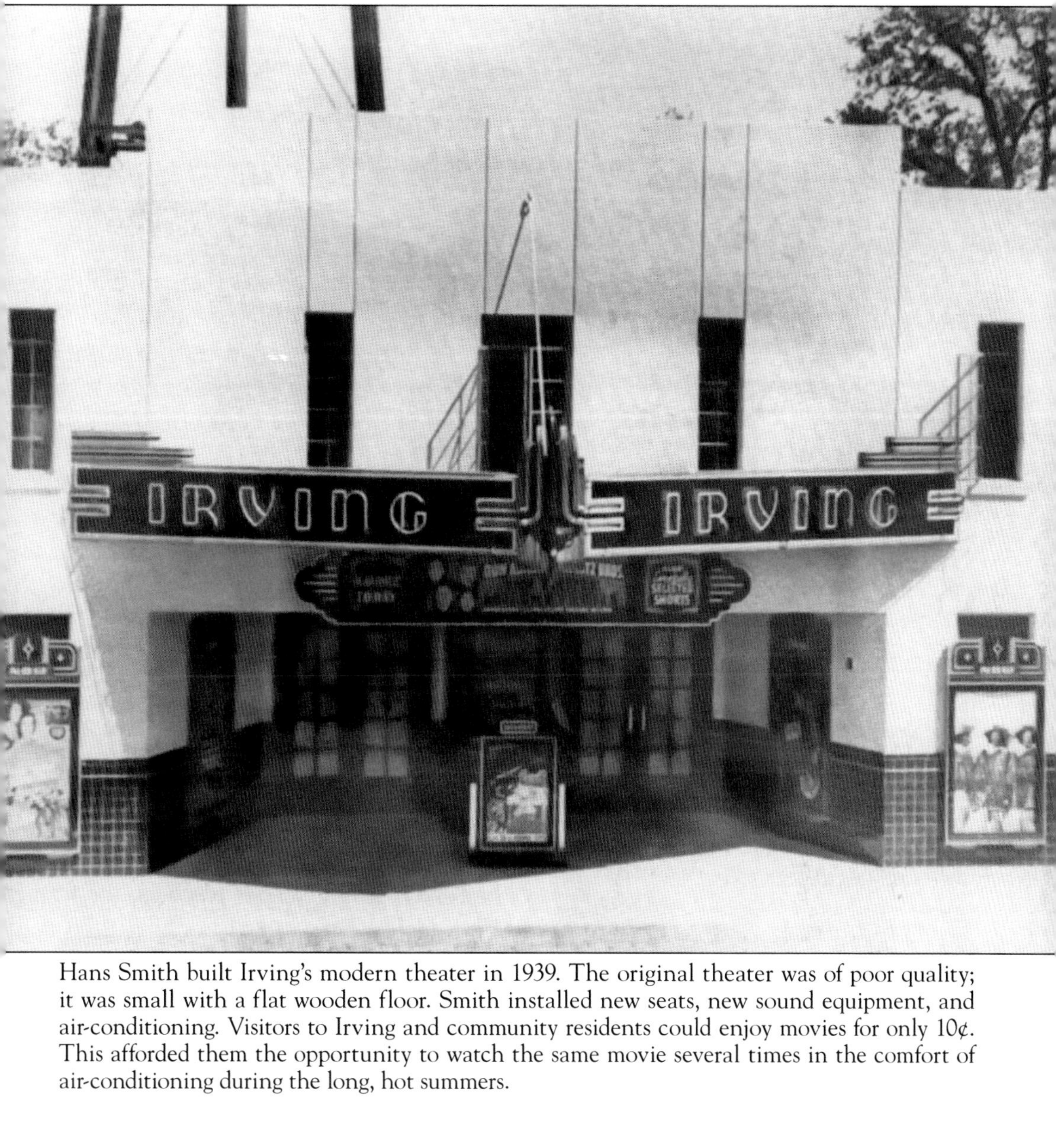

Hans Smith built Irving's modern theater in 1939. The original theater was of poor quality; it was small with a flat wooden floor. Smith installed new seats, new sound equipment, and air-conditioning. Visitors to Irving and community residents could enjoy movies for only 10¢. This afforded them the opportunity to watch the same movie several times in the comfort of air-conditioning during the long, hot summers.

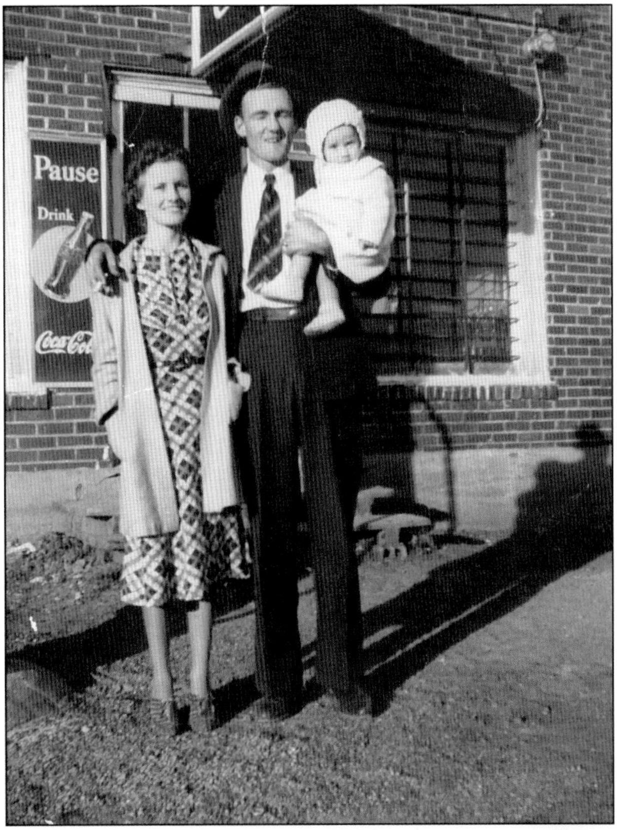

Bess and Tom Ramsey are pictured with their daughter Pat in front of the Estelle Grocery Store in 1939. Grocery stores were very competitive; thus, they had to stock merchandise that would entice their customers to keep coming back.

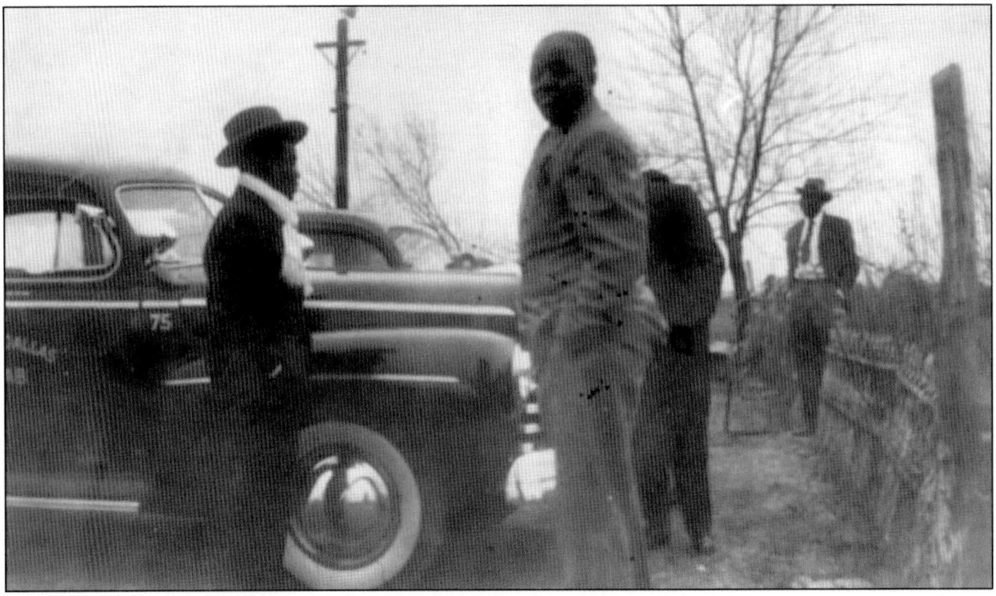

Bear Creek was a community of celebration, with birthdays, special days, and holidays. It was a happy community despite the discrimination that was endured during this time. Community members kept to themselves and gathered together to pray and sing. John Morton (left) and Walter Howard (right) are pictured on Thanksgiving Day in the late 1940s.

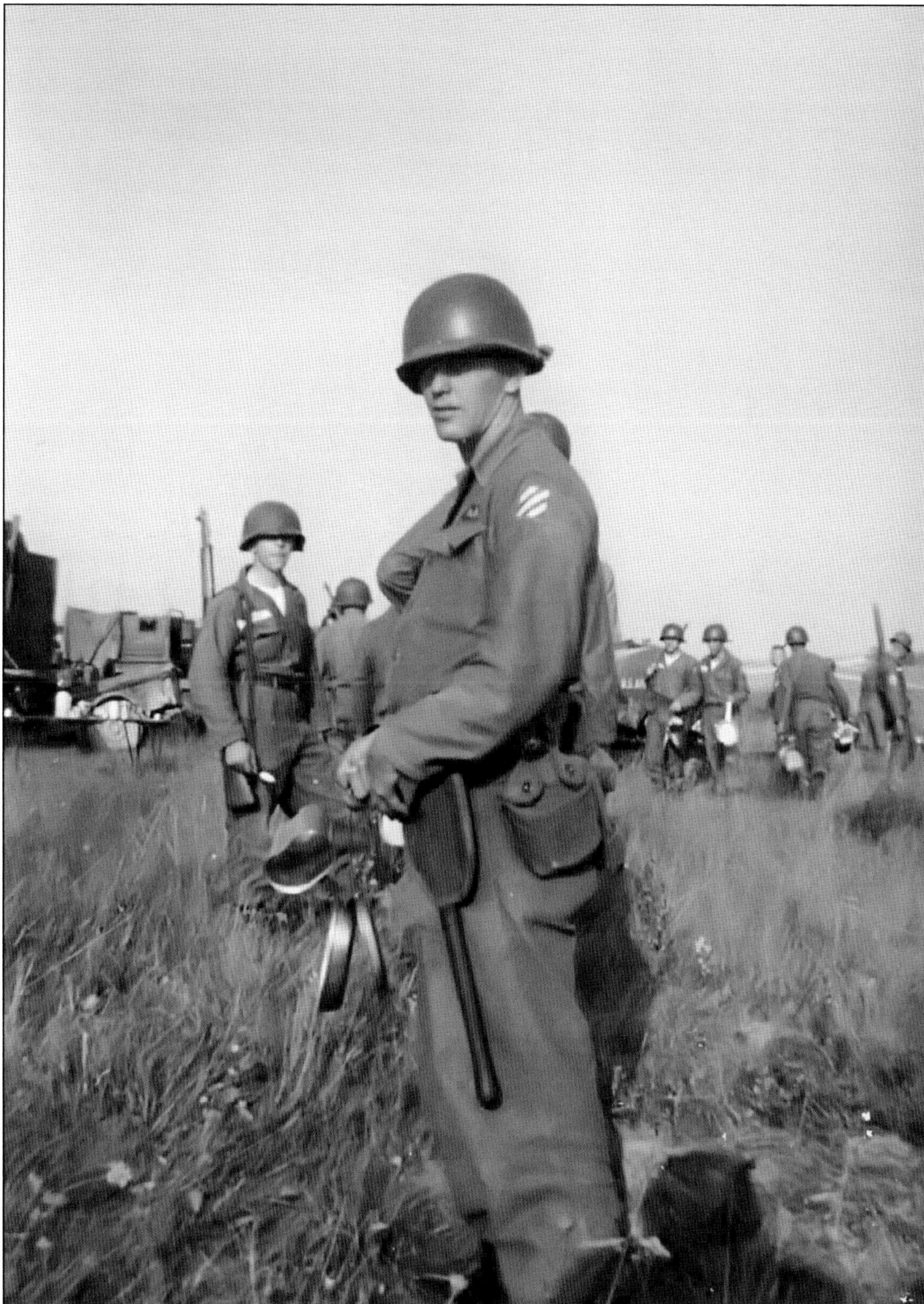

War was on the mind of many citizens in Irving during the early 1940s. This time brought about anxiety and panic for families and friends as many young men and women signed on with various branches of the military. Some families would welcome home their loved ones, while others would mourn their loss. Arthur Farine Jr. is pictured on the battlefield in 1945.

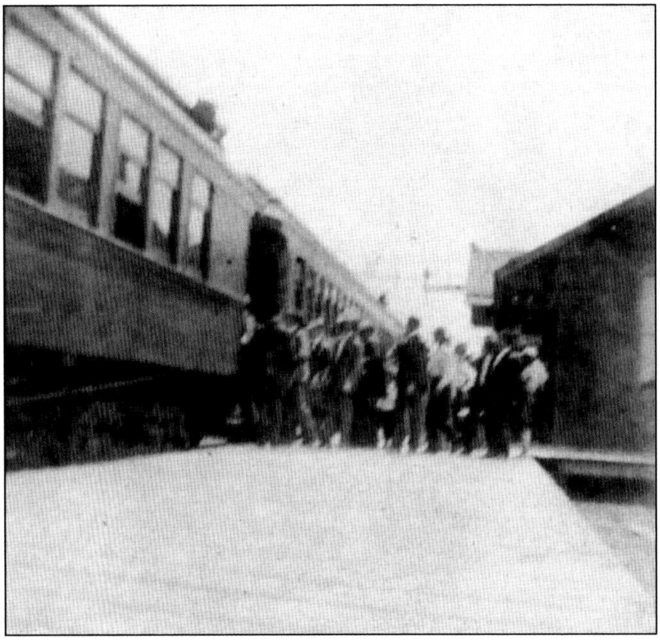

In 1940, trains from the Irving depot transported Irvingites to their jobs in the Dallas business district. During wartime, the Irving deport also served as a transportation hub for the military. Automobiles were prevalent during this time, and many citizens had at least one automobile. However, citizens were encouraged to ride public transportation to conserve gasoline and tires, which were prioritized for the armed forces.

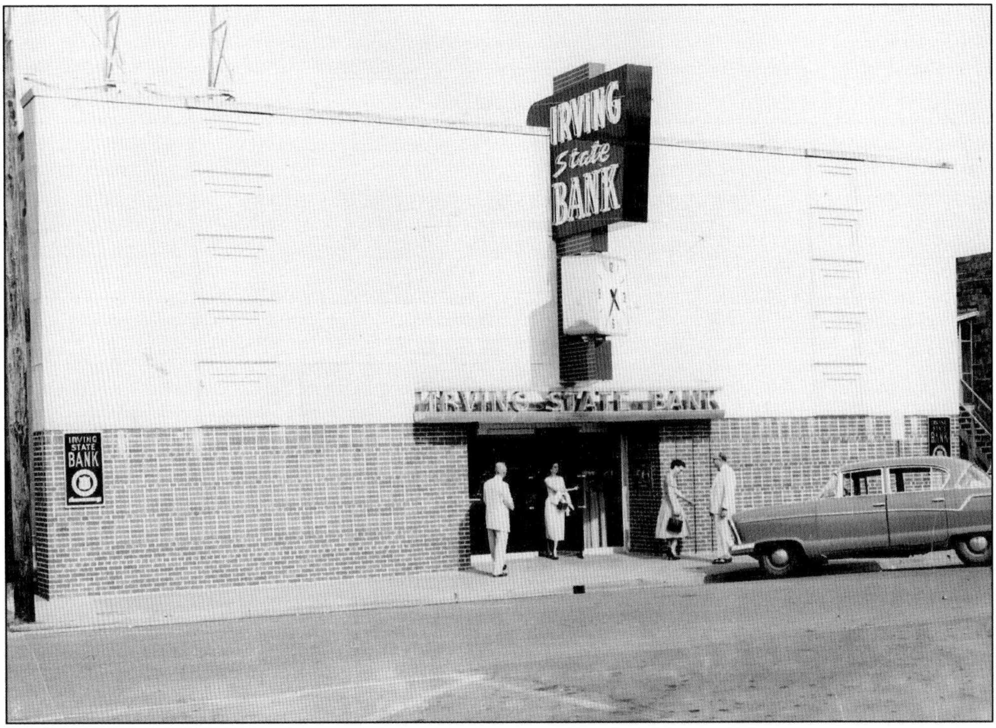

Pictured is the new Irving State Bank, built in 1947. This modern building served the growing commercial and industrial market. The population of Irving had increased and so had the level of sophistication of its citizens. In prior years, citizens lacked confidence in banks and thus would hide their money under the mattress. During this time, however, citizens became more confident that banks would take care of their money, so they began to use these services. Businesses also required additional banking services and efficient customer service.

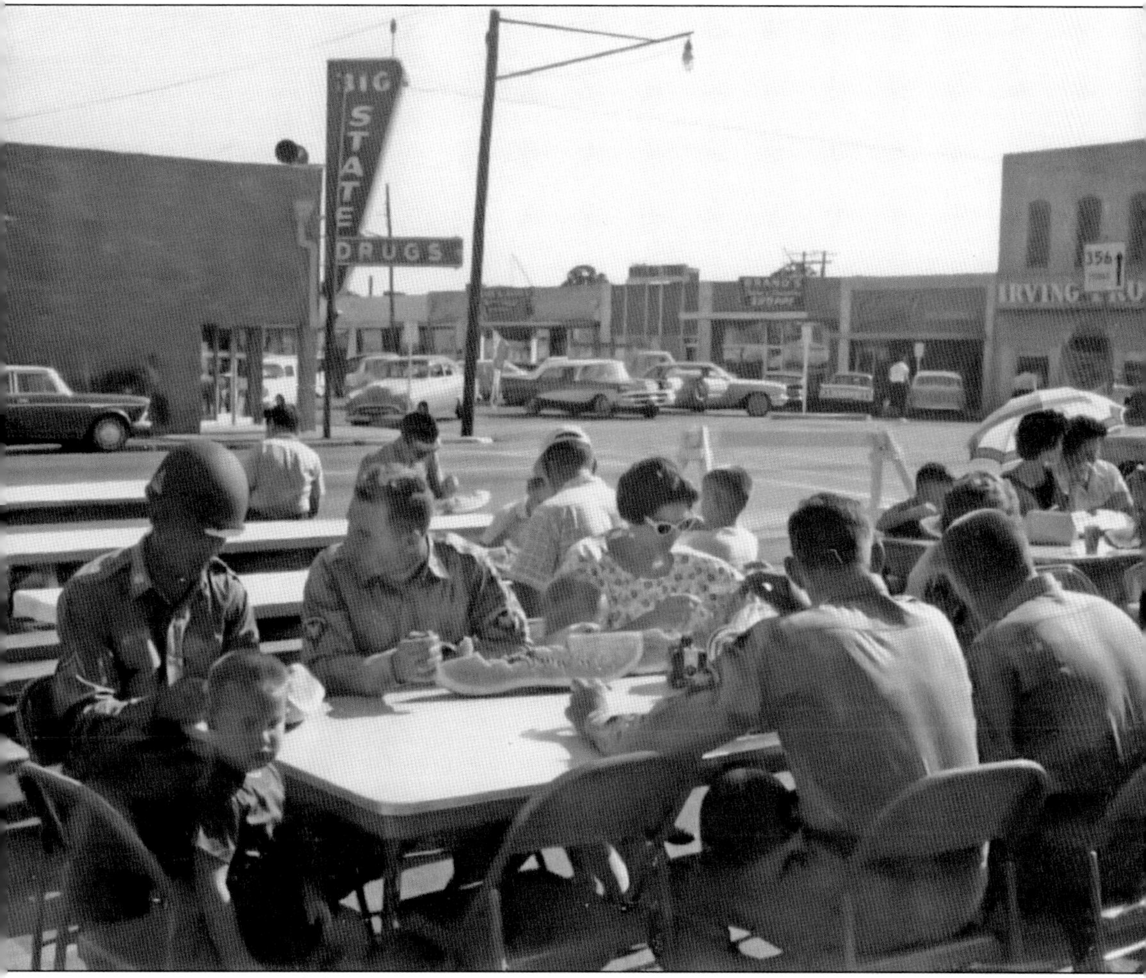

Big State Drugs graced the corner of Main Street in downtown Irving in the late 1940s. During wartime, families and friends would gather together to enjoy the company of their fellow military family members. Picnics were held outside the drugstore, especially during springtime.

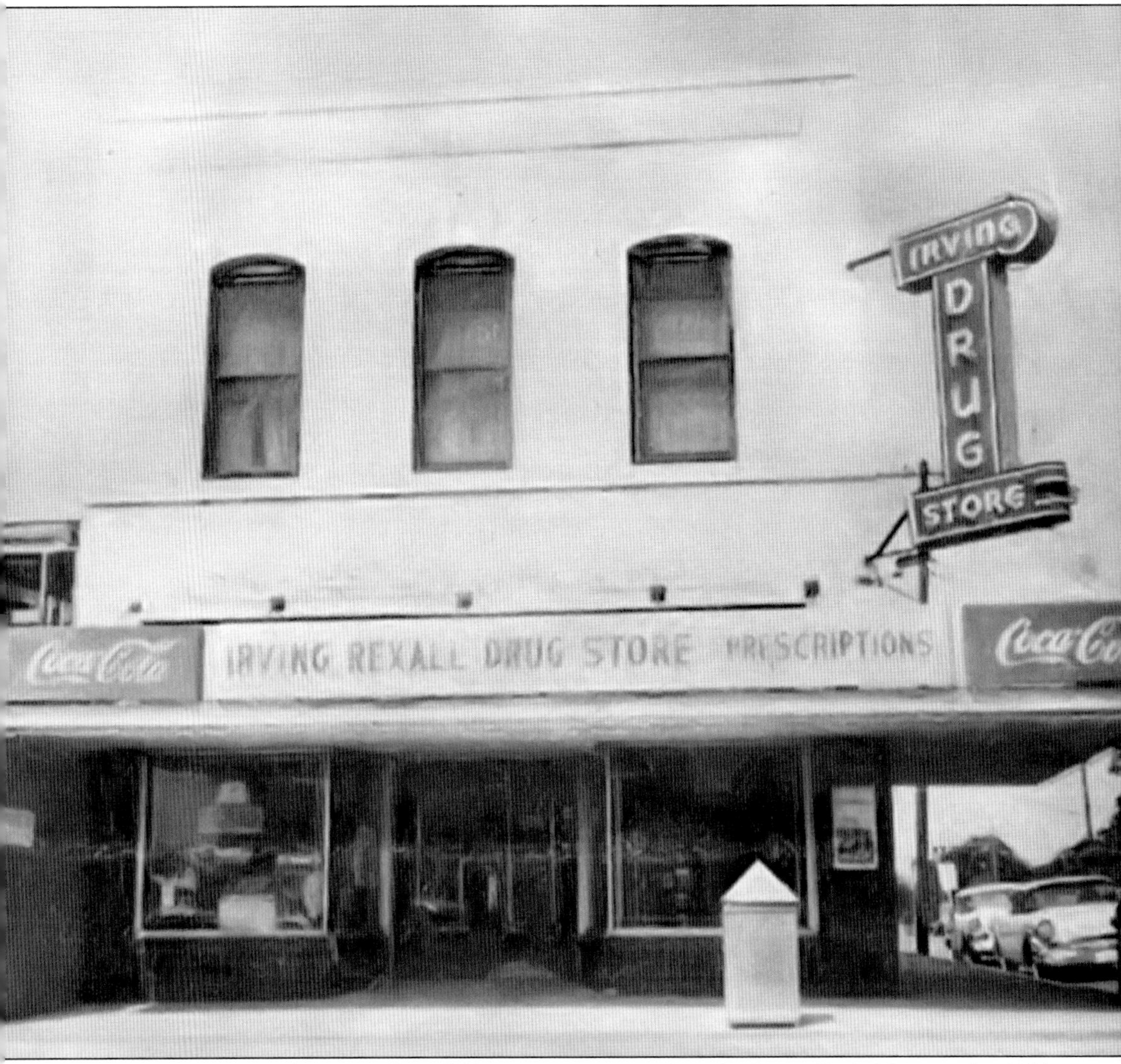

This front view of the Irving Rexall Drug Store appeared in the *Irving Daily News* in the 1950s. In addition to filling prescriptions, this modern drugstore on Main Street in downtown Irving had air-conditioning and provided its customers with a relaxing place to drink a soda on those hot Texas summer days.

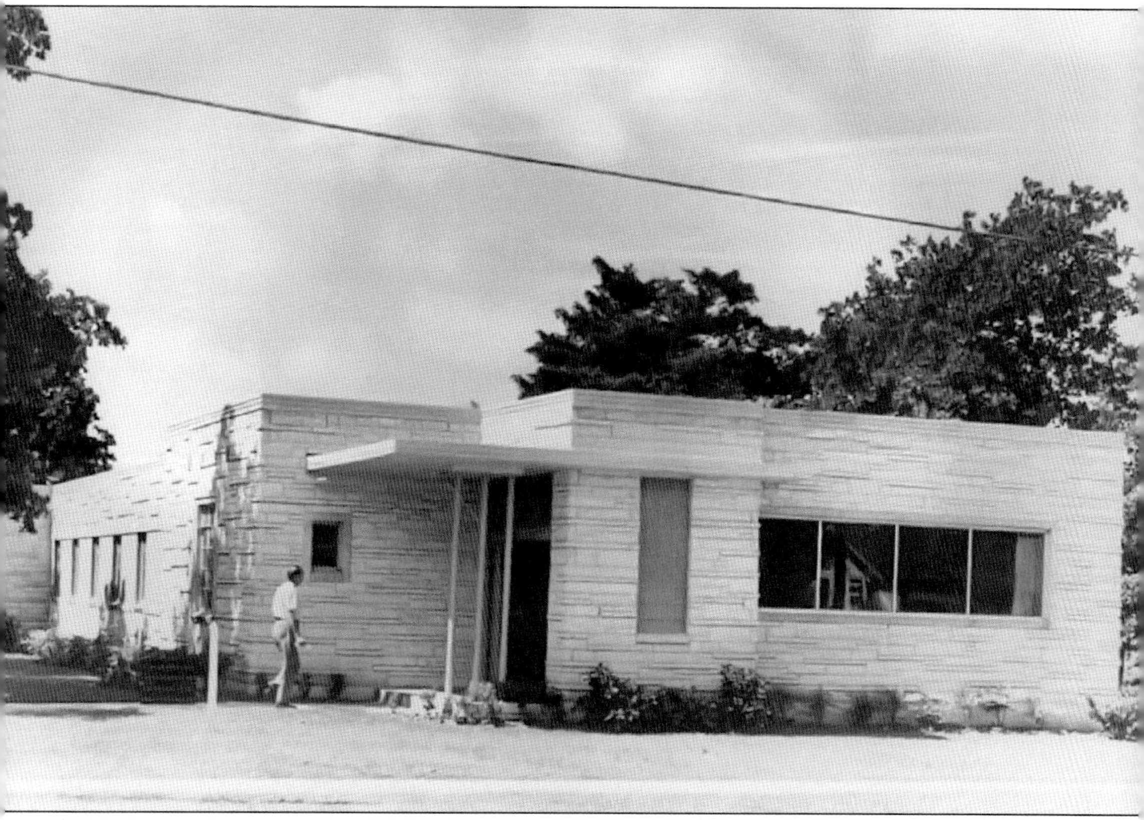

With the significant growth in Irving's population, doctors could no longer provide adequate medical care by making house calls. In 1946, the first medical clinic opened in Irving. The brainchild of Dr. F.M. Gilbert and Dr. Joe Roberts, the Gilbert Roberts Clinic provided citizens with necessary medical services. The clinic was strategically placed for convenient access. The Gilbert Roberts Clinic boasted modern equipment, professional services, and medical specialists.

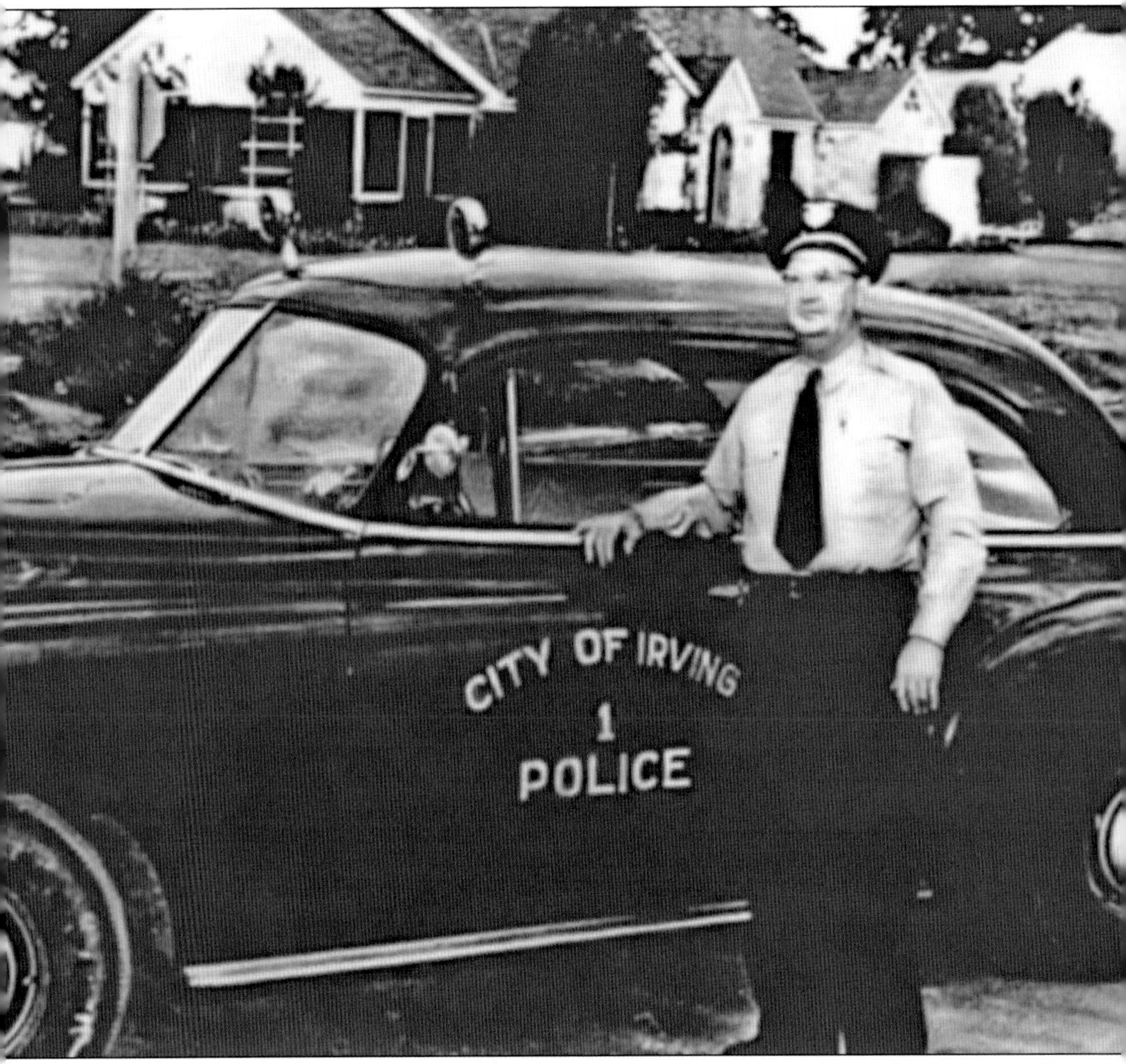

Irving's first police chief, Joe Reynolds, is pictured with the city's first police car in 1953. Reynolds was paid $145 a month. He replaced George Smith, who had retired as Irving's first foot patrol officer.

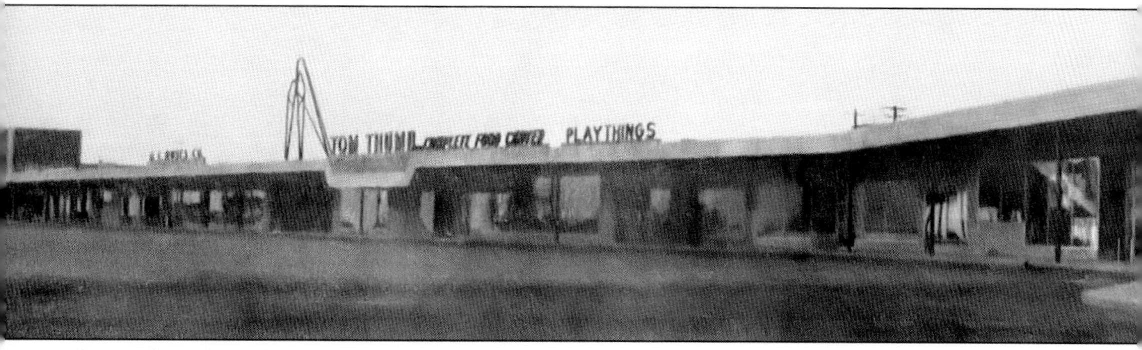

Plymouth Park was built at the request of Irving citizens and business leaders. Prior to the shopping center, Irvingites traveled to the surrounding cities of Dallas or Fort Worth to shop for specialty items, such as toys, upscale attire, and food, to name a few. After much debate, the Irving City Council approved the construction of Plymouth Park, built by the Mayflower Company. The shopping center included a grocery store, a toy shop, and a hardware store, as well as other specialty shops. Located on Story Road, the shopping center was surrounded by a large residential neighborhood. The center attracted residents from other cities as well, and soon additional stores were built in the center.

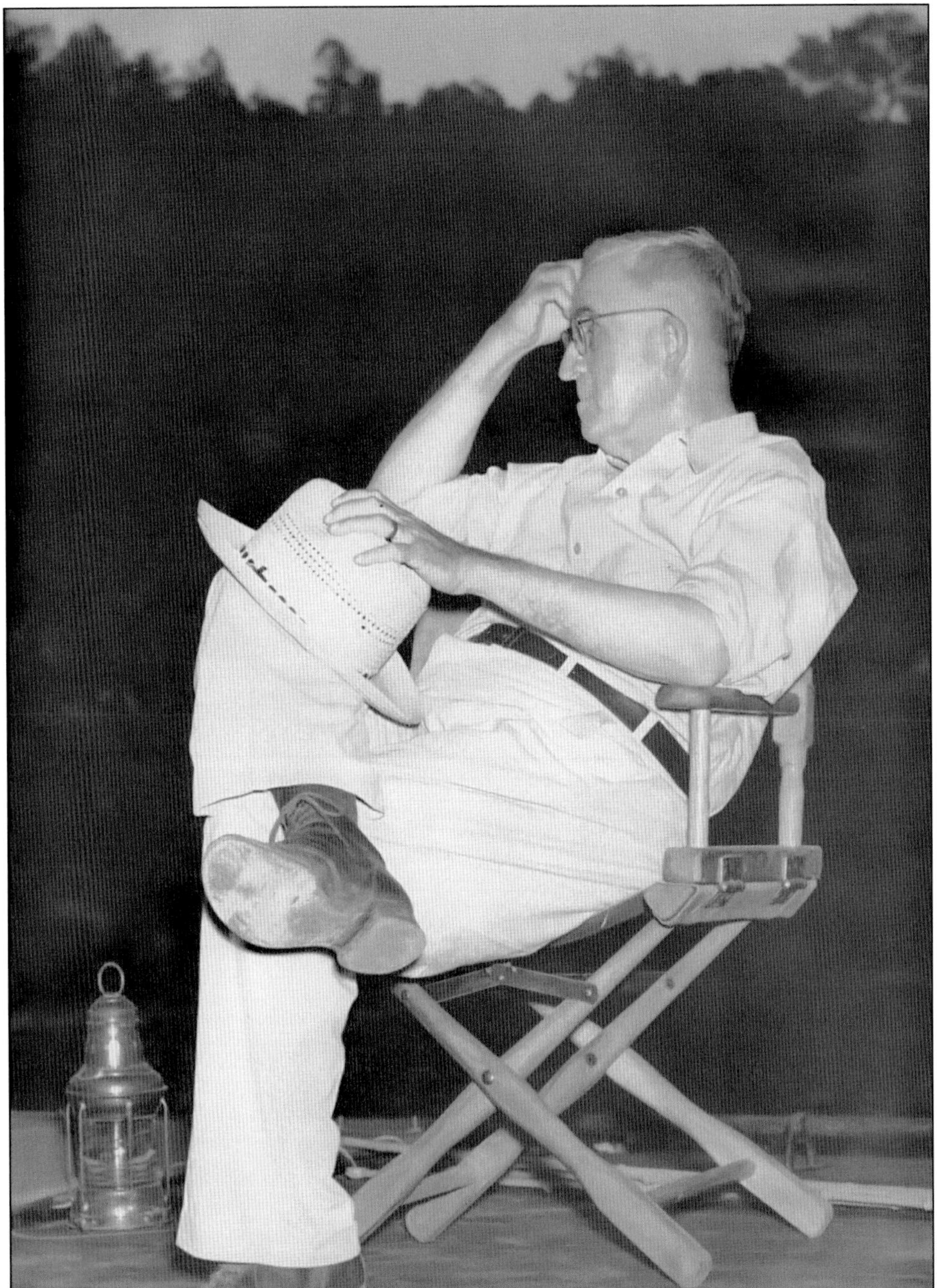

John William Carpenter is pictured deep in thought. During his lifetime, Carpenter was recognized as a utility and insurance executive and rancher. In addition to being the founder and first president of Lone Star Steel, Carpenter served as president of the Dallas Railway & Terminal Company (1927–1935) and the Texas Refrigeration & Ice Company (1945–1949). Carpenter managed and organized nearly 25 major companies in the Southwest, including 11 utility companies and the St. Louis Southwestern Railway Company. (Courtesy of LIZ Gillispie Genealogy Department Corsicana Public Library.)

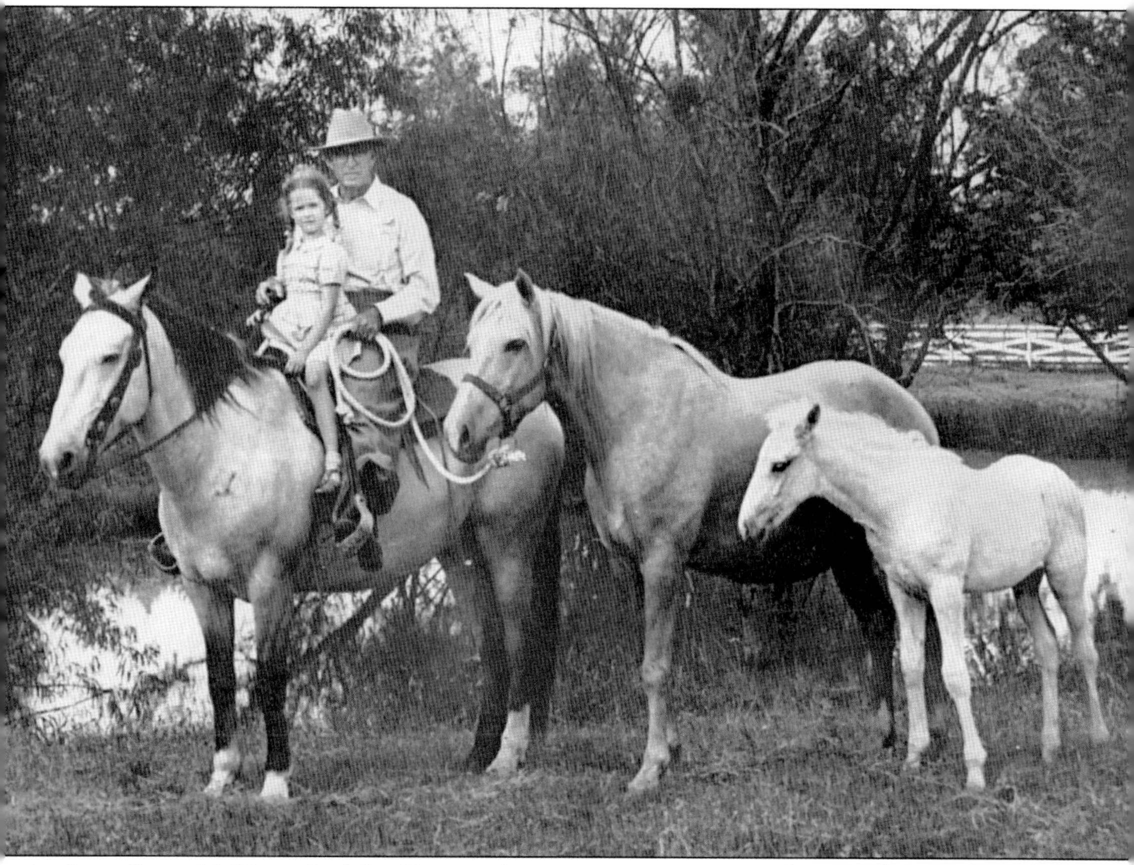

According to his biography, John Carpenter's major interests were agriculture and horse and cattle breeding. He owned and operated four ranches and one farm with the help of his son Ben. John introduced the technique of artificial insemination to Texas with a $5,000 grant to Texas A&M. (Courtesy of LIZ Gillispie Genealogy Department Corsicana Public Library.)

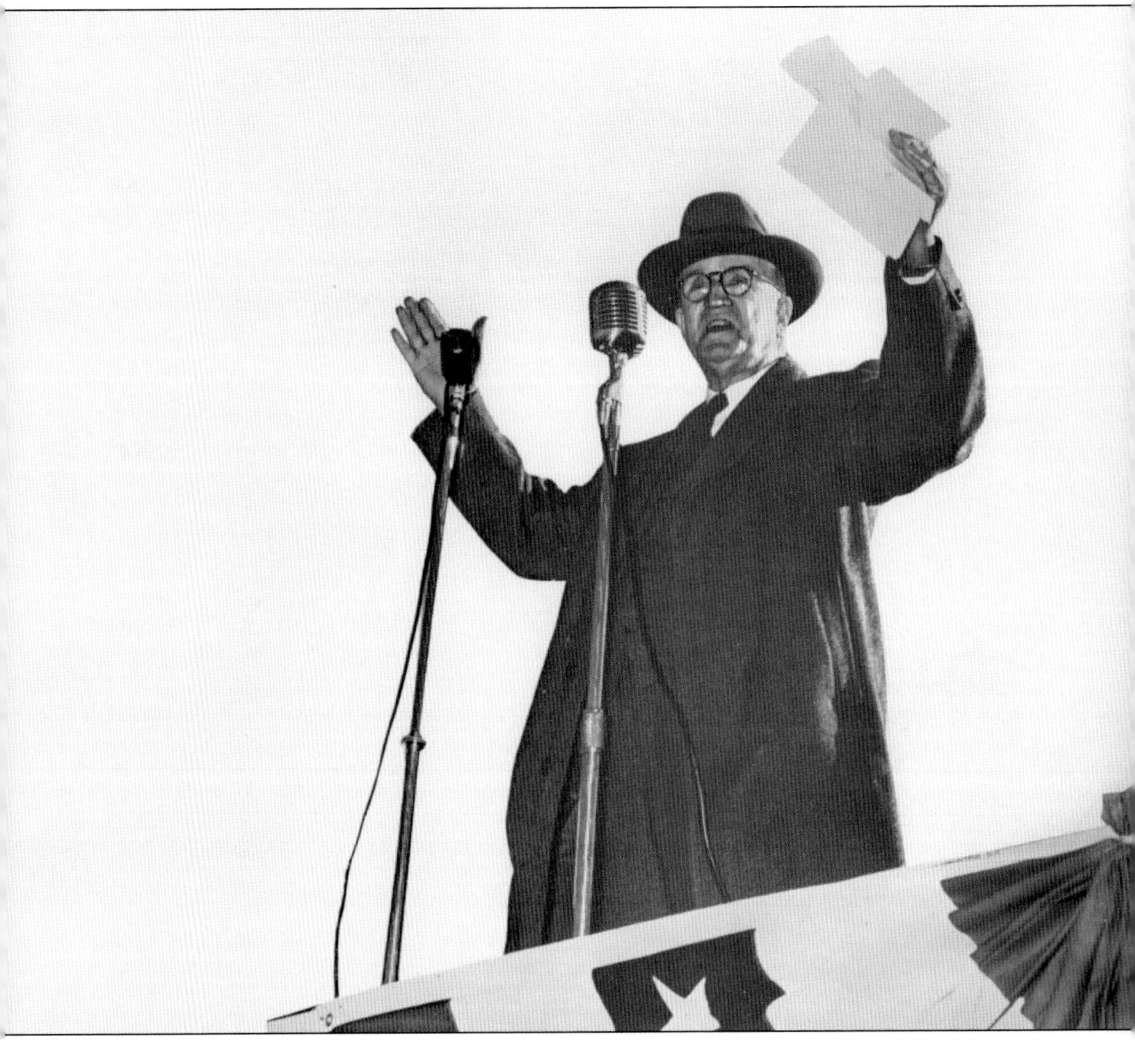

This photograph portrays how Texans will remember John W. Carpenter, as a true pioneer in the industrial world. He was a leader, developer, father, and husband. His 50 years of experience in business and industry led to a multitude of contributions to his community. He is known in Irving for donating his ranch land to further develop the city, thus making it one of the most thriving municipalities in today's metroplex. (Courtesy of LIZ Gillispie Genealogy Department Corsicana Public Library.)

Bibliography

"Between the Forks." www.cityofirving.org/1993/Between-the-Forks. Retrieved September 12, 2015.

"Clyde Barrow and Bonnie Parker." *The Portal to Texas History*. http://texashistory.unt.edu/ark:/67531/metapth78914/. Retrieved September 12, 2015.

"Digital Collections." www.cityofirving.org/1979/Digital-Collections. Retrieved September 12, 2015.

"From Humble Beginnings: A History of the Library." www.cityofirving.org/1990/From-Humble-Beginnings-History-of-the-Li. Retrieved September 12, 2015.

"Historical Sketch." www.cityofirving.org/1977/Historical-Sketch. Retrieved September 12, 2015.

"History of Bathing Suits." *Victoriana Magazine*. www.victoriana.com/library/Beach/FashionableBathingSuits.htm. Retrieved September 12, 2015.

"Iron Bridge Across the West Fork of the Trinity River Near Irving, Texas." *The Portal to Texas History*. www.texashistory.unt.edu. Retrieved September 12, 2015.

"Irving High School Football 1929." www.cityofirving.org/1994/Irving-High-School-Football-1929. Retrieved September 12, 2015.

"Mayors of Irving, Texas." *The Political Graveyard*. www.politicalgraveyard.com/geo/TX/ofc/irving.html. Retrieved September 12, 2015.

Perez, J. "John William Carpenter." www.tsha.utexas.edu.

Redding, Marie. "Hosiery Trends in the 1920s." *About Style*. www.lingerie.about.com/od/HoseCamiSlips/a/Hosiery-Styles-In-The-1920s.htm. Retrieved September 12, 2015.

Rice, Joseph. *Irving: A Texas Odyssey*. Windsor Publications Inc., 1989.

Rosenberg, J. "Flappers in the Roaring Twenties." Retrieved September 12, 2015.

Stanton, N. *Irving, Texas: From Rails to Wings, 1903–2003*. Virginia Beach, VA: Donning Company, 2003.

Thomas, Pauline Weston. "La Belle Époque, 1895–1914: Edwardian Fashion History 1." *Fashion-Era*. www.fashion-era.com/la_belle_epoque_1890-1914_fashion.htm Retrieved September 12, 2015.

Tindall, G., and D. Shi. *America: A Narrative History*. New York, NY: Norton, 2010.